Priest in the Pyrenees

A Mountain Walk across France

Dave Lewis

David Lewis

i

Priest in the Pyrenees
A Mountain Walk across France

by
David Lewis

Published by

Habakkuk Publishing House
The Rectory
Great Smeaton
Northallerton
North Yorkshire
DL6 2EP

Printed in the UK by

Antony Rowe Ltd
Eastbourne

iii

ISBN -   0-9550625-0-0
ISBN -   978-0-9550625-0-6

Contents:

Key to maps:

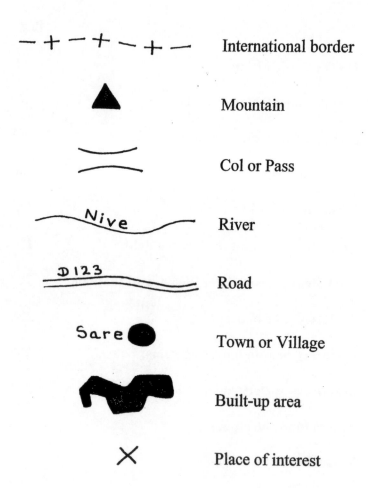

— + — + — + — International border

▲ Mountain

‿ Col or Pass

Nive River

D123 Road

Sare ● Town or Village

Built-up area

✕ Place of interest

List of maps:

Priest in the Pyrenees

A Mountain Walk across France

David Lewis

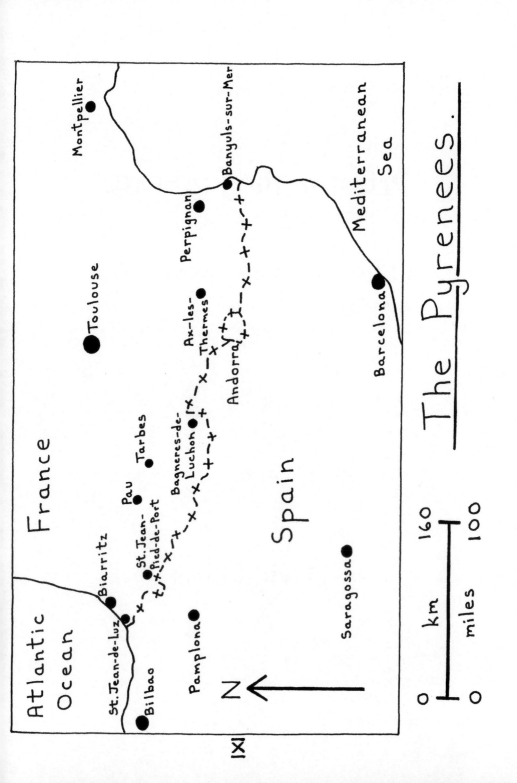

The Pyrenees.

Chapter 1.

The Yesterday Man.

Death had not been on my agenda for that particular day. Yet it found a way to impinge on my consciousness nevertheless. It did so ingeniously, invading from an unexpected direction and from a distance of eight hundred miles.

The accident happened on a steep and winding section of road, and it began with a skid. In a matter of seconds the horrible momentum of a bicycle was converted into the sickening impact of a man's head against a granite block. The viciously sharp edge of the bollard split the rider's skull open. No helmet could have saved him, and the attempts at resuscitation were futile. It was a Tuesday in July and tragedy had visited the *Tour de France*.

I was working in Carlisle in 1995 and knew nothing about this until the evening. At 6.30pm I performed a daily ritual, flicking on the television and switching eagerly to the Channel 4 Tour coverage, each day intoxicated by the beauty of rural France. But it was immediately clear that this day had been different. The commentator, Phil Liggett, was speaking gravely: "shortly after noon news came through on the Tour radio – there had been a crash on the descent of the Col de Portet d'Aspet." It swiftly transpired that the victim was Fabio Casartelli, an Italian who had been the Olympic Road-Race Champion. A young man at a peak of fitness had been claimed by the mountains.

As the programme drew to a close I snapped the TV off and left my house to go to a meeting. The Parochial Church Council was gathering at one of the local churches. The PCC held meetings regularly and they were guaranteed to be parochial. This evening was to be slightly unusual, as they were intending to choose a new musical setting for parts of the eucharistic liturgy. The organist performed the various options and different factions argued over the merits of the *Gloria in Excelsis* and the Lord's Prayer. I tried to show some interest but my heart was not in it. I was still surrounded by that awesome stillness you experience when an ambulance has just gone by and its siren is fading into the distance. More than that, something had stirred up my determination that one day I would return to the Pyrenees.

It was not just the beauty of the French countryside which drew me each evening to the Tour coverage. If sport can be a metaphor for life, then a journey can be an even more powerful metaphor, and what better than an event which combines both? The concept of the "Journey of Life" is so overworked that it is pretty much a cliché, but nevertheless there is a truth beneath it, and that truth is the foundation for pilgrimage. In the Tour I saw a sport which was also a journey, and which on occasions could lift me to a spiritual plane, in much the same way that good music can trigger our deepest longing to transcend ourselves and clutch at the immortal. Each day Channel 4 supplied a vicarious dose of this spirituality, in its superbly presented but miserably short thirty-minute slot.

It's possible that pilgrimage had been one of the motives behind my previous, and largely disastrous, venture to the Pyrenees. If so, I had barely recognised it at the time, and it was mixed in with other elements such as an adolescent desire for freedom. As a teenager I had taken easily to hillwalking, which offered healthy exercise and required little in the way of expensive equipment. The hills promised fresh air and were an

2

enticing outlet from a childhood lived mostly in a stable and secure Midland suburbia. Gradually I pushed harder against the horizons, usually in the company of my brother Graham and various friends. It became a tradition to head out of Birmingham for a day or two after Christmas, to burn off the calories and to rededicate ourselves to our quest for meaningful adventure during the coming year. Strolling on the Long Mynd near Ludlow somebody suggested the Pyrenees. In truth we knew nothing about them - other than their geographical location – and that was part of the attraction. Everybody had heard of the Alps, which were crowded, expensive and required rope-and-ice skills which were probably beyond us.

So Douglas and I began to plan for the Pyrenees. Douglas was four years my junior, being originally a friend of my brother's, but in many respects he was the senior partner in the enterprise. Easygoing and resourceful, he was a companion who inspired confidence. A vigorous upbringing, in which his parents had taken him camping in Europe from an early age, had imbued him with a resilience and strength which would serve us well as subsequent events played themselves out.

We had been together on various hikes in Britain, and even on one abortive walking holiday in Italy. Our attempt to travel by foot from Florence to Assisi in the heat of the summer had been a withering experience. It had started well enough. Waking up on a train that was sliding along the coast of the Mediterranean I was suddenly aware that the light had a seductive clarity which I had never experienced in northern Europe. The very air seemed to breathe Puccini. After a few days absorbing the glories of the Renaissance we left the Medici beside the River Arno and struck off across Tuscany in search of St.Francis. We saw no other walkers on the entire trip, and it didn't take us long to figure out the reasons. Anticipating high temperatures we had planned to adopt the local custom and have a *siesta* every day after lunch. That should have left plenty of time in the morning and evening to make progress whilst it was cooler. But we soon found that the plan was misconceived. By 9 o'clock in the morning it was too hot to move. If you ventured out of the shade you immediately felt that you were being fried by some great and merciless radiation.

It was also difficult to find suitable places for rough camping in a landscape which was relatively heavily populated and well cultivated. I spent one night in a plastic bag under a bridge. Douglas seemed to sleep well, but I was soaked in a suncream with a fishy and oily odour to it, and not wanting to pollute my sleeping bag I shivered through to dawn. In the end we resorted to walking at night, seeking to make progress by navigating across country in the dark, and then we resorted to not walking at all. A bus whisked us the last fifty miles to Assisi with ludicrous ease. The trip ended with mixed feelings, chastened by our failure yet inspired by the cleanliness of Assisi, which seemed to retain a spirit of peace whilst functioning happily as a tourist trap.

In spite of the Italian debacle we now approached the Pyrenees with confidence. It was 1987, Margaret Thatcher was still in power, and France had just lost to New Zealand in the final of the inaugural Rugby World Cup. I was twenty-six, and two-thirds of the way through a college course in Bristol, training to be ordained as an Anglican clergyman. Douglas was an undergraduate in Scotland, wavering between physics and philosophy. I was alarmed to see that his essential kit for the forthcoming assault on the mountains included two massive books, one written by Kant and the other by Nietzsche. We had no tent. He was cheerful in his intention to not only read the books during the trip but to carry them too. This sounded fine, except that we were piling up the kit in one heap and then

4

dividing it equally between our two rucksacks, so I began to sense a flaw somewhere in the logic.

The decision about the tent was part of our overall strategy. Our basic plan was beautiful in its simplicity – to walk from the Atlantic to the Mediterranean and thus to traverse a significant chunk of the map of western Europe. We had set aside seven weeks for the task. Speed would be one factor in our success, so in theory we were desperate to keep the weight of equipment down. We also needed to keep space in the rucksacks so that we could buy food to cook on our little paraffin stove. As usual we would be seeking our own places to camp in the wilds - *"camping sauvage"* as the French call it. Anticipating little rain, at least in the central and eastern Pyrenees, we had decided that goretex bivouac sacks would suffice to protect our sleeping bags from the damp.

I studied the remainder of our kit, which had been cobbled together and improvised as cheaply as possible. The most impressive items were our ice-axes, which could serve various functions besides offering security on steep ground, but we had no crampons. There were other shortcomings. Within days I would feel the back of my neck burning as my collarless tee-shirts became a liability. The solution was to buy some bright yellow dusters in a French supermarket and tie them to the back of my jungle hat. They were surprisingly effective, and I was proud of my invention, even if they conveyed an outlandish hippie-like image. But our biggest handicap, with hindsight, was simply lack of money. As impoverished students the budget was two pounds sterling per man per day, and beyond that we each had a cushion of about fifty pounds in reserve. It would be perilously little today, and it was not much more then, even allowing for the years of inflation in between. It was enough to finance a regime of monastic self-discipline with the cooking (which was largely Douglas' department) but it would not give us much flexibility if Plan A were to go badly wrong.

The coach from Victoria took ages to clear the outskirts of London, but after that it sped across Kent and a quick ferry ride put us on French soil. Then it was endless miles of motorway, traversing the vasty fields of France, dozing fitfully through the night but mostly alive with anticipation and sensing a growing liberation in the pure size of the country and the distances involved. Within 24 hours of leaving London the dark line of the Pyrenees became visible, and a degree of trepidation crept in. They looked a bit intimidating, even at their western end where they were supposed to be lower. In fact what we could see were little more than foothills. Getting off the bus was the moment of commitment. Our return tickets were dated fifty days hence, and they were from Perpignan which was on the other side of the country. As the bus disappeared towards Spain we shouldered the rucksacks. They seemed heavy and our legs were stiff from the journey. The first few steps into the town centre felt absurd. It was an existential moment with nowhere to hide.

We were in fact in St.Jean-de-Luz, a coastal town a few miles north of the Spanish frontier at Hendaye. Our basic intention was to follow the French long distance footpath, the GR10 (*"Route de Grande Randonnee"*), which runs from Hendaye to Banyuls-sur-Mer on the Mediterranean coast. But as the ambition was to get from one sea to the other the GR10 was a means rather than an end in itself. Deviations and variations would be allowed, provided we walked every yard of the way in a continuous line. Starting at St.Jean gave us the chance to save a mile or two by moving quickly inland to pick up the footpath proper near the towering peak of La Rhune, itself on the frontier.

Although it was July it was mercifully cool. I have still got a photograph of Douglas eating a sandwich on a bench on the seawall, and he is wearing a grey woollen jumper. It matched the sky. The water in the harbour had a heavy leaden quality to it. Beyond the breakwater there was nothing between us and North America. I shuddered. I have always found the sea frightening: it is simply so large and so cold. A human in trouble upon it is a puny thing and easily doomed to an unmarked grave. At the same time the coast is a spiritual place. The land seems solid and secure beneath your feet, but as the water extends away over the horizon to an unseen vanishing point it speaks to us of infinity. On a flat coastline I am always amazed at the sheer size of the sky, and conscious of the daily rhythm of the tides. So many of the early monasteries were built on coasts – Iona and Lindisfarne to name but two. Beyond them the sea stretches away with the curvature of the earth, mysterious in its moods of grace and menace.

"We'd better get going," said Douglas. We were both introverts and there was never likely to be a lot of sparkling dialogue on our expeditions.

With lunch completed there was nothing for it: no further excuses for delay. We strode a few yards down the beach and dipped our booted feet into the battleship-grey waters of the Bay of Biscay. Then we turned round and started walking. There was a brutal simplicity about it.

For the first couple of miles we trudged inland along the banks of the Nivelle, passing a few units of light industry, and by mid-afternoon we were into the village of Ascain. The neat houses and manicured lawns looked bizarre, juxtaposed with the enterprise on which we were now engaged – young men anxious for some desperate glory. It was hard to imagine that when Wellington's army had reached this point in 1814 his Spanish allies had ransacked the village, bent on revenge for the atrocities visited on their own homeland by the Napoleonic French. The Duke had sent the Spaniards home in disgrace, weakening his forces in terms of numbers but a vital move if he was to avoid antagonising the civilian population as he advanced into France. Beyond Ascain the track climbed and we climbed with it, sweating in the humid air. That evening we made camp on the Col des Trois Fontaines as thunder rumbled in the distance. We had survived our first day and it was a relief to be moving after the months of anticipation.

The first days went well and we made rapid progress inland through Sare and Ainhoa. It was surprising how quickly we settled into the routine of the march. There is an earthy pleasure in carrying all your possessions in one rucksack; a satisfying illusion of self-sufficiency. The concerns of the day are quickly reduced to simple ones – finding a suitable place to shelter for the night, buying food, locating clean water and dealing with blisters. We began to gain height in the rolling country of the *Pyrenees Atlantiques*. Somewhere above Bidarray there was a significant moment when we looked back and could no longer see the ocean. But we were still very much in the shake-down leg of the walk, and preferred not to think too much about the distance ahead. I said as much to Douglas.

"Banyuls and a bottle of wine!" he replied. "That can be our mantra."

"I prefer to think about one yard at a time," I said. "Let's remember that every stride is one yard further away from the Atlantic and one yard nearer to the Med."

On paper, and on the map, it is barely 240 miles from one coast to the other, as the crow flies. But in the Pyrenees such a statistic is meaningless. The GR10 rarely heads straight for any distance. As often as not its bearing is dictated by the anarchic geology of these mountains, with a crazy jumble of ridges and valleys going in all directions. Moreover hardly any of it is flat, and as it climbs and descends the inevitable zig-zags virtually double the distances. As the days rolled by we became aware of further subtle cruelties. Our self-sufficient camping meant we had to buy food, and naturally this was done in the villages

8

along the way. The villages, equally naturally, tended to be in the valleys, typically two days apart. So we were forced into a pattern of lugging our fresh supplies uphill, consuming the bulk of them at altitude, and then descending with relatively light packs to repeat the process.

In the meantime we were making progress. By the fifth day we were through St.Jean-Pied-de-Port, though that night we were nearly bitten to pieces by horseflies in the pleasant little valley we had chosen for a campsite. The next day a careless mistake in navigation had us marching towards Pamplona and we wasted a couple of hours before we were back on the correct path. We were both good map-readers and navigators – provided we concentrated and didn't just leave the responsibility to the other person. Constant checking of the compass was essential. Like most people we tended to delude ourselves that we had an excellent sense of direction, as though we were drawing on some primitive and long-buried evolutionary skill, but in reality the compass was far more reliable. On one infamous occasion in the Cheviots I had led us for miles along the wire fence which marked the Scottish border. It was a foggy morning but as long as I followed the fence I knew we were heading north. At noon the sun began to break through the mist and I sensed something was horribly wrong – the sun was in front of me. All morning we'd been going south and the fence was in fact the English frontier.

In the Pyrenees it was even more vital to concentrate, as there was the potential to get seriously and dangerously lost. Our maps didn't always help. By taking the "*Serie Verte*" at a scale of 1 to 100,000 we only had to carry four of them for the entire expedition. The drawback of the small scale was, of course, the lack of local detail. It also had the effect of reducing our map progress to a snail's pace. One centimetre on the chart represented a whole kilometre on the ground, so reaching a fold in the map became a major cause for celebration.

The cool temperatures were an unexpected ally in our campaign so far. However, the camping was damp and we were conscious that in continental terms we were still only a stone's throw inland from the coast. Depressions were moving in from the Bay of Biscay. Near the Chalets d'Iraty we received a good soaking during one night. The much vaunted goretex sacks failed to provide complete protection. In theory the breathable material meant that the occupant could zip the bag completely over his head, but I for one found this claustrophobic, and even when I tried it the zip proved to be vulnerable to the rain. By morning we were both wet and had no alternative other than to break camp during a further downpour. At least the soaking road to Larrau was downhill, but being cold and wet is notoriously bad for morale.

"This rain's obviously set in for the day," I grumbled. "Let's get to the next village and find a bed-and-breakfast or something to book into for the night."

"It's a bit early in the trip to start spending money like that," Douglas responded.

"I know, but we've got to dry this kit out before we catch pneumonia or something."

"Sounds fair enough to me. But the real problem is that three-thousand-mile-wide-puddle behind us. It could just blow depressions into here for weeks. Our best bet is to get as far east as we can, as fast as we can."

Douglas was right. The weather was propelling us east towards what we imagined would be drier and warmer conditions, to an imaginary point where the influence of the Atlantic would give way to a Mediterranean climate, to a healthier region in which it would be easier to camp. After a night under a proper roof in a small *auberge* run by an elderly couple we pressed on through Logibarria and into the Gorges of Holzarte and Holhedubi. At this point we seemed to be entering a Wagnerian world of knights and dragons, with foaming torrents surging over jagged rocks. It was impressive, but I was also finding the steep valleys and lush vegetation of the western Pyrenees oppressive, at least in the prevailing dull light. It was a relief to negotiate a precarious suspension bridge without mishap and to break out into slightly more open countryside.

It was at this stage, on about the tenth day, that we made the decisive mistake. As so often happens the destiny of a great enterprise can turn on a tiny detail. We were still going strong after ten days. All the minor problems had been ironed out, and we had survived some unpleasant weather. Also we were relieved to be through the gorges. We knew that in topographical terms we had barely begun. Far tougher challenges were waiting further east. But we had reasonable grounds for confidence. Another few miles and we would even be onto the second of our four maps.

Maybe we were over-confident. It was a Friday afternoon and a weekend mentality took hold. We succumbed to temptation. It came in the form of the local delicacy, the *gateau basque*, which seemed to be some sort of egg custard concoction. There was no other food available for purchase, and we figured that the extra calories from this local produce could only help our cause. The gateau turned out to be a disappointment, and within an hour we knew we had made a grave mistake. Less than a mile up the road Douglas was hopping over a gate into the corner of a field as he was overtaken by an attack of diahorrea. I was getting the first intimations of stomach cramps. For both of us the vomiting came later that evening, as we were camped on steep wooded ground next to a twisting section of minor road.

The sickness had passed by daybreak but we felt weak. The problem was the next section of the trail. It was only a few kilometres to Station d'Arette-la-Pierre-St.Martin, but this was an out of season ski resort and it was several thousand feet above our heads. We had plenty of water but no food. There was nothing for it but to walk up the road.

It turned out to be one of those exercises that makes the walker regret having ever taken to the hills or indeed regret having been born. A savage discipline, in which the pain is overwhelming but the mind largely censors it afterwards in an act of merciful anaesthetic. There was no alternative. Behind us the road ran downhill, but it offered a retreat to nowhere; merely to the miserable hamlets where we had purchased the offending *gateau basque*. Ahead of us the asphalt wound uphill. Very few cars passed, and even in our current plight neither of us would have dreamt of asking for a lift. So we dragged ourselves upwards, grinding out the yards, each man playing whatever private mental games were necessary to get himself to the next tree or the next bend on the road. At several points we were bewildered to see human names painted onto the tarmac; surnames such as Delgado and Roche, Fignon and Millar. Then it dawned on us that this section of road must have been used in the *Tour de France*. We were stupefied: the gradient was about one in three.

In our exhaustion the worst aspect was that we could not be absolutely confident that we would find a shop open when we arrived. After all, we were heading for a ski resort and it was July. So we plodded on. Occasionally we'd exchange the odd word of encouragement, but in these situations there is never much that's useful to say, and a mistimed comment can just become a further irritation. It is sometimes said that suffering brings people together, but I suspect that the bonding happens more when the survivors are laughing about it afterwards. At the time of trial each individual is alone, lost in their private wilderness of pain.

The ski station was a bleak place. There was no snow and the empty chairlifts creaked as they swung in the wind. It had the same ghost-town atmosphere as a British seaside resort out of season. But mercifully there was a shop open, a little supermarket no less. We threw off our rucksacks at the door, gagging for energy. On our first raid we bought two large tubs of yoghurt and a bag of sugar. Outside, with the sun glaring off the rocks, the sugar was poured feverishly into the yoghurt, given a quick stir, and wolfed down. Almost immediately strength began to return. A few more minutes and we were able to re-enter the premises and make some more sensible purchases, as we began to think rationally about the route ahead.

After a couple of hours rest we were ready to move on. We were aware that we had reached a significant point on the journey. For the first time we seemed to have risen above the tree line. At this higher altitude the light was brighter, and we sensed a change in the geology as we strolled through boulders, relieved to be on a limestone plateau where the path was virtually flat. There was vegetation around, but the landscape had assumed an almost lunar quality in our perception. To our right the Pic d'Anie rose to 8000 feet. The character of the country was changing as we were leaving the Atlantic end of the range and entering the higher and more arid central Pyrenees.

That afternoon we rejoiced that we were now onto the second of our four maps: it seemed to compensate a little for the trials of the preceding twenty four hours. We were aided by the fact that the first map, "Pau-Bayonne", overlapped with "Pau-Bagneres-de-Luchon" by a good few miles on their common edge, but we weren't complaining. However, even as the topography was changing the gateau basque incident had been a watershed too, and its significance was greater for the eventual fate of the expedition. Steaming downhill to Lescun on that bright Sunday morning it was easy to believe that all was well, but in truth the food poisoning had weakened me. In those days I was a thin man, with little fat in reserve. Douglas seemed to have a more robust constitution: his strength was rapidly restored whilst mine ebbed away.

Over the next few days I argued for a change of tactics. Surely it was best to use some of our reserve money to lie up for a day or two in decent accommodation, get the last germs from the *gateau basque* misadventure out of our systems, and then continue refreshed? At the cost of a few pounds and a couple of days the odds on our eventual success would be restored. Douglas, a man of iron self-discipline, argued for the opposite: he was reluctant to buy even a bar of chocolate in France if it was more expensive than its equivalent in England, and he felt that any softening of our regime could undermine the entire effort. In his opinion we had made a cracking good start to the project; now was the time to keep up the momentum. Who is to say which of us was right? In our own terms both of us were, and it was proved when we reached a point where Douglas could go on and I could not.

In the meantime we were walking. Beyond Etsaut we came to the spectacular Fort du Portalet. Instead of ascending to the Col du Somport on the frontier we beamed off to the left, along the dizzying *Chemin de la Mature*, dutifully pausing to read a noticeboard warning us about bears in the National Park. We entered the Park higher up the valley, and beyond the jagged pinnacle of Pic-du-Midi-d'Ossau we negotiated a dangerously narrow section of track as we skirted the Pic-de-la-Sagette. The path was cut into the cliff face with a low ceiling of rock overhanging it in an irregular fashion. A collision between the top of a rucksack and the rock itself might have been enough to send an unwary walker spinning off the path and over the edge. A token guardrail, set barely above knee-height, would have served little purpose other than to invert the victim in midair and turn his final fall into a spectacular dive. The poor man would have gone into the abyss screaming like a Stuka.

In my exhaustion it probably seemed worse than it truly was. Lunch was a good-humoured joke as we discovered that the bread we had purchased that morning needed to be toasted: eaten cold it was foul and unpalatable. I was still holding my own, more or less, on level ground or going downhill, but the slightest incline meant that my performance tailed off dramatically. Later that afternoon I sat on a boulder, eating an apple as I tried to force some energy into my system, fighting back hot tears of anger and frustration as Douglas steamed on effortlessly towards the next pass. My emotions were not directed towards him as much as to myself – an infantile raging at my own impotence.

At Station-de-Gourette we assembled a decent picnic and ate it sitting on a grassy knoll a few feet above the road. To our right a signpost pointed to the Col d'Aubisque, which ranks alongside the Tourmalet as one of the truly classic passes used regularly over the years in the *Tour de France*. In pleasant sunshine, digesting our lunch, all seemed fine again. It was easy to be positive about pressing on. Our route was not, in fact, over the Aubisque, because the GR10 saved a couple of miles by cutting across the hillside in a series of steep zigzags. Heaving my rucksack up the hill I was soon dreaming of food again. My culinary fantasies were not ambitious ones. I was simply telling myself what I was going to do, if and when I got back to England. It all centred on a ham salad, (something light and easily digestible), with plenty of water in the cucumber and tomatoes. Besides lettuce there would be cottage cheese, and slices of brown bread, fresh and wholesome. Potato crisps, with plenty of salt, were essential, and all this would be washed down with white wine, cold and sweet. After that I would indulge in desserts, an area where my imagination could really run riot. And then I dreamt I would lie down in the shade of a garden, digesting my meal at leisure whilst gorging on coffee and chocolates.

The weight of my rucksack and the soreness of my feet brought me back to reality. In truth I was starving: that was the diagnosis I came to with hindsight. I had hit the barrier which marathon runners refer to as "the Wall". I was also learning that the male instinct of attraction towards women, which so many people assume to be an essential in life, is really a trivial thing compared to the desire for food. To be truly hungry, as opposed to experiencing slight discomfort because one has skipped a meal, is an awful prospect. Since the sickness incident I had simply not been consuming enough carbohydrate for the task in hand. Carrying a rucksack up and down mountains is seriously heavy work. Nor was I eating enough protein: in spite of all the exercise my muscles, far from growing larger, were wasting away as my body consumed them in its relentless quest for energy.

On the face of it the problem had a simple solution – eat more food. But it was not so straightforward. We were cooking rice and pasta, but having been ill once I never really had the appetite to consume large volumes of these, whereas Douglas seemed to ingest them fairly comfortably. Constant exercise in a hot climate doesn't necessarily confer a healthy appetite. No doubt dehydration plays a part. Without sufficient water the body's efficiency tails off sharply, and so does its ability to digest food and to convert it into energy. Appetite is easily satisfied with a few sweet snacks rather than by the bulky carbohydrates which are really required. Again one might think it would be easy to solve this problem – just drink more water – but unfortunately it's not so simple. A dehydrated body can't cope with a large intake of liquid. It needs the correct balance of salts and minerals to be restored before it can absorb further fluids happily.

So a series of vicious circles were operating: fatigue, hunger, heat and dehydration were reinforcing each other. My memories of the next few days are patchy, as we struggled over several ridges and descended through further poor weather to emerge above the rooftops and building-cranes of Cauterets. Repeatedly we had difficulties getting out of towns: it was easy enough to find your way into them but harder to pick up the correct footpath on the way out. Beyond Luz-St.Sauveur a stream of weekend traffic was heading up to Bareges and the Col du Tourmalet. Saloon cars with families in them swept past like tanks. We, the poor bloody infantry, trudged along in their exhaust fumes until our route struck out across country and towards further ridges.

And so the ordeal went on. Douglas remained cheerful and he seemed to be strong. He sought to encourage me. "Remember the words of Nietzsche," he intoned. "Whatever does not kill a man strengthens him."

"Thanks pal," I grunted. We were struggling to remain positive and to remain friends. But countless expeditions to the Antarctic and elsewhere have demonstrated that a two-man team makes for poor dynamics. Almost inevitably the protagonists will move at different speeds. One will end up angry and frustrated because he's being held back, whilst the other will be angry and frustrated because he's being left behind. In our case my rucksack was starting to assume an impossible weight. To put it on was exhausting, and to carry it ten paces uphill was becoming a Herculean endeavour. Somewhere around the Vallee d'Aure and the Vallee du Louron it became obvious that I wasn't going to make it to the Mediterranean, and indeed was struggling to make progress at all. It was not a case of making a decision as much as simply acknowledging a reality. One night I crawled from my sleeping bag to vomit again, in a painful dehydrated sort of way. The next morning I buried my hiking boots, scraping at the topsoil with my ice-axe. From now on my training shoes would suffice. I was adamant that I would never go near another mountain again. When I got home I would give the axe away to my brother.

So we agreed to abandon the march at Bagneres-de-Luchon and to use the railhead there to flee the mountains. Briefly we discussed the possibility of splitting up: I could return to England whilst Douglas continued alone to the Mediterranean. This idea was quickly discounted. We felt it was too dangerous for one man to travel alone in these mountains – an ironic perception considering that years later I would be attempting to do precisely that. There were also practical issues. Our coach tickets were dated several weeks hence and were from Perpignan, and we were not at all sure that our remaining money would be enough to change the tickets or buy new ones. We had embarked on this expedition together: all in all it looked much better to stick together.

Our retreat from the Pyrenees was ignominious and painful. Having made the decision we settled down to doze through the warmth of the afternoon. For the first time on our trip we had the perfect excuse to be lazy. I was wary of the sunlight, having always burned easily, and made sure I was well covered by my tracksuit. Up here, above Superbagneres, we were still over 6000 feet, and the thinner atmosphere gave us less protection against the sun's rays. But I was not careful enough. As I slept the legs of my trousers rode up a few inches, and the sensitive skin of my ankles was exposed to the radiation.

Descending to Bagneres the next morning I was troubled by soreness in my ankles, and to a lesser extent across my stomach, which had also been inadvertently exposed. Later, in the town and wearing no socks, I glanced down and noticed a dirty yellow thing on the top of my foot just above the tongue of my training shoe. For half a second I assumed that it must be some dog's mess that I'd trodden in, then a sickening realisation kicked in and I saw the blisters for what they were. The largest was a good half inch across; an ugly yellow hemisphere sitting on the surface of my ankle – on the surface of me.

It was the beginning of an anxious time. The next day I hobbled onto the train and it whisked us down to Bordeaux, where we hoped to pick up a bus reversing the route which had brought us out to south-west France. There should have been a coach every evening, heading back to London Victoria, but we had no tickets and for all we knew there would be no empty seats available. Meanwhile our calculations suggested we could scrape together just enough cash for the journey, but it would be a close-run thing. We spent the afternoon in the café at the railway station, buying only bread rolls and glasses of water, as the temperature on the station's digital thermometer climbed to the mid-thirties centigrade. Of course if we could not get on the bus that evening then we would have to eat something and spend the night somewhere, and then we would have less money for tickets tomorrow.......and so on. The heat was appalling and I felt frightened. The blisters on my ankles were not particularly painful, provided I sat still with my feet up, but the real damage was in my mind.

In his 1952 book Maurice Herzog gave a classic account of the struggle to ascend the Himalayan giant Annapurna. It was the highest peak conquered up until then, and Herzog had led the French expedition which had achieved it. The book ends with an unforgettable description. Returning from the mountain the team travel by train across northern India, and as they travel the expedition doctor progressively amputates Herzog's frostbitten fingers and toes. As the train stops at each station the doors are opened and the newly dismembered digits are swept out onto the platform with a broom. Herzog's indomitable spirit shines through, and his book closes with the line "there are other Annapurnas in the lives of men". The author managed to climb again, and was elected mayor of Chamonix. But I was no Maurice Herzog, and as I sat sweating

19

through that suffocating afternoon in Bordeaux my spirit was subdued by the dangerous combination of inactivity and sickly fear. I was still only 26 and felt that skin cancer was one Annapurna that I did not particularly need.

Eventually the bus drew up in the square outside. Mercifully there were a couple of empty seats and we had enough money to secure the tickets. Once on the move the endless miles of French motorway held nothing of the anticipation or excitement of the outward journey. By the time we reached Dover my stomach problems were being compounded by a fresh dose of food poisoning, easily traced to a plate of sausages I had consumed at a service station somewhere in the heart of France. Or maybe the sausages had provided a further lease of life for the germs originally absorbed from the *gateau basque*? Either way the retreat had degenerated into a rout.

My burns were sufficiently serious to warrant three or four outpatient visits to the Birmingham Accident Hospital. For a week or two I rested with my feet up, hobbled around as my gastric problems were gradually overcome, and healed up quickly enough to captain my college's football team through the ensuing winter.

Meanwhile the old mental anaesthetic was doing its work too. I reneged on the promise to myself to give away the ice-axe. Douglas and I were still firm friends, and neither of us was satisfied about the way our trip had ended. We had set out to do a job and we had left it unfinished. More than that there was a lingering suspicion that without the fatal egg custard we might well have succeeded anyway. The last ten days of our walk had been dreadful, and for me at least they had been dominated by suffering and defeat, but in spite of that we had actually walked half way across France in just twenty days. There was no reason to suppose we couldn't do the second half in the same time. Some decent planning, better equipment and a bit more money should all help to tip the scales in our favour. Within a few months the plan was settled. The following year, 1988, we would return to Bagneres-de-Luchon, to the very spot where we had boarded the train, and we would walk to the Mediterranean.

By the following summer I had completed my theological studies and been ordained as an Anglican deacon, going to serve in a large parish covering housing estates on the eastern edge of Birmingham. The vicar, my new boss, drove me and my large red and blue rucksack to the railway station next to the National Exhibition Centre, and he wished me well for my three weeks of vacation. He was a good man who had already suffered one heart attack: I sensed that he would have loved to have been young and fit again and to be heading for France himself.

I had arranged with Douglas that we would meet in London, where my brother Graham was living and working. We hadn't seen each other for months, and both of us had been assembling equipment between our various exams.

"I've got that tent I was thinking of buying," Douglas announced sheepishly. "But you're going to hate the colour."

He was as good as his word. The tent was tiny, and it was bright yellow and magenta pink. "For goodness sake," I blurted out, "we're supposed to be serious walkers! Anyone who sees us with that thing will think we're off to some gay carnival or other".

"It's not that bad," Douglas retorted. "It was the lightest one I could find, and the colours are in fashion this year. Besides, it looks sort of, well, French."

"It looks absolutely hideous."

"Don't worry. It's so small nobody will see it from any distance in the mountains."

As usual Douglas was right. In spite of the ghastly colours his tent actually obeyed one of the basic rules of camouflage - the colour scheme broke up the familiar shape of the object. In

21

practice it was a bit cramped, but it proved to be an asset as it provided a measure of psychological security at night. As it turned out we encountered little rain on this, the eastern half of the journey, and the tent was more valuable as a shade against the sun. Besides, I could hardly complain too vigorously about the tent when my contribution to the fashion parade was a pair of bright orange cotton trousers. I had picked these up in India for a few rupees several years before, and they proved to be ideal in the Mediterranean climate – light, baggy and surprisingly tough they gave total protection against my deadly foe, the sun, whilst also allowing sweat to evaporate easily.

There was further good news. Douglas had completed his studies in philosophy and was now training to become a dentist. This time Kant and Nietzsche would not be on the team.

The coach tickets were simpler too - a straight return to and from Perpignan. From there it was a train to Toulouse, a quick change and we were back in Bagneres-de-Luchon. As an added boost for morale we mused on the fact that this year we were starting at an altitude of a couple of thousand feet. From here to the sea must be, by definition, more downhill than up. We set off and by the second day we were onto the third of our four maps. Everything seemed to be on our side for once.

In the end we reached the Mediterranean in seventeen days. Compared to the previous year it was an easy holiday, almost idyllic. Hardened by experience and bolstered by better gear and more cash we simply sped across the countryside. The strange thing is, I can hardly remember it at all. The previous summer had degenerated into a hellish ordeal. Yet as I looked back on our overall achievement in subsequent years my most vivid memories, and indeed my greatest nostalgia, were for the first year of our expedition.

I have often wondered what that tells us about the human psyche, or about the human experience of living. Obviously my mental anaesthetic had been at work, dulling the worst of the agony from that first year and telling me that it could not really have been that bad after all. But there was a second factor at play. The pleasant walking of the second year had not been anaesthetised: it had simply not registered. It was agony and relief that were etched into the soul: simple pleasure had left little impression.

I have some recollections of course. Looking up at the imposing bulk of Mt.Valier in blazing sunshine. Crossing a couple of patches of snow in an area of upland tarns as we skirted around the northern edge of Andorra; the only time in either year that the ice-axes were used for anything approaching their proper purpose. Onto the fourth and final map and I remember pleasant easy strolling near Mt.Canigou, and struggling to sleep properly in Arles-sur-Tech because it was too hot. Approaching the coast we ate a picnic within sight of the frontier toll-booths on the motorway at the Col du Perthus. It wasn't a pleasant view, but frontiers have always fascinated me. The muted thunder of the traffic was incessant, as thousands of cars and trucks poured down into Spain and a seemingly identical number of vehicles toiled up the opposite carriageway towards France. I felt that I was observing some bizarre dynamic equilibrium, as though a law of nature was operating to prevent the Iberian peninsula becoming too heavy and tipping into the ocean. Where were these countless individuals going? Why were they so desperate to get there? A multitude was on the move, but I was not sure I could detect a pilgrimage in the noise and fumes. It was a relief when we could pack up from our lunch and resume the walk, and the thunder faded into a distant hum behind us.

Eventually we camped on a ridge which ran along a peninsula, jutting out into the Mediterranean. We were still quite high, and Perpignan was again visible, this time in the distance to the north. It was our last night on the GR10. I sat outside the tent, watching a cow a few feet away as it chewed contentedly on the grass. Behind the cow was a low fence, and beyond the fence was Spain - the frontier again. The next day we followed the ridge to a simple road which wound downhill into Banyuls-sur-Mer. Beyond Banyuls I could see nothing that wasn't blue. We had crossed from one sea to the other in 37 days of walking. The exact distance was impossible to judge, but we reckoned we had covered 500 miles. It must have been the best part of a million strides each. We tried to calculate the total ascents involved from our four maps. The result suggested we had climbed and descended Everest, from sea-level, four times over. But it was a muted triumph. After all, we had originally set out to do it in one go, and we had failed miserably in that purpose. I knew deep down that one day I would have to return and prove to myself that I could have done it.

Years slipped by and the day never came. A series of exhausting jobs took me from the Diocese of Birmingham, via Guildford, to Carlisle, and from there I went to work in Scandinavia. This brought an unexpected delight, in that the Eurosport TV channel gave me day-long access to the mountain stages of the *Tour de France*. Each year, as the race entered the Pyrenees, I would contrive a couple of days off work. Those same four maps would be brought out and I would trace the cyclists' progress, sometimes identifying each twist and bend on the road. Again I was plugging in vicariously to the spirituality of the journey, seeking to experience the pilgrimage which is ostensibly about travelling across a landscape but which is, in reality, a discovery of the self and of the soul.

At last in 2003 I thought I could see a chance to return. Douglas was now a successful dentist and had been married for several years. So had my brother. So had everyone else. This time I would be going alone, but in some respects that suited my purpose. The concept of pilgrimage was one motivation, and so was curiosity about the monastic life. My love of history had overflowed into extensive reading about the Peninsular War of 1808-1814, a conflict which had eventually boiled over the western Pyrenees into France itself. I was equally interested in the Cathar heresy and the Albigensian Crusade which had so affected Languedoc and Roussillon at the eastern end of the range. And there were other attractions, of which the beauty of the mountains and the refreshing pleasure of simply walking were the most obvious.

All these were factors. But deep down the strongest pull came from the feeling of unfinished business. There was a score to settle. That's probably not a good reason for doing anything, and it is certainly a dangerous motive for venturing into the mountains. But in so many ways we are all the prisoners of history. I also knew that when I had gone to the Pyrenees with Douglas I had been a young man. Now in my forty-third year of existence on the planet I was no longer young. In fact I was an old-fashioned person with traditional values, doing a job which virtually defined me as an anachronism. One might think in terms of a mid-life crisis, though in my perception there was no such thing: merely a continuation of the same crisis of living with which I had been preoccupied for the last four decades. It is so easy to let life slip away, consumed with regrets about the past or preoccupied with fears for the future. It can be so difficult to simply be alive now; to know the sacrament of the present moment; unique and unrepeatable in its gift to us. And so here I was, heading once more for France, *a la recherché du temps perdu*.

June 20th 2003 was a Friday. At Stansted airport I checked in and handed over my large green rucksack. I experienced that strange sensation you always get when you have checked in your luggage - relief at being liberated from the weight of it combined with curiosity about whether you will ever see the stuff again. Once through the security check and into the Departures area I headed into the toilets for a cold wash. With water dripping from my face I stared into the mirror for a long minute, hoping to detect strength and courage in my own eyes. Then I saw my features soften as a wild grin spread slowly across my face. It was time for the Yesterday Man to walk again.

Chapter 2.

Dinner with Doctor Parrot.

For the time being I was not walking anywhere. I was lying on my bed in a hotel in St.Jean-de-Luz, staring at the ceiling. It was the middle of the afternoon, and I was luxuriating in the fact that whilst there was a telephone next to the bed I knew it would never ring. None of my friends or enemies knew exactly where I was. I had no mobile 'phone and I was beyond the range of electronic mail. It felt beautiful.

Abraham Lincoln once said that people are more or less as happy as they decide they are going to be. Months previously I had resolved that this was going to be a happy day. My first full day in France: a day of rest to recover from the flights: a day to slow down mentally as I pottered around the town buying up some food and a few final items of kit. I understood Lincoln's wisdom to mean that happiness has little to do with circumstances, and I was inclined to agree with him. I was convinced that a person facing a firing squad could be perfectly happy, if he genuinely believed it was the correct thing to be doing. Conversely a man sleeping with the most beautiful actress in Hollywood could know himself to be a wretched thing, if the relationship was somehow not right. Of course I could not claim to have had either of these experiences myself, so my philosophy may well have been just idle speculation. In my situation there was every likelihood that suffering lay ahead – walking the entire length of a major mountain range was unlikely to be a painless exercise – but for the moment I was in a state of blissful anticipation. The next few weeks would reveal whether it was genuine hope or merely a fool's paradise. In *"The Prophet"* Kahlil Gibran says that the hope of heaven is heaven itself. (He also says that the fear of hell is hell itself, but for the moment I was choosing to focus on the positive half of his equation).

I rolled onto one side, meditating on the details of my journey out to south-west France. The flight from Stansted had been remarkably fast, and sitting next to a window on the starboard side I was treated to some phenomenal views. The sky was totally cloudless, and at 37,000 feet I felt vulnerable to the sun's radiation and wished that I had had the foresight to grab a seat on the shaded port side of the aircraft. Approaching Bayonne the pilot announced that the temperature was 34 degrees centigrade. I had to translate this into fahrenheit to make it meaningful, and my mental maths told me it was about 93 degrees. I fumbled for my British passport, for I was intending to enter France using one of my real identities.

As soon as I stepped off the plane the heat hit me, and it was appalling. Having reclaimed my rucksack I found a taxi and was soon shooting down the motorway towards St.Jean-de-Luz. The taxi driver was friendly and talkative, switching easily to English as my rusty French failed me. I felt reassured: in the aftermath of the second Iraq War I had been unsure what sort of attitude I would encounter in France as a representative of perfidious Albion.

The Hotel Ohartzia was located in a narrow street only fifty metres from the seafront. It was a pleasant place but didn't serve evening meals, so once I had freshened up I slipped out and headed into a restaurant around the corner. I was struggling to come to terms with the currency in the Euro zone, but I found that 35 euros was enough to secure a three-course feast consisting of red peppers stuffed with cod (a local Basque speciality), followed by veal kidneys and a vanilla dessert. I ate all of this in an atmosphere of heat and sweat, but there was nothing much anyone could do about that. I was used to the high cost of living in Scandinavia, and reckoned that my meal was pretty good value by comparison.

St.Jean-de-Luz was crowded and noisy, and it was obvious that some kind of carnival was in progress. Whilst I had been eating several brass bands had passed nearby, their music contributing to a cheerful and anarchic cacophony. After dinner I wandered around the streets. Most of the local population seemed to be wearing black tee-shirts with red scarves or neckerchiefs, and several black dogs went past, also decked out in red collars and scarves. A fair was operating and children played games whilst several massive fireworks went up and the town centre shuddered with the explosions. I made a few enquiries and established that the black-and-red colours represented the town, as opposed to anything else. Apparently I had wandered into the middle of a four-day fiesta which marked the summer solstice and led up to the Feast of John the Baptist on June 25th.

By now I was tired, and I retreated to the relative calm of my hotel room. The television had a small selection of channels, one of which was showing France playing a tedious football match against Japan in some meaningless tournament. I flicked over to another channel, which appeared to be a film set during the Second World War. I strained to get my ear tuned to the French dialogue, and after a few minutes I had fathomed that the Resistance leader Jean Moulin was about to be captured by the Gestapo. Actually had I surmised this, in part, from the fact that he was looking miserable and was trying to eat his diary. The film was drawing to a close, and the final scene had the camera closing in on the dead face of Moulin, now at peace and lying in a pile of straw on the floor of a railway truck next to a pair of jackboots. A subtitle explained that he had succumbed to his injuries whilst being transported to Germany. In the background the soundtrack played a dirge which, it

29

transpired, was "the Song of the Partisans." Reading the local newspaper at breakfast the following morning I learned that Moulin had been arrested in Caluire on 21st June 1943. It was the sixtieth anniversary of this dismal event - hence the screening of the film.

With Moulin gone there was nothing else worth watching, and I had dozed off in spite of the noise outside in the town. I woke in the early hours of Saturday morning, troubled by a disturbing dream in which I was back in school and about to sit an examination without having done any studying or revision. In fact I suffered from these anxiety-inducing dreams fairly regularly and this was a typical example. Other variations would be the dream in which I was about to represent the school at sport and had forgotten my kit, or the one in which I was going to a meeting and failing to reach the correct place at the appointed time. Invariably the harder I strove in my dream to correct the situation the worse my predicament became.

The return of daylight had made me a lot more positive. I had enjoyed a substantial continental breakfast, which was served in the open air in a large and secluded garden behind the hotel. After this I had set out to explore the town. St.Jean-de-Luz means "Saint John of the Marshes," with the John in question being John the Baptist as opposed to John the Evangelist. In Basque the place is called Donibane Lohizune, and its destiny has always been tied to the sea. Indeed the Basques have a proud history as resourceful seafarers, claiming to have discovered Newfoundland a hundred years before Columbus reached the Americas. Whale and cod were their main targets in those days, but during the 17th century English and Dutch whalers gradually drove the Basques out of their Arctic ports. The Basques responded by devising a method for boiling down blubber at sea, in effect inventing the first factory ships. However, they suffered a further blow during the 18th century with the Treaty of Utrecht and the loss of their cod-fishing waters off Newfoundland. Increasingly Basque skippers turned to piracy, and when they resumed fishing in the 19th century it was more for tuna.

Meanwhile the Basques had endured their share of problems on land too. St.Jean-de-Luz suffered the typical fate of border settlements the world over, with countless invasions. Most of these were Spanish incursions, and the one in 1558 resulted in a serious fire which destroyed most of the town. It was both symbolic and appropriate that when France and Spain signed the Treaty of the Pyrenees they did so here in St.Jean. The Treaty was negotiated, on the French side, by Cardinal Mazarin, and agreement was achieved in November 1659, with most of the 124 clauses being about the ceding of territory by one side or the other to tidy up the line of the frontier.

The Treaty included the ceding of Roussillon by Spain to France, but it left one or two anomalies. The most curious is probably the Spanish enclave of Llivia, just to the east of Andorra. It is part of the Cerdagne, a largely flat area measuring sixteen miles by four and located at an altitude of over a thousand metres. Under the terms of the Treaty Spain ceded the villages of the Cerdagne, all thirty-three of them, to France. However Llivia was classed as a town, so it remained part of Spain and does so to this day. The enclave, which is only a couple of miles across, is difficult to find, owing to the refusal of the French authorities to mention it on any roadsigns. Maybe it is surprising that the negotiations of 1659 did not produce more bones of contention. As it was the discussions were fraught enough, and the complexity of the Pyrenean topography and the crudity of the maps available did not make the task any easier. At one point in the discussions an official complained that the mountains were not as straight as their depiction on the maps.

St.Jean-de-Luz was chosen for the signing, and for the marriage between Louis XIV and the Infanta of Castile, the

Austrian princess Marie-Theresa. With a population of 12,000 the town was at the peak of its prosperity as a maritime centre. The seafaring profits had been transformed into large houses for the merchants and shipowners, and it was in one of these that Louis XIV stayed when he entered the town in triumph on 8th May 1660. In fact this building, now called the "Maison Louis XIV" had been built for the Lohobiague family in 1635. I paid a few euros to wander around it and saw some good examples of period furniture. The wedding was not scheduled until 9th June, but in the meantime the Sun King had to sign the treaty with Philip IV. At some point Marie-Therese also arrived and lodged in the Italian-style "Maison de l'Infante" which is little more than a stone's throw away from Louis' lodgings.

Of course the marriage was arranged as a matter of political convenience, but oddly enough the couple seem to have fallen in love too. The Sun King was still only twenty years old. The wedding took place in the Church of John the Baptist on the Rue Gambetta, which is now a pedestrian precinct and just down the street from where I was staying on the Rue Garat. Apparently it is the largest French Basque church, and its tiers of dark oak galleries give an extraordinary impression of height. I estimated that the highest gallery was about fifty feet up, and the massive nave roof added to the effect. On 9th June 1660 even this imposing building was too small for the hordes of dignitaries who turned up, and unseemly conflicts over protocol had to be resolved before the ceremony could proceed. Eventually Mass was celebrated by the Bishop of Bayonne, Jean d'Olce d'Iholdy, and the happy couple left the church through a door which was subsequently sealed up. This door is still clearly visible from the street, about twenty metres to the right of the existing entrance. The wedding had certainly been an extravagant occasion: Cardinal Mazarin alone had presented the new queen with a gold dinner service, a pair of sumptuous carriages and a quantity of pearls and diamonds.

A morning of wandering around as a tourist, interspersed with historical research and shopping, had left me feeling hungry again. I found a small restaurant and lunched on squid, before summoning my courage and ordering a dessert of *gateau basque*. I had decided that I needed to do this as a sort of exorcism ritual. Indeed, if I didn't do it I would be spending the rest of my life prejudiced against this dish. My memory from the 1980's was of a kind of egg custard dessert, but the version I now received was more in the form of an apple and almond flan, and it tasted good. Nevertheless, I ate it nervously, and having finished my meal I strolled aimlessly in the fresh air and sunshine, waiting to see whether I would be overtaken by vomiting. Happily there was no problem at all, and I figured that I had laid a ghost to rest. I was now back outside the Maison de l'Infante, which is itself a rather sickly pink colour, and I took a few photos of the fishing boats tied up in the harbour with the summit of La Rhune prominent in the background. Across the harbour lay the suburb of Ciboure, and on the quayside I could make out a distinctive Flemish-style house which had been the birthplace of the composer Maurice Ravel. I was familiar with his "*Bolero*," and I hummed this gently to myself as I wandered back towards my hotel, flushed by my triumph over the dreaded *gateau basque*.

So here I was, back in my room and being lazy. As I idled away the afternoon lying on the bed my mind wandered back to my dream of the previous night, laden with its anxieties from my schooldays. If the fear of hell is hell itself I had had plenty of experience of the sensation, at least during my first years of secondary education in Birmingham.

The school I attended had academic standards which were not high so much as stratospheric. In most schools a pupil who went to university was regarded as a notable success. In this one, merely going to university meant you were a failure. You were expected to go to Oxford or Cambridge, and preferably with an entrance award. These awards, called "Scholarships" or "Exhibitions", were pretty much tokens in financial terms by the 1970's, but they were greatly coveted as a matter of honour for the school. Winning an award at an Oxbridge College meant that your name would be inscribed in gold leaf on the walls outside the school hall. This hall, the so-called "Big School", doubled as an examination room during the clammy months of the summer term when tension hung heavily in the air and fear stalked the corridors.

To get into the school in the first place was difficult enough. At the age of eleven you had to endure a double round of entrance examinations. I still retain vague memories of the experience. Coming from a reasonably comfortable little junior school this new place seemed enormous. The corridors were long and cold and reeked of polish. The other candidates, of whom there were hundreds, appeared confident and all seemed to know each other. Indeed, many of them did, having spent years together in private preparatory schools training for this very ordeal. Each was carrying a burden which is particularly cruel for a child – that of a great potential. The classrooms in which we took the various tests were bare and bleak. Half way through one of the papers I looked at the large clock, ticking away high up on the wall above my desk. It was one of those significant moments in life, when you know things have changed irrevocably and can never be the same again, and you are powerless to do anything about it.

In many respects I had enjoyed a sheltered childhood, in Liverpool and Birmingham, and notwithstanding the normal fights in school playgrounds my education had been in places which were basically warm and friendly. But for a few years the suspicion had been growing in the back of my mind that the adults were not telling us the whole truth – the suspicion that life in this world is really a pile of excrement and that only the strong survive and prosper. And now, staring at that clock and feeling abandoned in this hostile environment, my suspicions were confirmed.

Somehow I passed the entrance exams and thus gained access to several years of pain, which is not to say that I would have been any happier anywhere else. The school was single sex, of course, and whilst technically financed by "direct grant" from the government it was to all intents and purposes a fee-paying public school, albeit one with only day-pupils and no boarders. The atmosphere was designed to intimidate, and some of the staff seemed to have little purpose or pleasure in life other than to terrify the wretches in their charge. Pressure pervaded everything, and at the age of twelve I was doing three hours of homework per night just to survive. This was the place which had educated Tolkien and produced Field Marshal Slim of Burma fame, as well as the chess grandmaster Tony Miles and other luminaries such as Enoch Powell and the comedian Bill Oddie.

To be fair most of the teachers softened into something more akin to humanity as one advanced up the school. Once I reached the Sixth-Form and could concentrate on subjects I instinctively understood I really began to enjoy it, and at this level the education was excellent. Standards of achievement were maintained and raised not only by the staff, many of whom were superb teachers, but also by the spirit of competition amongst the pupils. Of course some of the latter were frighteningly intelligent. Every year there were chess competitions, one of which was a knockout for a trophy named after someone called Pugh. One year I reached the quarter-finals of this Pugh Cup – which was inevitably known as the "Puke Up". At that stage I was demolished by an opponent called Borcherds, who was already some sort of Midlands champion. The next time I saw him was on television, decades later. Now a Professor of Mathematics in the United States he had been awarded the Fields Medal, which is more or less the mathematical equivalent of a Nobel Prize. It made me feel a little better about my defeat in the Puke Up.

Whilst the school had incredibly high standards and expectations it was not academic to the exclusion of all else. On the contrary there was a vast range of other activities on offer, many of them making use of some excellent sporting facilities. Rugby was compulsory for the first few years and I took to this new game with relish. My parents had come from working-class backgrounds in South Wales, and arguably I had inherited some of the depression which stemmed from centuries of domination by the English. In the valleys of the coalfield life was easily characterised by drizzle and dominated by cheerless nonconformist chapels. However, if the Welsh national psyche was predominantly one of doom and gloom there was one arena where this patently did not apply: on the rugby pitch. This was a golden era and stars such as Gareth Edwards and Barry John, who were born in villages just a few miles from my mother's, had contributed massively to the British Lions team which had at last defeated the mighty All Blacks in a series out in New Zealand. I found I had some aptitude for the game, and more importantly had the imagination to use it, but physically I was a late developer and never had the weight or bulk to truly excel. I eventually represented the school ninety times at the various age-levels, playing as a lightweight half-back, but only appeared twice for the First Fifteen.

I also joined the Army section of the Combined Cadet Force, which was definitely the best decision I made in the place. I liked the self-discipline and the camaraderie, and there were plenty of comic and absurd moments. We dressed in uniforms which were always too large or too small and which had been recycled after several years wear in the regular army – I recall that one of my friends was issued with a khaki pullover that still had a bullet-hole in the chest. There was plenty of drill on

36

the paradeground whilst on the sports pitches we practised outdated infantry tactics with ageing weapons. Typically this meant "section attacks": half a dozen people weighed down with Lee-Enfield bolt-action rifles running across open ground, covered by a Bren gun which was represented by somebody swinging a football rattle. I was not the only person left bemused by the philosophy and tactics. We were supposed to be training to defend our country, which would in practice mean trying to halt the twenty thousand Soviet tanks reckoned to be in East Germany, so it was difficult to see how this particular training was going to be helpful.

Initially I had been attracted to the Cadet Force by the prospect of adventure training. Yet I also found the military side of the experience stirred a terrible nostalgia in me, a harking back to a time when Britain had been Great and had been responsible for an Empire, to a time when the Nazi enemy had been easily defined and the cause undeniably just, and to a time when there had been a broader basic concensus in society about values, standards, decency and so on.

But in reality these things were eroding fast, of course. Besides the backdrop of the Cold War the Birmingham of the 1970's had a poisonous foreground of class struggle, much of it focussed on the Longbridge car plant. Personally I was proud of the fact that my parents' generation had put paid to Hitler, but winters of discontent and the power of the Trades Unions convinced some of my schoolmates that the wrong side had won the Second World War. The city rumbled with racial tensions, and to top it all off came the IRA pub bombings. A public school teaching Latin and set in leafy parkland a couple of miles from the city centre made for a bizarre island on which to be marooned.

I was at the school for seven years and one term. By the time I left I had piled up nine O-levels and four A-levels, all at Grade A, and I was half-way to being burned out. I sometimes wonder what happened to my contemporaries. Roughly one hundred of us had been fed into the machine at the age of eleven: of those forty went to Oxbridge. It was the highest such percentage for any school in the country that year. Our names joined the ranks of gold leaf on the boards outside Big School, many of them basket-cases doomed to be forever successful. I went back once to see my own name, newly inscribed. It was a strange sensation, standing outside the examination hall where I had seen so many people filling their pants with fear. It was like reading your own name on a war memorial.

Thinking about my schooldays was an unnerving experience as it transported me back thirty years. But when all was said and done I was thankful that I had received a privileged education, even if I was spending the rest of my life recovering from it.

By now I was beginning to feel hungry again. It was already early evening and the prospect of French cuisine beckoned. Leaving the hotel I strolled lazily in no particular direction, at one point going past the house on the corner of Rue Mazarin where Wellington had established his headquarters during the winter of 1813-1814. Eventually I found a cosy-looking restaurant in a backstreet and settled at a small table in a quiet corner. Saliva flowed as I perused the menu. I knew that in theory I ought to be packing pasta into my body ready for the trials ahead, but I was in no mood to spend the evening simply eating to satisfy a sense of duty. In this Basque fishing port the local tuna, sardines and anchovies would have been appropriate, but I have always been a bit of a carnivore and the steak au poivre was tempting, albeit as the most expensive item on the menu. "Why not?" I murmured, uttering the eternal mantra of the glutton down through the ages.

Having taken my order the waiter reappeared with an excellent bottle of claret. It looked a little extravagant for a single diner, but I was used to eating and drinking alone and had long since ceased to be self-conscious in a restaurant. I held up the first glass, relishing the dark warmth of the liquid as it refracted the light. I resolved that a toast was in order – to the success of the expedition.

As several other toasts followed I became aware of the empty chair on the other side of the table, and I decided to drink one to Doctor Parrot. Indeed, I reckoned that he would make an interesting companion for dinner. Frederic Parrot was a German explorer, and in 1817 he became the first person to walk the length of the Pyrenees. He had started right here, in St.Jean-de-Luz, and he had reached the Mediterranean at Canet-Plage, just east of Perpignan, after fifty-three days. His traverse of the mountains had included some notable summits, such as the Pico-de-la-Maladeta at just under 11,000 feet. As a dining companion he could have been helpful, even if he was speaking in German. I was not well acquainted with the Teutonic tongue, but nevertheless it would have been useful to hear Parrot assessing the odds on my success. I was reasonably confident that I would beat his time of fifty-three days. Indeed, if I failed to better Parrot's time I would be in serious trouble, as my flight home from Perpignan was dated only forty-five days hence and I would have to get back to Scandinavia for work.

The steak arrived, large and succulent and sizzling on the plate. I poured another glass of wine and surveyed my dinner with relish. "If this is a mid-life crisis, give me more of it" I thought. The conversation with Parrot was put on hold as I attacked my food. Nevertheless my mind was still working, and still weighing up the odds. There were a number of factors which gave me confidence. For months I had been assembling equipment, testing it out and refining it as I conducted punishing training walks with an ever-heavier rucksack. The forty-five days set aside for the project should be enough, and travelling alone meant I could be flexible and adapt my plans as I saw fit. I had enough money to stay in reasonable accommodation for most of the time, which should help me to recuperate quickly, and I could afford decent food. Moreover walking is not technically difficult: you just put one foot in front of the other and then you repeat the process. Repeat it often enough and eventually you will arrive. Of course my previous Pyrenean experiences demonstrated that there is a bit more to it than that - at least on the logistical side – but the problems should be soluble if I tackled them with determination and patience.

However, as I dug into my steak I could sense that Parrot had some reservations. He pointed out that whilst my training had been good it had not, and could not, replicate the actual reality of carrying a rucksack up and down mountains for eight or ten hours in a day, followed by the same the next day and the day after that. Most of my recent walks had been a couple of hours snatched every other afternoon, and they had been on relatively flat terrain. Parrot also reminded me that whilst I had accumulated a lot of walking experience when younger, I had not done much serious walking at all since my previous Pyrenean adventure.

This was true. Having completed the GR10 in 1988, I had found that shorter hikes – the odd afternoon getting cold and wet in the Peak District or wherever – held little attraction. I had been drawn to cross-country skiing as a fresh challenge, but had done little walking. The exception had been back in 1991 when I had gone on a short expedition to the Picos de Europa area of northern Spain. It had been a memorable experience. It was remarkable that the trip had happened at all, as it had been a nightmare to organise. It had involved Douglas again, my brother Graham and a friend of ours called Jim. All four of us were working in difficult jobs in different corners of England, so each of us had to negotiate dates off work and the whole thing had to be organised by telephone. Until a fortnight

40

before departure we didn't even know where we were going, and Corsica was a strong alternative possibility. I mentioned these difficulties to a Bible Study group I was leading in my parish in Birmingham.

"Not a problem," announced one of the members, who was something of a local wide-boy. He whipped out his wallet and produced a dog-eared business card. It had a picture of an aeroplane on it, and an address in the inner-city. "Go to this house," he said seriously, "and ask for Rasheed." Then we were treated to that immortal line: "mention my name and he'll give you a discount."

I took the card but looking at the picture, which was a drawing and seemed to depict an old Dakota or some such, I decided we would stick with British Airways. The following day I booked four tickets to Bilbao. In spite of the chaotic preparations it turned out to be a hugely enjoyable trip. Our team was harmonious and strong: in fact I was clearly the weakest link in it. Douglas obviously had great stamina whilst Graham was six feet two inches and fourteen stones of solid muscle. Indeed, he regularly opined that anybody less than six feet two and fourteen stones was "a mere shrimp." Jim was blessed with extraordinary natural fitness: his heart and lungs could possibly have carried him to an Olympic medal if he had ever found a sport which truly fired his imagination. He jokingly described himself as "the expedition asset", but there was a measure of truth in this because he had enough experience of genuine mountaineering to lead us over snow and ice to a couple of summits. He also had a superb sense of humour; not that the rest of us were deficient in that department. The dynamics of the group worked well, leading us to conclude that four is the optimum number for such an enterprise. I remembered how we had huddled happily in our three-man tent at a bleak spot called Mega Huerta. It was a bit cramped but it was fun to sit there, experiencing no rain but listening to the thunderstorms as they circled around the valleys below the massif. At one point the tent had to be evacuated in a hurry. Douglas had bought some of the local cheese and stored it in a metal cooking pot deep in his rucksack, trusting that the proximity of his damp socks and pants would keep it cool for a day or so. When he opened the pot our tent was suffused with a noxious odour: his precious cheese was now a seething mass of maggots.

The Picos proved to be a beautiful location. Compared to other mountain regions the area was tiny, but the huge range in altitude ensured a startling variety of climate and vegetation. Moreover this corner of Europe, roughly half-way along the northern coast of Spain, seemed to be a well-kept secret. We met few other walkers, and hardly any of these were Europeans. Most were in fact Australians, enjoying sabbaticals from their jobs and exuding health, energy and purpose. The majority were great company and extremely pleasant, with the odd exception. We were resting in one café when it was invaded by a middle-aged Antipodean lady. She was very loud, and her persona seemed to expand instantly to fill every corner of the premises. She was announcing that she intended to climb a hill she had heard about called El Naranjo de Bulnes. (It is actually a famous and picturesque rock pinnacle, and something of a mecca for serious Spanish climbers). We had seen El Naranjo a couple of days previously. It was about 1500 feet high, it was vertical, and it had as many handholds on it as the surface of a polished mirror. As the Australian rattled on I exchanged quizzical glances with my companions. We sat in silence. Nobody was going to risk getting into an argument with this menopausal marsupial.

Doctor Parrot was certainly giving me plenty of food for thought. Meanwhile the food on my plate had been devoured and the level of wine in the bottle was dropping fast. I did not wish to appear rude to the good doctor by dismissing his reservations, but the alcohol I was imbibing was bolstering my confidence and suppressing the niggling doubts which Parrot had introduced. Then a shadow slid across the table between us and the waiter hovered into focus, brandishing his notebook.

I was no longer hungry but I was still greedy, and my order for chocolate mousse and coffee bought me a few more minutes to continue my argument with Parrot. The dessert duly arrived and I fixed my concentration upon it. The calories in the mousse did not worry me: I had already calculated that my body would need to consume and process about three hundred thousand of them to get me to the Mediterranean. I poured the last glass of claret from the bottle, but realised that I didn't really want it after all. Maybe I should carry it down to the beach and pour it into the sea? In just twelve hours I would be starting my walk, at the edge of the North Atlantic, and maybe a libation to Neptune was in order? After all, the Church of England is terribly broad these days.

Fortified by the coffee I paid my bill and thanked Doctor Parrot for his company and advice. Staggering back in the general direction of my hotel I found the sea air salty and sobering. In my hotel room I flopped onto the bed, enjoying the pleasure of a full stomach. It was still too early to turn in for the night, and levering myself up onto one elbow I surveyed my kit, of which there seemed to be an alarmingly large amount.

My giant green rucksack was propped up in the corner of the room, and had been lurking behind the door when I entered. I eyed it suspiciously. A walker's relationship with his rucksack is an ambiguous thing. The object is simultaneously a trusted old friend and an instrument of torture. This green rucksack seemed strong and reliable, but I doubted I would ever feel the same affection for it which I'd had for its predecessor, my old red and blue pack. As I thought about the latter I still felt a pang of bereavement.

43

The red and blue rucksack had come to a sad end. It had been bought originally for an expedition to Norway in 1980. Since then it had seen action on many fronts, travelling around India in 1982 and serving on the two Pyrenean trips of the late 1980's. It was fitting that when it died it did so back in Norway. Graham, Douglas and I were intending to have ten days of cross-country skiing, whilst camping out in the wilds. It was the middle of February and when we got off the train at Geilo it was the middle of the night and the thermometer on the station platform was registering eighteen degrees of frost. Within a couple of minutes I was aware of a strange feeling in my nose as mucus began to freeze and crackle – an odd but not unpleasant sensation. We set off on our skis into the darkness, heading along a pre-cut trail beside a frozen lake. Carrying ten days of food and fuel, plus enough clothing and camping gear to survive in an Arctic climate, we were heavily laden. After less than a kilometre I suddenly heard something snap. The world span upside down and I found myself on my back with my head in a snowdrift. My companions, who had been behind me at the time, said I had gone down as though I'd been shot. A few minutes of examination by torchlight revealed the problem. The waistbelt of the rucksack had parted company with the pack itself on the right-hand side. Presumably years of rain and sweat had worked on the stitching to rot it away, and the current horrendous load was, almost literally, the final straw.

So I had been forced to buy a new rucksack, and I was hoping it would prove to be a loyal servant over the coming weeks. It was clearly a more sophisticated design than its predecessor, with straps, buckles and zips all over the place, and it was even larger. However, I was desperate not to use its capacity to the full. The lighter my load the less I would feel like a beast of burden. I was haunted by the words of Reinhold Messner, the famous mountaineer who once dragged a sledge of supplies to the South Pole. He wrote that as he advanced, gradually consuming his rations, his sledge became progressively lighter, "but light it never became."

In my attempt to reduce the weight I had decided to leave behind my trusted old ice-axe, the same one which had served in the Pyrenees previously. In Britain I always slept with it under the bed – a habit I had picked up in my first parish in Birmingham where burglary was a constant threat. On this current trip it could have served various functions, especially that of providing psychological security as a defence of last resort. I was not worried about burglars but about dogs. In France dogs are an absolute curse on the walker. Every village and farm has them and they are not friendly pets; they are kept to deter intruders. The standard advice is to carry a stick, but that is unlikely to stop a Doberman or Alsatian which really means business. I remembered an odd experience I had had in Bombay, where I had found myself in a street which was suddenly empty of people. In India of all places that should have told me something was wrong. Then I saw the dog limping along, and at the same moment it saw me and stopped. The dog and I stared at each other. I should have been thinking about the threat of rabies, but strangely the thought that came to mind was how similar the scene was to a gunfight in a spaghetti western. I wondered about turning to run but discounted the idea: the dog had only got three legs but that was still one more than I'd got. Instead I moved a couple of feet sideways to a pile of rubble and picked up half of a broken brick. Fortunately the dog decided to skulk off. In spite of this experience I had decided to leave my ice-axe at home for this trip, realising that it would be impossible to carry it on my rucksack and also get it out quickly enough to use it as a weapon.

Leaving the axe behind saved some weight. There was also the fact that to benefit from its proper purpose I would need to take other equipment too, principally a pair of crampons. The whole business illustrated how the selection of kit inevitably becomes a series of compromises. In theory there are any number of items one would like to have which could improve the comfort, or even the safety, of an expedition. But the other side of the equation is that you have to carry them. Weight itself is a safety factor, as it limits the speed with which you can move and thus reduces the flexibility and energy with which you can respond to a crisis. I have always enjoyed planning and packing for expeditions, trying to assess the probabilities and the risks involved in taking different combinations of kit.

One department where I could afford no compromises was with my feet, and lying next to my rucksack were numerous socks and a couple of containers of foot powder. The socks were mostly goretex but included two woollen pairs. Wool is quite effective as it retains warmth even when wet – presumably this is the reason so many sheep seem to use it. I knew that trouble with my feet could literally stop me in my tracks. My mother had always claimed that my father's family "died from the feet up", which was not an encouraging thought. Indeed, when I was younger I had suffered from athlete's foot and septic toes at various times, and had had one minor operation to remove excess bone from a little toe. My feet are quite broad and (like most people) my left foot is slightly larger than the right. I had never found it easy buying shoes, and it was possible that my Celtic genetic inheritance was a factor. Foot shapes vary between races, and in Britain shoes are traditionally manufactured in Northampton, in the Anglo-Saxon part of the country. My goretex boots, purchased in Norway, were comfortable but felt large and they allowed a lot of space for the instep: apparently that is a distinguishing feature of Scandinavian feet. I had also been seeking to toughen my feet, and often after long training walks I would

46

submerge them in buckets of freezing salted water. It was quite therapeutic. At any rate I found that if I had any other problems in life it made me forget about them pretty quickly. All the same, I was conscious that my feet were my Achilles Heel, so to speak, and I would be on the lookout for any symptoms of trouble with them.

The rest of the kit was a hotch-potch of bits and pieces, mostly clothing. I had my old goretex bivouac sack and a fibre-pile sleeping bag, for whilst I was intending to get a roof over my head most nights I knew that I had to be able to survive a couple of days in the open. One useful innovation was a two litre plastic container with a tube attached, called a "platypus." This would be filled with water and would fit neatly into a side pouch on the rucksack. It meant I could drink small amounts regularly by sucking the end of the tube and thus avoid dehydration. If you have to take the rucksack off every time you want to get at a water bottle you tend not to bother, as it wastes time and energy and puts extra strain on the pack's harness, to say nothing of your spine.

I decided I had had enough for one day. Technically, as a clergyman, I should probably have been reciting the words of the Daily Office again, either Evening Prayer or Compline, praying for protection from the ghouls and phantoms of the night. I was, after all, a serving priest, though probably not a particularly good one. In my own perception I saw myself as a fanatical Anglican – in other words I was willing to die for what I believed but I often had difficulty remembering what I believed.

It took me a while to drop off to sleep, and again I woke in the early hours. Often it is during the darkest part of the night that doubts and fears close in. I sat on the toilet feeling uneasy and sensing that the inactivity of the previous day had begun to erode my morale. I was sure that I would feel better when daylight returned and I could get cracking with the walk. In the meantime I had to face the fact that there were genuine dangers to frighten me. What if I got appendicitis out there? On my own in the middle of the mountains it would be a nightmare trying to get help and medical treatment, and paying for them, and all the time guarding my possessions too. There was an element of risk about the whole venture. Being on your own multiplies the risks, and also makes it easier for fear to work on you. On the wall of the bathroom a large notice warned me not to flush my tampons or sanitary towels down the pan, as the toilet worked on some sort of vacuum device and could easily get damaged. Eventually I got tired of staring at the notice and decided to return to bed. The key thing was not to panic. There is a sense in which there is nothing to fear except fear itself, for fear and worry drain your energy away like nothing else.

I slept fitfully for another couple of hours and was awake well before dawn. That is not to say that I felt like walking. My head had the ill-defined ache of a mild hangover and my mouth was dry. After a hot shower I made my way downstairs for breakfast, and ordered plenty of strong coffee. Picking up the newspaper I turned to the sports pages and searched for the rugby reports. It seemed that England had achieved another notable victory, for Martin Johnson and his merry men had pummelled Australia into submission in Melbourne. This came on the back of a somewhat narrower victory over New Zealand in Wellington the previous week, and England were now looking like serious contenders for the World Cup which would be contested in the Antipodes in October. Meanwhile France had lost to Argentina by a single point in a high-scoring game, and New Zealand had bounced back from their defeat in Wellington to demolish Wales.

I finished my breakfast quickly, for in spite of myself the impending prospect of the walk was making me nervous and I was anxious to get going. The weather looked ambiguous. The sky was heavily overcast with a thick haze, and whilst this would provide merciful protection against the sun's rays it was also raising the humidity. Even at this time in the morning the temperature was 22C (70F). Back in my room I was sweating profusely as I packed my kit. By the time I had finished the green rucksack was hideously heavy. Previously I had been congratulating myself on keeping its weight down, but I had just added the contents of a small purple daysack which had functioned as handluggage on the flight. I had also loaded up with three litres of mineral water and some food. The result was a pack of well over forty pounds. It seemed I had fallen into a trap which I had been determined to avoid.

I struggled downstairs with my burden and settled the hotel bill. Then I heaved the rucksack onto my back and stepped out into the street. The idea of walking to the Mediterranean was appalling. I didn't feel fit enough to get to the Atlantic, and that was only one hundred metres away. In the grey light the town had a definite air of the morning after the night before, and there were few souls to be seen. I wondered whether it was about to start raining.

Reaching the seafront I saw that the tide was halfway out. A large cruise ship, the *"Silver Cloud,"* was lying at anchor in the bay, but I could not detect any signs of activity on board. It was still only ten minutes to nine. For the second time in my life I walked down the beach at St.Jean-de-Luz to dip my feet into the Bay of Biscay. It seemed appropriate to offer a few short prayers at the beginning of the coming ordeal. Crossing the sand on the way back the rucksack felt heavier than ever. I clambered up the steps onto the seawall. "Only another million strides to go", I thought absurdly. The prospect was grotesque. But I knew that if I kept going steadily I should eventually get there. In approximately six weeks I should reach another beach, this time stretching down into that great tideless pond which had spawned Western civilization. And then I could worship on another shore and, I trusted, in a greater light.

I always feel a great peace at the beginning of a long journey. The road seems to stretch so far ahead that you are conscious of nothing else, and there is a sense of being in harmony with the task. On occasions I have spent a day driving the length of England, and have enjoyed achieving the necessary balance of concentration and relaxation. If you don't concentrate enough you'll probably have an accident, but conversely to concentrate too hard can leave you exhausted before you are half way there, which is equally dangerous. Likewise with the walk I knew it was important to pace myself, both physically and mentally. If there were really a million strides between here and the Mediterranean I would take note of the fact and then try to forget it. I knew that my journey could end on any one of those strides. It would not take much - just a boot coming down carelessly on a stone at the wrong angle. Damage to a ligament or tendon, or even a bad sprain, and it would all be over. To take an analogy it was like embarking on a military campaign where you could not possibly win the war on the first afternoon but you could easily lose it. I had run the marathon a couple of times when I was younger and I knew that in any endurance event the secret is to find a speed, or actually a rhythm, which you can maintain indefinitely. A sprint at the start, fuelled by adrenaline, could serve no purpose.

So I set off through the streets at a slow plod, with sweat dribbling everywhere. I began to wonder whether I would simply melt into a puddle before I had cleared the outskirts of St.Jean. After a few minutes I was heading south-east alongside the turgid brown waters of the Nivelle. I passed a grassy area where two women were throwing a ball to a dog. Then I overtook two men with a child in a pushchair. I met a few pedestrians who were strolling in the opposite direction. Some of them could not avoid eye contact, and I noted that their faces betrayed a mixture of pity, incomprehension and fear. I supposed that it was the size of my rucksack and the streams of perspiration which were having that effect, and I tried to smile and exchange a *"bonjour"* with each of them. Then a jogger pulled up just in front of me and seemed to be nursing a knee injury. It was a salutary reminder that my journey could end at any moment and without warning. Then I'd be spending the remainder of my life thinking "if only." "If only it wasn't for that bit of bad luck and that injury maybe I would have made it – who knows?" I grimaced. However unpleasant the climate might be and however much I had to carry, these irritants were as nothing compared to the crushing disappointment that failure would bring. Immediately I felt lighter and more determined.

During my long months of preparation I had tried to imagine this very morning, and the moment when I would leave St.Jean. Mostly I had envisaged a heroic sunrise, with those first strong bars from the *Tannhauser* Overture sounding across the hills in front of me. The reality was somewhat different, for the sun was obscured by cloud and there was no sign of the Pyrenees at all. I had to continue on the assumption that they were still out there, somewhere beyond the mist. And already I was looking for a place to relieve myself as the morning's coffee worked its way down through the system. But it did not matter. I felt deliriously content, with the joy that you can only experience when you know that you are in the right place at the right time and doing exactly the right thing. Not for years had I felt so alive. I was moving at last, and advancing east out of St.Jean-de-Luz. I was walking in the footsteps of Doctor Parrot.

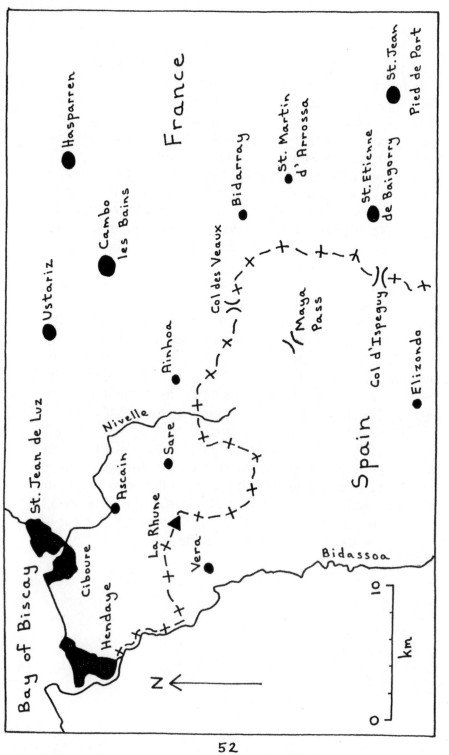

St. Jean-de-Luz to St. Jean-Pied-de-Port.

Chapter 3.

French blisters and a Spanish ulcer.

My euphoria lasted just long enough to carry me to the foot of the first ascent, which was at the village of Ascain. The road alongside the Nivelle had been pretty flat and I had made steady progress in spite of the humidity and the burden of my rucksack. However, the instant that my route began to ascend it seemed that the rucksack doubled in weight. Immediately I was face to face with the cruel physics of expending energy in order to raise the pack, plus my own bodyweight, up the incline. If the walk is a metaphor for life then it's on the uphill sections that the metaphor really begins to bite.

My tactic was always to tackle a hill by trying to establish a rhythm which I could maintain. The task was to get my body into first gear and my brain into neutral. There are various mental tricks which one can employ, but basically you have to find a way to think about something other than the pain. I was often disappointed to find that I could not use these ascents to think methodically and fruitfully about a serious topic. I would start climbing determined to put the "free" time to constructive mental use, but invariably a stream of consciousness would take over and lead my thoughts away down numerous false trails. Trivial and silly thoughts came much more easily than deep philosophical ones. For example, running my mind over football and rugby teams from yesteryear and assembling "dream teams" worked quite well for me. On occasions, and provided I am fairly fit already, I have found it possible to drift off into something akin to a mild trance whilst walking or running: at least in as much as I would suddenly "wake up" and realise I had just run half a mile or climbed a couple of hundred feet without really being aware of it. Anything that blanks out the pain for even a short while can be a useful ally.

Thinking about music can help, humming it softly if its rhythm happens to match your progress over the ground. But it can also be a mistake: the downside of music is that once you get it into your head it is very difficult to get it out again. The same tune is liable to return throughout the day, welcome or otherwise. And so it was that I found myself singing my old school song. I suppose that my mind was still churning over memories of the place, in a mildly traumatised state, and I latched onto the school song for inspiration. This composition was a sort of parody of the ethos of a 19th century public school, and I recalled somebody telling me that it had won a competition, run by a national newspaper, which was seeking to establish the worst school song in the country. Even Kipling would have squirmed with embarrassment at parts of it. My favourite part consisted of the sort of invocations one might expect to hear in a classical Greek temple, combined with some ferociously muscular Christianity:

"Those who gave our school its laurels, laid on us a sacred trust;

Forward therefore, live your hardest, die of service not of rust."

It occurred to me that on my current expedition there was a good chance that I could live out these demands to the full. If this first morning was anything to go by then rust would not be a factor. Dissolving completely in my own sweat seemed a far more likely fate. By noon the sun had finally burned off the mist and broken through with a vengeance. I stopped to dig my hat and sunglasses out of my pack, slapping on the first of my suncream and chatting briefly to a middle-aged couple from Cape Town who were on holiday with their cousins from

Northampton. The South Africans revealed that they had also lived in Australia and had interests in the wine trade. Shortly after this I realised that when I had left Ascain I had made a slight mistake with my navigation. I was still struggling to get used to the cartographic scale, and to make matters worse the decisive point had come (as is so often the case) on a fold of the map. The result was that I followed the wrong lane and got held up behind a flock of straggly sheep which a Basque teenager was moving up the road with no real sense of urgency. When I came out on the open hillside I was about a kilometre east of my intended route. Having lost a little time getting my bearings I used my compass to set a course which intercepted the correct path, which was now heading southwards and upwards to the Col des Trois Fontaines. It was a relief to come around the flank of the hillside and finally see the summit of La Rhune, with its ugly collection of buildings and radio masts.

La Rhune looked close in the bright light, but I knew that the summit was at least two miles away. By now I had eaten a snack for lunch, and had continued with the ascent. The heat was appalling. The sunlight was reflecting off the rocks of the path, seemingly adding to the crushing weight of the rucksack. I sensed I was already staggering from side to side as my body began to obey the selfish instinct to seek out any route which was less steep, even by a few inches. Everything seemed to be hurting - legs and hips worst of all – and I was fighting for breath. Again the lyrics of that wretched song came back to haunt me:

"Oftentimes defeat is splendid, victory may still be shame;

Luck is good, the prize is pleasant; but the glory's in the game!"

"So come on," I spluttered to myself. "Play up! Play the game!" I had already resolved that I would have to create some luck for myself by giving the rucksack some radical treatment, throwing away everything superfluous in an attempt to save weight. I knew from past experience that there is also an art to how you pack the contents. Ideally you want to get the heavier items near the top so that you can walk upright. If the pack's centre of gravity is too low it forces the walker to bend forwards, which is even more tiring. I thought my rucksack was packed quite well, but I discovered that adjusting the straps by the odd inch (which usually meant tightening them) made a remarkable difference to the ease with which I could bear the weight.

Often on a long expedition the first day is not too bad. The walker is full of energy and excitement and has not yet got any problems with stiffness or soreness. The second day tends to be the worst. The third day is the worst too. By the fourth or fifth day most people experience a slight improvement as the training effect of the walk begins to come through. However, the current expedition seemed to be an exception. The first day was proving seriously tough, and it was giving me a brutal reminder of several of the good reasons for avoiding hillwalking.

During the ascent I stopped a couple of times and stepped off the path to sink into the grass in exhaustion. It was good to rest, but there was no shade. In my mental battle I was already trying to encourage myself with the prospect of my first rest-day, which I intended to take after about a week of effort. Indeed I had earmarked St.Jean Pied-de-Port as a possible stopover. On the previous Pyrenean expedition Douglas and I had reached it after five days, so I thought it would be a natural spot for me to halt and regroup at the end of the introductory "shake-down" leg of the trip. I also reckoned that the monastery at Roncesvalles could be even better, if it were possible to stop there for two nights and rest for the day in-between. I had mixed feelings about the physical effects of rest-days. A long-distance walk depends on rhythm and routine, and as soon as the stress of the exercise is taken away the body tends to follow its natural impulse and starts winding down, which can leave you weaker rather than stronger. On the other hand the prospect of an impending rest is such a psychological boost that it's worth having for its effect on morale. At least with the town of St.Jean and the monastery at Roncesvalles I had got a couple of good options for a restful day and I could remain flexible as to which one I used.

Of course neither St.Jean Pied-de-Port nor Roncesvalles would be of any relevance if I failed to survive the first day. I heaved myself back onto my feet and continued towards the col. On the way I drew inspiration from the efforts of Miles Morland. His 1992 book *"The man who broke out of the bank"* described how he had walked across France with his wife. Their route had been some way north of the Pyrenees, and they had travelled from east to west, in the opposite direction to myself. It took them less than a month to cover 350 miles from Gruissan Plage, near Narbonne, to Capbreton just north of Biarritz. It was a fine achievement, but what interested me most was the motivation. Morland, an Oxford graduate, had spent 22 years in merchant banking until he resigned at the age of 45. It was clear from his book that he could have continued his banking career successfully, but nevertheless he dropped it and went for his walk. His reason was "because I had stopped learning. And when you stop learning you start to grow old fast."

At last I reached the Col des Trois Fontaines, where a dozen brown horses were grazing in the shade of a few trees. They looked contented enough and were seemingly unperturbed by their numerous escorting flies. Before I set out from St.Jean-de-Luz I had considered ascending to the summit of La Rhune, which now lay on my right and was about a mile away. However, it would have meant a further thousand feet of ascent, all of it without shade and trudging up the track of a little rack-and-pinion railway. After my struggle to reach the col I was not going to expend further energy on a detour, particularly a detour taking me up the side of a mountain which, from many angles, had a profile resembling a volcano. In earlier centuries the top of the mountain had been considered to be witches' territory, and until the French Revolution of 1789 the mayors of the surrounding villages were still paying a volunteer monk to live on the summit and keep the witches at bay. It would have been a lonely vigil but at least the monk would have had a good view, stretching over twenty miles to the twin spires of Bayonne Cathedral.

Even without ascending La Rhune I had plenty to think about because I knew that here, on the Col des Trois Fontaines, I was standing on historic ground. By September 1813 the Duke of Wellington's Anglo-Portuguese army had swept through Spain and driven the French back over the Pyrenees. However, the Duke was cautious about entering France whilst a French garrison remained in his rear, albeit under siege in Pamplona. He also knew that it was not inconceivable that Napoleon might yet win a great victory in Germany. If the Emperor were to defeat the Prussians, Austrians and Russians somewhere east of the Rhine he could then transfer his attention, and his forces, to southern France.

Wellington's more immediate opponent was Marshal Soult, who by this stage had 60,000 men defending a line from the mouth of the Bidassoa River to the town of St.Jean Pied-de-Port. Wellington had slightly more men in his own army, plus 25,000 Spanish allies, so he decided to make a limited advance. On 7th October his Fifth Division crossed the Bidassoa at low tide, using the fords at Fuenterrabia, and then stormed into Hendaye. To their right there was heavier fighting as the famous Light Division sought to force the French from the steep ridge above the village of Vera. On the left flank Colbourne's Brigade made for the stone redoubt called La Bayonette, with the Fifty-Second (Oxfordshire) regiment flushing out the defenders and sending them scurrying from the ridge. Further to the right there was less success, with Kempt's Brigade struggling to get up a steep spur as they tangled with trees, rocks and brambles. Further right again were a couple of Spanish divisions from Andalusia, whose task was to capture the summit of La Rhune itself. Their failure was not too surprising, as the steepness of the ground would have made it a formidable obstacle even if it had been undefended. However, the following day the French abandoned the summit, fearing that any troops left up there would be rapidly encircled.

In this way Wellington's forces became the first Allied army to enter France. He was established on French soil and in a good position to make a further advance, if and when he judged it to be prudent. In the meantime there was a curious stand-off, with the British on the top of La Rhune and the French holding the ridge of La Petite Rhune, which was a thousand feet lower and a mile or so away to the north-east across the saddle of the Col des Trois Fontaines. (The geography, and the descriptions of the fighting, can seem confusing because modern maps ascribe the name "Petite Rhune" to a feature west of the main mountain. This was the case with the 1:50,000 map I was using, where the Napoleonic ridge was marked with the Basque name Altxanga). As I looked up at the summit of La Rhune the jagged ridge that the French were defending lay behind me, and whilst not as high as La Rhune it was nevertheless a formidable obstacle with a precipitous crest. Indeed, the defenders had added to its natural strength by constructing a series of three stone redoubts along the summit: from west to east these were named the "Place of Arms," the "Magpie's Nest" and the "Donjon."

From the top of La Rhune Wellington could see the French soldiers toiling like ants as they constructed further earthworks and redoubts across the countryside behind La Petite Rhune. However, he was confident that he could out-manoeuvre the defenders and flush them from their fortifications. For all the natural strength of the positions held by the French, Soult simply didn't have enough defenders to man all of them adequately. Nor could he move reserves quickly enough to counter an attack if Wellington chose to concentrate his forces against a few key points. On 30th October the French garrison in Pamplona finally surrendered, and this was followed by encouraging news from the east. Napoleon had been heavily beaten at Leipzig, losing 100,000 men and 300 artillery pieces. This was the cue for Wellington to put his next plan into operation: he would drive down the valley of the Nivelle and seize the high ground around St.Pee.

For the plan to work properly it required the Light Division to storm the Petite Rhune, thus breaking a key hinge in the French defences. They could then continue into the Nivelle Valley, assisting the main offensive by taking further French defenders in the flank. On the night of 9th November the Allied troops slipped silently into position and shivered through the night on the slopes of La Rhune as a full moon came out. At dawn the firing of three guns signalled the assault. Swarms of British skirmishers from the legendary 95th Rifles spread across the col on which I was now standing, supported by yet more from the 17th Portuguese Cacadores. Behind them came the formed battalions of light infantry. On the right the 43rd Monmouthshires would attack the enemy ridge, working their way along it from west to east. To their left the 52nd Oxfordshires headed across flatter ground towards the Mouiz redoubt, thus cutting off the natural line of retreat for the defenders on the ridge itself.

The Monmouthshires were under the command of William Napier, who would later write the first comprehensive history of the Peninsular War. On the morning of 10th November he had other things on his mind as he led the assault on the first of the three stone "castles" which his men had to overcome. For a while Napier's progress was obstructed by a gallant French officer who was hurling rocks down at him – indeed one of them caused the British commander a painful injury to his thigh. The French were defending some formidable strongpoints, but the ferocity of the Monmouthshires' attack prised them out and they were soon put to flight. Possibly the sight of the Oxfordshires moving to cut off their retreat demoralised the defenders. In any case, by this stage in the Peninsular War the French had simply got into the habit of losing whereas the British knew they would win. A broadly similar pattern played itself out in the other sectors of the Nivelle battlefield. Soult was outnumbered about four to three in infantry, but the natural strength of the French positions should have more than offset that weakness in numbers. However it was the difference in morale which was of greater significance and ultimately proved decisive.

Many years later Wellington was asked which of his battles had been the best planned and executed. The man who had won victories stretching from Assaye to Waterloo thought carefully before replying, "I think that the battle of the Nivelle was my best work."

I crossed the little railway line and started down a narrow path. The irregular stones made this descent just as tiring as the ascent had been, and more dangerous. At one point I stopped for another snack, resting in the shade of a lone tree and leaving my sweat-soaked tee-shirt to dry on a rock in the sunshine. I had been walking for five hours, and it felt an awful lot longer. Higher up the hillside one of the little trains rattled past on its slow ascent, and higher still eagles were circling around the crags of the Petite Rhune – the very crags where, two centuries earlier, a desperate French officer had been throwing stones at his British adversary.

I suppose it was that sort of curious and bizarre incident which had first fired my interest in military history. It was always fascinating to follow the sweep of historical events and learn how it came to pass that two individuals from different countries should find themselves fighting each other at a particular place at a specific time. Often it would be a case of people who were far from home, caught up in momentous events which were way beyond their control and probably beyond their comprehension. And yet there is a sort of paradox, in that however momentous and significant the battle may be, it still comes down to individuals to do the fighting. In the most extreme cases, such as at Leipzig in 1813 or at Stalingrad a century later, there are literally hundreds of thousands involved, and yet at the end of the day it all comes down to individuals who need to be motivated to die or to kill.

Military tactics are interesting in any age, but personally I had always been drawn more towards strategy, and the interaction of politics, diplomacy and the military on the grand scale. No doubt this dilettante interest is an outworking of the male instinct to use power to control and direct events towards some grandiose purpose. Like many other armchair generals I could derive great pleasure from moving flags on a map, though I was well aware that war is not a game of chess and that clever manoeuvres are far less significant than logistics to a professional soldier. And like many men who have not been exposed to the reality of battle I had the latent personal question, of wondering how well I would react and perform faced with a real enemy intent upon securing my destruction. Moving flags is fun, but in real life it is real people who have to pay for the miscalculations and do the dying.

My specific interest in the Peninsular War had started innocently enough. In the course of my various studies in school and college I had touched on many periods of history, but not the Napoleonic era. So I started reading about it simply to find out what happened. The interest grew and within a few years several feet of bookshelf were groaning under the weight of the volumes I had accumulated. I had plenty of literature on the Emperor's career and on the battle of Waterloo, but it was the campaign in Portugal and Spain which really got to me: the business dubbed by Napoleon himself as "the Spanish Ulcer."

When the first British troops waded ashore at Mondego Bay on 1st August 1808 the struggle against Revolutionary and Imperial France had already been going on for the best part of fifteen years. In an age which predated aircraft this first global struggle was played out on land and sea, and with no radios or telephones any communication was limited to the speed of a man on a horse or a ship under sail. With two-thirds of the earth's surface covered by water it was the power of the Royal Navy which was vital in enabling Britain to survive and prosper, for the relatively small island-nation depended on trade and on its ever-increasing number of colonies. Britain could never hope to muster the numbers required to confront France directly on land, and so the wealth generated through the Industrial Revolution was directed towards subsidising one or other continental power (usually Austria) to fight on Britain's behalf. The French for their part could not challenge British power at sea – certainly not after Trafalgar in 1805 – but on land the massive French conscript armies reigned supreme, and all the more so once they were under the command of the Corsican Ogre.

By 1808 Napoleon was at the zenith of his powers. His continental rivals were all defeated and subdued, and following the Treaty of Tilsit even the Russians had been drawn into his "Continental System," which was an attempt to weaken Britain by totally excluding its goods from European markets. A form of stalemate had been reached, with the French elephant dominant on land and the British whale ruling the seas. It was French intervention in the Iberian peninsula which gave the British an opportunity to engage the enemy on European soil. The British commitment was somewhat tentative initially and, like many of the wars Britain has fought, it got off to a couple of false starts. Wellington defeated Junot in Portugal before his superiors, Dalrymple and Burrard, negotiated the notorious Convention of Cintra. All three men were recalled to London to explain themselves, and in their absence Sir John Moore led the army into Spain. Moore's retreat to Corunna ended in his own death and the humiliating evacuation from Spain of the British forces.

When Wellington returned to the Peninsula he liberated northern Portugal and advanced to Talavera, realising during the latter campaign that it would be extremely difficult to cooperate with the regular Spanish forces. The strategically brilliant construction of the Lines at Torres Vedras enabled Wellington to retreat to Lisbon before forcing Marshal Massena out of Portugal for good. The action then revolved around the various forts on the Spanish-Portuguese frontier, and early in 1812 Wellington succeeded in taking Cuidad Rodrigo. This was followed by the siege of Badajoz and by scenes of horrific carnage when the breaches were stormed. Having taken the town discipline amongst the British troops broke down completely as they embarked on an orgy of rape and looting which went on for several days. It was one of the darkest and most disgraceful episodes in the entire history of the British Army. Having restored order Wellington went on to win a significant victory over Marshal Marmont at Salamanca before liberating Madrid. He then overstretched himself by laying siege to Burgos, and by the end of an eventful year he had been forced to retreat once more to Portugal.

However, 1812 is not remembered for Wellington's retreat from Burgos. At the other end of the continent Napoleon had entered Russia with half-a-million men and came back a few months later with barely twenty thousand. The legendary disaster on the freezing steppes meant that the Emperor was forced to reduce his forces in Spain in order to build an army for the campaign of 1813 in Germany. When Wellington advanced yet again from Portugal he at last had parity in numbers. A series of outflanking marches turned successive French defensive lines until Marshal Jourdan and Joseph Bonaparte, (who was Napoleon's brother and the nominal King of Spain), had been forced back to Vittoria. This strategic pattern was more or less repeated at a tactical level in the subsequent battle. Wellington's victorious troops seized a fabulous quantity of loot in the closing stages of the fight, and the shattered remnants of the French army were driven back over the Pyrenees.

I regarded Wellington as something of a hero, though I was not blind to the fact that he had some unattractive traits. He was cold and aloof; he was notoriously reactionary; he was a womaniser and he hunted foxes using hounds. However, he embodied many of the best qualities of a general and a leader. As far as leadership goes I reckoned that it has three essential elements. The first is simply to know where you are going. Beyond that the second element is the ability to communicate. A large part of leadership boils down to calm clear concise confident communication, and Wellington was a master of that. The third ingredient is more difficult to define, but it's the ability or charisma that inspires people to follow. After all, in the last analysis nobody is a leader unless they can persuade other people to follow them.

Wellington had a superb grasp of logistics, with skills that he had honed in India organising bullock trains. In the Peninsula he used this experience to keep his troops fed and supplied, at least most of the time. The French armies were expected to advance on a broad front and live off the land – a policy which worked up to a point in the relatively rich countryside of central Europe but which failed miserably in Poland, Russia and Iberia. It was said that "in Spain small armies get beaten and large armies starve." In the Peninsula the French logistical problems were reinforced by the hostility of the populace, which became a factor at every turn. Indeed, the French soldiers in the Peninsula only really controlled the land on which they were standing: beyond their garrisons their ever-lengthening lines of supply and communication became vulnerable to all sorts of guerrilla attack. Conversely the activities of the guerrillas could furnish Wellington with fresh intelligence even as they intercepted French couriers: Wellington's ability to "see what was happening on the other side of the hill" was not wholly attributable to his powers of logic or some weird psychic ability. The conflict has been described as the first "modern" guerrilla war, and it is certainly the case that the French and Spanish were sucked into an escalating spiral of violence and retribution with horrible atrocities being committed on both sides.

The overall effect of the guerrillas is difficult to assess. The extreme Spanish view would be that "*la Guerra de la Independencia*" was a purely Spanish victory and owed little to the British, who had a propensity to turn and run for the coast and the succour of the Royal Navy whenever danger threatened. On the British side Wellington was conscious that he was commanding "England's last army" – it would only take one defeat and the entire campaign would be lost. The truth is surely that the British Army and the Spanish guerrillas needed each other if they were to continue the struggle, let alone achieve victory. Had there been no guerrillas the French could (in theory) have concentrated their forces to drive the British back into the sea. Likewise, had there been no British forces the French could probably have subdued and dominated the Peninsula.

The guerrillas were not the only factor mitigating against a concentration of French forces. Rivalry and jealousy between the various marshals constantly undermined the French cause. This was not a problem when Napoleon was present in person,

66

but this condition only pertained for the brief period during which he drove Moore back into Galicia. For the rest of the time the Emperor's subordinates bickered amongst themselves.

So there were numerous factors at work which enabled the relatively small British army to outmanoeuvre its foe. By the time the British reached the Pyrenees their forces had built up to something like 60,000. Besides the English regiments many of the units were Portuguese and the rest of the army was a colourful and romantic mixture of Scottish, Irish and Germans. The French troop levels in the Peninsula varied over time but peaked at almost 350,000. For me it was Wellington's ultimate success in the face of this discrepancy which was the fascinating thing. Of course it was also a reminder that it would not be honest to study the Peninsular War in isolation, without reference to the far larger numbers of Austrians, Prussians and Russians which were engaging the Emperor's attention at different stages.

Ultimately the satisfaction which I had derived from studying Wellington came down to his tactical genius in battle. In an age when infantry, cavalry and artillery each had clearly defined strengths and weaknesses they tended to dance around each other on the battlefield in a sort of macabre waltz. Clearly Wellington had a masterful grasp of the tactics and possibilities. He has often been derided as a purely defensive commander, but his battles in the Peninsula do not bear this out. Certainly Busaco was a classic defence of a steep ridge. But Salamanca was a bold piece of opportunism, judging the point at which his opponent had become overstretched and using the advantage of what was, in effect, a strong central position to seize the initiative and "defeat forty thousand Frenchmen in forty minutes." Torres Vedras was a complete contrast, and almost constituted a bloodless victory: Wellington's army grew stronger behind its defences whilst the French were reduced by hunger, exposure and disease. The boldest offensive battle was probably at Vittoria, and it followed a campaign which bears comparison to Marlborough's march to the Danube and victory at Blenheim a century earlier.

The thought of marching brought me back to my immediate situation. To walk to the Danube would be a fine thing: I had struggled to get myself a few miles inland from the Atlantic and it had taken me five hours to do that much. I donned my dirty tee-shirt once more, heaved the rucksack onto my back and continued down the path. I was now on the official GR10 route, which meant that every so often I passed its distinctive waymark of two parallel lines, one red and the other white, each about four inches long and painted on rocks, walls, trees or whatever else. This sequence of comforting markings should, in theory, be unbroken all the way to the Mediterranean, but I knew that in practice the long-distance path was poorly marked on some sections. By now I was descending pathways with some resemblance to sunken lanes, and mercifully I was able to benefit from the shade of thicker vegetation. At one point I went past a couple of secluded gardens and could hear a large family enjoying a pleasant Sunday lunch in the open air. Food and wine were an enticing thought, and I wondered how much they appreciated the privilege of the company and friendship they were enjoying.

By three o'clock I had struggled into the hilltop village of Sare and found an open bar. There was no food on offer but the cold beer was refreshing. I drank it slumped in a plastic chair on the pavement, hoping that none of the other drinkers – innocent civilians enjoying a lazy Sunday afternoon – would be able to smell my steaming carcase. In fact I was opposite the Hotel Arraya which, I learned, used to be a hospice on one branch of the St.Jacques pilgrimage route. That sounded like the right place for me: a hospice was what I felt I needed. However, it seemed to be full, along with the other couple of hotels in the place. I was not surprised that Sare attracted tourists. It was a pretty place, with the typical Basque combination of a church and a pelota court. The writer Pierre Loti had used the village, disguised as "Etchezar," as the setting for his 1897 romance "Ramuntcho." (He actually wrote it whilst staying in a hotel back in Ascain). There could be no doubt that I was in the heart of the Basque country here. The Basque flag, with its green and white crosses on a red background, was ubiquitous in these parts, and there was plentiful evidence of the distinctive Basque language with its predominance of "k", "x" and "z". I saw several advertisements for *gateau basque*, but these were less intimidating now. However, at no point was I aware of any militant or aggressive Basque nationalism of the sort which has spawned the ETA organisation on the Spanish side of the border.

With no accommodation on offer in the village I would have to try my luck further on. Sare is surrounded by a ring of satellite hamlets, and I headed off towards the one called Lehenbiscay. My route took me down a paved Roman road and past a couple of wayside shrines before it ascended again. In Lehenbiscay a couple of enquiries led me to the Hotel Pikassaria. I had not made a reservation because I had had no idea what sort of progress I would be making on my first day of walking. The hotel was full: "*complet*" as the lady at the reception desk put it. No room at the inn. Given my condition, (there was not a stitch of clothing on my body which was not soaked in sweat), she was probably relieved to have a good excuse to direct me down the road to a campsite. The proprietor at Camping-La-Petite-Rhune was friendly and quickly ushered me into a spacious room with an adjoining shower. I had been on the move for only seven hours, but it felt like days since I had left St.Jean. The intensity of the day's experiences had slowed time down as my mind had struggled to take it all in: the opposite of the commonly-observed

69

phenomenon of time speeding up as you grow older. The first day had born out Miles Morland's wisdom – when you stop learning you age faster.

After my shower I felt vaguely human again, and I had the strength to set about a savage reduction of my kit. I had two black army water bottles, in addition to my "platypus" equipment, so one of them went into a bin-liner. So did my thermal underwear, plus a perfectly good pair of thick socks. That left me with only three pairs, but I reasoned that if three pairs, used in rotation, were not enough then a fourth pair wouldn't make any difference. I found that some of my kit was duplicated. I had two whistles, so one of them went. I had two ball-point biros, so one of those went after I had removed the refill from inside it. I also got rid of several packs of toilet paper. On the day's march I had barely passed any water, let alone anything else, and this fact suggested that for toilet paper I should just pick up a few pieces every so often in the places where I would be staying. Various plastic and metal eating utensils also went into the bin-liner. By the time I had finished I could lift the bin-bag and feel pleased that I was dispensing with a few pounds of dead weight. But I had not enjoyed the exercise much. I hated throwing away good kit, and of course I wondered whether I would come to regret it if I needed any of the stuff later in the trip. Be that as it may; I knew that without some weight reductions there would not be any "later" in any case.

It felt marginally cooler when I left my room and dumped the bin-liner in a dustbin. I knew that the famous "Grottes de Sare" caves were nearby, inhabited as long ago as fifty thousand years, but I was more interested in finding some serious food. I strolled the short distance back to the Hotel Pikassaria, feeling incredibly liberated without the rucksack. The lady at the Reception barely recognised me in my new and more hygienic incarnation, and she confirmed that I would indeed be welcome to dine in the restaurant when it opened in half an hour. I killed the time by sipping a cold beer outside the front door of the hotel, resolving that I would treat myself to a feast. I seemed to think I deserved it for coming through the ordeal of the day. I was told that the temperature had reached 38 or 39 degrees centigrade, which is touching 100 fahrenheit. No wonder it had seemed tough! It occurred to me that if the weather remained this hot for the next six weeks I would have no chance of getting across France. In fact I would be fortunate if I made it as far as Roncesvalles.

I shrugged. There was no point spending the evening thinking about what the weather might or might not decide to do. It was better to concentrate on getting some substantial food down my neck. When the restaurant opened for business I despatched a magnificent salad, followed by a steak with half a bottle of claret and finally a plate of profiteroles. Even with the coffee it came to less than thirty euros. At barely six feet tall and twelve-and-a-half stones I was not the largest man in the world, but I needed fuel nevertheless.

It was clouding over as I left the restaurant and staggered back to the campsite, feeling slightly sick. However, I slept well and when I woke I was pleased to see that the sky was overcast. It was still humid, but according to the campsite's proprietor the temperature was not forecast to exceed 24 centigrade all day.

It turned out to be another hard day, though it was a mercy to be under the cover of cloud for most of it. I did not bother with my sunglasses, hat or suncream, but in spite of the overcast conditions my head still burned a little in the course of the day. My rucksack was better packed and felt marginally lighter, though, as Messner would say, "light it never became."

On the whole the morning's walking was not difficult, though I made another map-reading error after a couple of miles as I approached the frontier. For a few minutes I was totally disorientated until I worked out that I had missed a turning on the official GR10 route, continued too far down a lane, and come back to the red and white markings at a point where they seemed to lead straight back to Sare. I was standing outside a café which was solidly closed, and I subsequently realised from the map that I was right on the frontier. I attempted to talk to an elderly Basque gentleman who was walking his dog and who tried to help me get my bearings, but it was difficult as we had no language in common. When I eventually got going in the correct direction the route took me along lanes and farm tracks and eventually down through pleasant oak woodland to cross a road. On the other side of the road I passed a number of parked cars and caravans which were dispersed amongst the trees, with groups of people hanging around them. I was surprised when I came across one youth who was pointing at me and jeering aggressively in some language which I could not recognise. This rapidly drew the attention of others, of course, and I wondered whether I had wandered into some kind of gypsy settlement. The atmosphere was not entirely pleasant, and I did not stop moving until I was clear of the place and could rest on a narrow section of path – a good defensive position – next to a fish farm.

Another mile or so brought me into the village of Ainhoa, where a few tourists were strolling around and schoolchildren were having their P.E. lesson on the pelota court. I had already realised that this game existed with numerous variations. In many cases the players would use their bare hands, or possibly gloves or bats, but the most sophisticated version involved the use of a wicker basket attached to the forearm, and this was employed to catch the ball and hurl it back against the wall at great speed. Every Basque village has its own court, but these seemed to have various dimensions and markings. A proper match has two players on each team, and the game is even played professionally in Florida, having been carried there by Basque exiles.

Ainhoa was a thin village, strung out along one street. It did not take me long to establish that there was no food easily available, so I contented myself by dissolving sugar cubes into two large cups of *café au lait* which I purchased in a bar. The coffee was delicious, and I consumed it whilst talking to a pair of tough-looking French hillwalkers, both of whom were short powerful men in their fifties. I was finding that food, or rather the lack of it, was emerging as a serious problem. The previous day I had eaten little during the day, and then enjoyed an outsized dinner which had left me feeling slightly ill. Now I was having my second day in a row without any proper lunch. Breakfast that morning had consisted of a few mouthfuls of muesli, moistened with water because I had no milk. The little shop at the camping site had not opened during my stay there, and I had not passed any other shops all morning. When I had finished my coffee I set off again, heading uphill out of Ainhoa, but during the afternoon I would again experience a slightly sick sensation, and I took this as a sign that my body was starting to burn fat in its quest for energy.

The route out of Ainhoa consisted of a savagely steep road which swung back and forth as it zigzagged up to the Col des Trois Croix. (The previous col I had crossed was the Trois Fontaines, so they seemed to like names with "threes" in this part of the world). The ascent seemed to be designed as some sort of penance, for on every hairpin stood a plain white cross, each six feet tall. At the top of the climb I had a brief rest next to a small chapel. More impressive were the three life-sized crucifixes (so large that they had been visible from the village far below) and these stood above a cluster of gravestones on the open grass of the col. The central figure was a gruesome spectacle of blood and nails, for liberal quantities of red paint had been expended on this depiction of Christ. The two thieves were fastened to their crosses by ropes rather than nails, and both seemed to have contorted themselves into bizarre foetal positions.

At least the next section of the path followed a contour and then it came out on a lane, just east of Mont Ereby, which I could follow for several miles. Half way up the next ascent I stopped for an exhausted rest and met a couple from Wiltshire who were passing in the opposite direction. They were heading downhill, of course, and their little daysacks looked beautifully light. At the top of the climb I came out on a col where the cloud seemed to be closing in, but it lifted again as I trudged south below the ridge of the Gorospil. In this way I completed the final two miles of the day, ending up back on the frontier at the farm on the Col des Veaux. The farm included a "*gite d'etape*", ie some basic overnight accommodation which enabled it to function as a staging-post on the long-distance footpath.

After drinking a cold beer in the farmhouse I negotiated my way across the farmyard between pigs and horses. The proximity of the animals made me slightly nervous but they seemed docile enough. At the bottom of a steep field lay the hut which would be my shelter for the night. It had fourteen beds, arranged as bunks in a single room and, according to the elderly lady who had booked me in, ten of them were already taken. So I had arrived at an auspicious time: doubly so because none of the other guests were around so I got first crack at the shower. It had two taps, which I reckoned was something of an extravagance as both of them yielded only cold water.

Having cleansed myself my thoughts turned to food. Later in the evening I would be eating at the "restaurant" in the farmhouse. I hoped that there would be some decent carbohydrates on offer. I had a little pasta in my rucksack and could have cooked it in the hut, if I had possessed a saucepan

74

and if the gas supply to the stove had worked. It did not, so I contented myself by consuming a small tin of sardines in olive oil, thinking that at least the protein should go some way towards repairing any tissue damage in my body. In my First Aid box I had some sachets of powder for treating diahorrea, and even though I was not suffering from that particular complaint I decided to dissolve one in water and drink it anyway. It tasted grim but it meant that some salts and minerals were going into the system.

I was surprised at how little I had thought about anything during the day's walk, except for the weight of my pack, the blisters developing under my feet, the roughness of the stones on the trail, the sweat pouring from my body, the lack of food and my general weakness. But my advance from Ainhoa had granted me the prospect of a shorter day to follow. It was meant to be three hours to Bidarray, but even if I took five it would still be an easy day. There would be no point pushing on beyond Bidarray because there was no prospect of anywhere to stay on the nine-hour march to St.Etienne-de-Baigorry. I was weighing up this strategy when the first of my fellow-guests appeared. He was a tall Frenchman called Pierre, and he came from Perpignan. He had travelled to the Atlantic by train and granted himself 45 days to walk back to the Mediterranean and to home. His intention was to follow the GR10 as far as the Refuge de Pombie under the Pic-du-Midi-d'Ossau, which he should reach in about a fortnight. After that he would be onto the High-Level Route, which more or less follows the watershed and frontier all the way. Pierre looked like an athletic and fit young man, and I had no doubt that the odds were on the side of his eventual success.

I tried to talk to Pierre in my broken French, but after a few minutes we were forced to switch to English. Half way through our conversation the main group staying in the gite appeared. They were a party of eight middle-aged friends who were travelling by horse. They seemed to have ridden up from Bidarray by a circuitous route and had stabled their animals in a large shed across the farmyard. I had a brief talk with two or three of them. An attractive brunette had drawn the bunk above mine, and was looking rather dismayed at the prospect. I offered to swap but she refused, pointing out that there were no guard-rails of any sort along the sides of the top bunk. Then she took the mattress from it and dragged it out into the kitchen, explaining that she liked to sleep under an open window for the fresh air. After a few days in France I reckoned I could assemble enough French vocabulary to make a joke: *"peut-etre c'est votre dernier chance a dormir au-dessus d'un pretre."* ("Maybe it's your last chance to sleep on top of a priest"). But I thought better of it: humour does not always translate the way you want and it would be awkward if she made a joke in return which I failed to understand.

At the appointed hour I meandered back up to the farmhouse and settled myself by the enormous window of the dining room. I had a good view of the yard, where a couple of small children were playing in a sandpit. The place turned out to be a veritable Animal Farm. A troupe of five pigs (sows actually) were rooting around, and they were soon joined by five donkeys. There was a dog – the first friendly one I had met in France judging from the fact he declined to bark at me – and at least three rough-looking cats. In addition there were numerous hens and ducks.

The group of horse-people staggered into the dining room in high spirits and arranged themselves around a long table, laughing and joking in loud voices. Clearly their throats had already been lubricated with alcohol. There was no sign of any menu, but after a while a basket of bread was placed in front of me along with a whole bottle of wine. I had not ordered any, and I protested to the elderly lady that I would never drink all of it. *"Au meilleur dormir"* ("to sleep better") was her reply. In

76

fact I was beginning to understand why every man in Wellington's army had been issued with a pint of wine per day. It helps to dampen the pain in one's feet, and eases the aches and pains everywhere else. Presumably the alcohol helps the blood to circulate, bringing healing warmth to the joints and muscles. So I started on my bread and wine, and presently a small child came in with an enormous bowl of soup. It included potatoes, kidney beans and onions, and was exactly what I felt I needed. The next course, a tasty omelette with two massive slices of bacon, was more than I could manage.

Meanwhile the horse-people grew more and more animated as their food and wine were devoured in industrial quantities. It was pleasant to see a group who were clearly good friends enjoying each other's company. From my solitary table I watched the animals in the yard as the farmer's wife laboured to manoeuvre a large tractor, using the spikes on the front to skewer and shift large bales of forage. After a while the farmyard was obscured in mist as damp clouds rolled in across the col, blowing on a chill wind and seemingly coming from two different directions at the same time.

After a coffee I retreated to the hut and to bed. The horse-people rolled in some time later, laughing and giggling. Their chatter kept me awake but it was pleasant lying there, and I wished I could have joined in with their intimacy. Of course I could not impose my company uninvited, and in any case I barely spoke a word of their language. I was dropping off to sleep as two or three prolonged rumbles of thunder, each of them fifteen seconds or so in length, echoed across the hills, and then I heard the sound of rain.

The following morning was bright and sunny. After breakfast I was settling my bill at the farmhouse when the two tough-looking French walkers I'd seen in Ainhoa appeared. We had another conversation and I learned that Laurent and Fabian were actually brothers, though they did not particularly look alike, and they had been training for two years prior to tackling the GR10. The brothers' efforts made my preparations sound amateurish by comparison.

I set off and a few hundred metres to the east I found a man crouching at the foot of a post. I was wondering what on earth he could be up to, and whether I should offer him some of my toilet paper, but then I spotted his box of paints. The man was touching up the red and white waymarks along the path. He explained that the responsibility for this tends to devolve onto local walking assosciations or individuals, and these have varying amounts of money and enthusiasm, which accounts for the variations in the quality of the route-marking along the GR10.

The next section of the route was steeply uphill, and when I paused to look back and photograph the farm I realised that I could see the horse-people again. By now they were tiny specks on the skyline, moving along the ridge north of the Gorospil and the best part of two miles away. It was already getting hot, and at the Col de Mehatche there was not a scrap of shade. I hurried on to the east, aware that I was being pursued by a flock of sheep. The tinkling of their bells was interspersed with the aggressive shouting of the Basque shepherd.

With the sheep closing in I came to a steep and rocky descent below some towering crags. Apparently this is one of the worst spots on the entire GR10 for anybody suffering from vertigo, with steep grassy slopes dropping into a ravine, and it is a bit of a shock when it comes on only the third day. Strangely I had only the vaguest recollection of the place from my previous trip sixteen years earlier. I did not find it too difficult, but then my rather lazy start to the day had given the sun time to dry the rocks. In wet conditions it could have been treacherous. Inevitably I was on the steepest part when the sheep finally overtook me. They were an added hazard but also a source of amusement as the flock of fifty or so animals tumbled over each other along the path. It was a comical sight, especially when the track narrowed between a couple of rocks and the pressure of this great scrum of wool lifted one or two creatures clean off their feet as the current carried them through the gap. Two sheepdogs followed, and finally the shepherd himself. He paused and said something incomprehensible to me in gruff Basque, waving a large stick in my face. When he repeated the message I realised that he was asking why I was not equipped, like himself, with a similar implement as an aid to balancing on the steep ground.

This was the third day of my walk. It was short, but it was by no means easy. I was beginning to wonder whether I was simply not fit enough. My feet hurt and so did everything else. The rucksack was intolerably heavy, but I had thought a good deal about its contents and it was difficult to see what else I could jettison. Indeed, I had already made use of most of the items inside it. I was also concerned about my knees. The right knee in particular was complaining by means of nasty twinges, as though it was contemplating giving way altogether.

After four hours of walking I reached Bidarray and staggered into a hotel bar in a horribly unhygienic state of sweat. The barman, who had worked in London and spoke excellent English, affected not to notice and served me a cold beer. I eventually located the *gite d'etape* (in fact there were two and I ended up in the one further from the centre of the village) and after a shower I felt a little bit more presentable. Pierre, who had set off that morning ahead of me and had reached Bidarray earlier, told me that he had been listening to the radio. Apparently a storm was brewing up for later in the afternoon. Certainly the clouds were coming down and the wind seemed to be freshening. I decided that I would prepare my own meal that evening, packing myself with pasta ready for the long haul to St.Etienne-de- Baigorry.

Again it was time to take stock of my progress. I realised that I was still struggling to get used to the style of the map, and that the map didn't tell you everything. Sections of the route would look fairly harmless on the map until you realised that they were crossing a dozen contour lines in half a kilometre. And I had already found that features which were significant on the ground might barely appear as wrinkles on the map: the steep descent towards Bidarray would be one example and so would the rocky crags of La Petite Rhune. The Basque hills can be unbelievably steep. In mist or low cloud they almost take on the character of Chinese watercolours, with near-vertical sides.

I carried out another drastic cull of my equipment. Of course I did not enjoy it, for I hated throwing away decent kit, but I knew I had to be ruthless in getting the weight down. I talked it over with Pierre and felt a little better about it: he had reduced his pack to 18 kilos by taking some fairly drastic measures. (He had previously owned a small two-man tent weighing two-and-a-half kilos, so he had replaced it with a one-man effort weighing only one-and-a-half. He thus saved a whole kilo: ie two pounds). Inspired by his example I ditched my karrimat, which was virtually new, and the two straps around it. I threw away a compression-sack which had been holding my sleeping bag. Next to disappear was a one-pint plastic cup, which had been on top of the water bottle which I'd thrown away previously. These were followed by a Petzl headtorch with battery, a quick-dry towel, a bandage, numerous plasters, a packet of soup and two tins of fish, and finally a near-empty tin of foot powder.

Really it was ridiculous to worry about losing these items, as I could afford to replace them after the expedition. But I was loath to part with them. My training as a hillwalker had taken place when I was a teenager and student with little money: to throw anything away had been a heinous crime. It raised the question of what a man actually "needs." I could see that my planning for the expedition, or my packing, had been based on a false premise. I had approached it by asking "what might I need?" and then packed accordingly. So I had fallen into the trap of trying to cover every possible contingency. Obviously certain items were genuinely necessary – the water bottles, maps and sleeping bag for example. However, for many of the other items I would have done better to say "I might need this but it's unlikely, so if it turns out that I do need it I'll just make do for a few days until I can get to a place where I can buy it or something like it".

Having once again sorted through my kit I prepared a basic meal in the *gite* kitchen: pasta cooked in a little soup powder, sardines in olive oil with salt and pepper, a peach and a chocolate nut bar. By now Laurent and Fabian had appeared. I had seen them from a distance during the tricky descent that morning. When the sheep had overtaken me the flock had then halted almost immediately whilst the shepherd rounded up one or two strays on the steep hillside. So I had taken the chance to get back in front of the animals, with a clear path ahead of me. Looking back some time later I could see the two brothers stuck behind a traffic jam of heaving wool. They were joking about it now, and the punchline which kept getting repeated was *"jetez le mouton!"* (literally "throw the sheep!"). I surmised that they had suggested to the shepherd that he could clear the log-jam by tossing one or two of the animals down the mountainside. This joke had enabled them to cope with their frustration: they must have been baulked by the sheep for a long time because they had never caught up with me on the path into Bidarray and I had not been moving at all quickly myself.

When I retired to bed thunder was again circling around the hills. It seemed to be coming from at least two different directions, but it might simply have been echoing. I woke early and after a simple breakfast I was underway by 7am. My

French friends had been sleeping in different parts of the building and of them there was no sign. They had probably departed even earlier.

The cloud was right down over the mountains, so I decided not to attempt the long ridge of the Iparla which runs due south for several miles along the border. In good weather it would have yielded spectacular views, but in the mist I would not have seen anything and it could easily have been dangerous. I resolved to navigate across lower country to the east, following some sort of horse track for the sections that were not on country lanes. By 7.15 I had felt a few drops of rain. To put on my waterproof jacket would have been futile, for the humidity was far too high and indeed I was soon sweating profusely. I managed to get past some aggressive dogs at a couple of farms, but when I reached the point where the horse track should leave the road there was nothing there. I could have tried to follow a compass bearing, but ascending through mist on an unfamiliar hillside held little appeal. So I stuck to the lane and eventually it twisted down some steep gradients into the village of St.Martin d'Arrossa.

It was a depressing morning - grey and misty with the air dank and the trees dripping moisture. It was easy to be aware of my isolation and of the absurdity of the project on which I was engaged. The blisters under my feet were becoming desperately painful. Why was a middle-aged man crucifying himself trying to trudge across a foreign country? I decided to cut my losses for the day and follow the main road to St.Etienne-de-Baigorry. It would not do my feet any favours, but then they were going to hurt whatever surface I walked on. On the main road at least I knew where I was going and how to get there. A couple of hours of foot-slogging and I could rest at my intended destination, which was the *gite d'etape* at the northern end of St.Etienne.

By now my feet were hurting badly. When you have got blisters they hurt whilst you are walking and they hurt even more if you stop. And they hurt most of all when you resume walking after a rest. I was aware that on my expedition I ought to be thinking profound and intelligent thoughts – spiritual insights which I could bring back to my masters in the Church to justify my existence and my continuing employment for a little longer. But on this day all I thought about was the pain in my feet. I tried to rationalise things, and realised that if my feet were discounted then pretty much everything else was going well. The rucksack did not seem unduly heavy, and the cooler temperature meant that I did not have the same raging desire for water that I had experienced on the first day. If I could take away the pain in my feet I would be in a state of mind which could almost be described as approaching happy.

But in practice I could not entirely ignore the soles of my feet. I told myself that the ordeal was working to toughen them up, hoping that I could convince my brain to reinterpret the pain as pleasure. I wondered why no other walker ever appeared to be in real pain with blisters, or even to be unduly sweaty. Hiking books and magazines always show photographs of attractive views; they never show pictures of a walker with his face twisted in a rictus of pain. You don't see groups of hikers surrounded by flies as sweat gushes from every pore, coursing in streams over their tortured bodies.

Gritting my teeth I made it to the *gite*. Within an hour I had showered, washed my hair, cleaned up my feet, washed my revolting kit and hung most of my worldly possessions on a clothes line to dry out. It might rain during the afternoon, but then again it might not. The sky had looked much the same all day, and if my clothes got wet again I had not lost anything. It was still only the early afternoon, and armed with my wallet and passport I set off into the village in search of food, revelling in the fact that my feet were now comfortable in a pair of training shoes.

The first hotel I passed was closed for refurbishment, but in the centre of the village I found a bar which was doing a good trade. The "*plat du jour*" turned out to be excellent value at seven euros. By the time I had got outside some lasagne, salad, melon, bread and wine the world was looking like a much more positive place. It was the first time I had had any real lunch in four days. Besides restoring my strength it would make it easier to go on and ingest a large meal in the evening.

Wandering through St.Etienne I crossed its spectacular old bridge and entered the church. It was unassuming from the outside and dark when I entered, but when the lights came on they revealed three tiers of galleries with virtually every inch of the walls and ceiling decorated in Baroque – a style I found both impressive and sickly. Indeed, for somebody coming from an English background it was notable to find a church open during the day, but this seemed to be the case with every church building in the Basque country.

Outside the church door was a memorial listing the dead from the conflicts of the previous century. It is always salutary to see the massive impact of the First World War in particular. To me this was just a list of names, but of course they represented real lives extinguished in a welter of waste and grief. 1914 had ten names and the following year had fifteen. Surprisingly 1916, the year of Verdun, had only nine, and for 1917 there were a mere four. The final year of the Great War had eleven, and then there was one name for 1920, presumably for somebody who had succumbed to his injuries at that stage. And all of this in a village which was not particularly large. In fact St.Etienne, like many of the Basque villages, was more a series of independent hamlets loosely strung together. But even taking into account the farming settlements out on the surrounding hillsides this was not a large area to absorb such traumatic losses, even if the rural population was higher before 1914. Apparently some Pyrenean villagers did not even know whether they were in France or Spain until they were called up to go to the trenches.

Today it is difficult to appreciate fully the massive psychological impact of the First World War on a Europe which had previously been perceived, rightly or wrongly, to be a civilised and Christian place. One of my grandfathers had been a machine-gunner in the Welsh Guards and was involved at Passchendale. I had been told that on one occasion he had been sitting in a trench talking to a friend when a German shell had landed in the mud between them, but it had failed to explode. At that point he had not met my grandmother, so it follows that a simple detonation would have spared me and my blistered feet from the pain of existence.

The list outside the church door showed that the 1939-45 war had taken a lighter toll, with fourteen names in total. And then there were two victims of the Algerian conflict, dating from the late 1950's. Of course I would never know who any of these people were. But every time a man dies so does a universe. With each corpse tossed into a mass grave there goes a whole world of self-awareness and perceptions, a unique set of memories, and a particular collection of hopes and fears and relationships. Such is the pity of war.

Chapter 4.

To be a pilgrim.

Back at the bar in the centre of the village I teamed up with the brothers Laurent and Fabian. It transpired that they had left Bidarray at some unearthly hour, and had followed the Iparla ridge. They had not seen anything much in the mist. But Laurent at least had been up there twenty times before and could be confident of finding his way safely. It seemed that he knew much of the Pyrenees intimately. He had been a fellrunner and a serious climber. After a while Pierre joined us, having also crossed the Iparla. He was brandishing a walking book with a photograph of some impossibly steep rock pinnacles on the front. Laurent recognised these immediately as the Aiguilles d'Ansabere. He was laughing that as a young climber he had pioneered a new route up one of them, and he traced the line of it on the picture. The joke was that the person who subsequently wrote it up in a mountaineering guide-book had forgotten Laurent's name, and attributed his new route to "Jacques." Laurent had written to the author pointing out the error, but by then the book was in print and it was too late to correct it.

A few minutes later we were joined by a Belgian walker who introduced himself as a computer programmer called Philippe. As we drank our beer there was much laughing and joking in French, which I could barely follow, and periodic interjections of the new slogan *"jetez le mouton!"* It seemed that Philippe had experienced serious difficulties coming down the steep section where I had encountered the sheep. It had frightened him, and he had resorted to descending much of it on all fours, which had left him aching and exhausted. The group also told me repeatedly that I was carrying too much weight, which was true. Living in France and Belgium each of them was carrying only a couple of maps and a thin guide book. Whenever they finished with a map they would post it home. Likewise maps required later – ie further east in the Pyrenees – had already been mailed ahead to Post Offices, from which they could be collected in due course. By way of contrast I had a complete set of eleven 1:50,000 maps plus the four original 1:100,000 maps dating from my previous expedition in the 1980s, which added up to a ridiculous duplication. I was loath to part with any of these as they had sentimental value, and as a former geography student it would feel like a sacrilege to lose a map. However I resolved that I would have to cast sentiment aside. When all was said and done these maps were only "things" and they were there to serve my needs: I did not want to be serving them.

We finished our drinks and split up, having made arrangements for the evening meal. I was going to eat with Philippe in the eccentric little hotel in which he was staying. When I arrived at the front door for dinner a few hours later there was no sign of activity and the restaurant had a "*Ferme*" sign on it. I knocked on a side door and was granted access to a back room, where Philippe soon joined me. He reckoned that the owners of the place fancied a quiet evening so they had simply put up the "closed" sign on that basis.

The young man and the elderly woman who were running the establishment set to work and soon began to serve an excellent dinner of *pate* with salad, followed by chicken, potatoes and *ratatouille*. It was an entertaining meal with good company. Philippe described himself as a restless character. A couple of years previously, aware of a general dissatisfaction with life and work, he had resolved to go on a pilgrimage to

Compostella. He had cycled from his home in Belgium, right across France and through the pass at Roncesvalles before continuing across northern Spain. We discussed the whole concept of pilgrimage, in English more than in French, and came to the fairly mundane conclusion that the choice of journey is arbitrary but that it provides an opportunity to learn more about life and about oneself.

Philippe had some useful information about the pilgrim route, but not all of it was encouraging. He had found that during the height of summer the pilgrim *refuges* along the route were full, and that pilgrims would get up early and race each other to the next staging-post to secure a bed for the following night. This unhealthy spirit of competition was not the worst thing he had experienced. It seemed that some of the travellers had base motives and would steal each other's clothes. Philippe had lost a treasured sweatshirt off a clothes line at one point, and this had left him depressed. A Belgian woman had had her passport and money stolen. It sounded like things had not changed much since the Middle Ages, when pilgrims could easily fall prey to bandits and vagabonds along the route.

Philippe had brought his diary from that previous trip on his current walk, in which he was aiming to wander as far as he could along the Pyrenees. He had set aside three weeks for this project, but he was already finding it hard going. His diary reminded him of how depressed he had felt after three or four days on the cycling journey. Paradoxically this information seemed to be encouraging him now, because it told him that the previous trip had been seriously discouraging at times, but that he had got through that and had eventually reached Compostella. By extension his journal encouraged me, for it told me that other people also feel "low" after the first three or four days on the march. The initial euphoria of the start has evaporated and you are facing the realities of fatigue and pain.

It was helpful to know that other people feel the same: being tired and footsore did not mean I was some sort of freak.

The conversation moved from pilgrimage to other esoteric topics. Philippe had been doing martial arts for twelve years and had been impressed by some of his Japanese teachers. On one occasion he had personally felt the sharp end of a knitting needle before it was pressed with great force into the neck of one of these masters. The knitting needle had bent. As I said to him, it was a case of "don't try this at home, kids!" We found we had both seen intriguing films of Buddhist monks meditating in Himalayan monasteries whilst wrapped in wet towels. In spite of the bitter cold these characters were soon giving off steam, such was their apparent ability to control their bodies with their minds. Philippe was cheerful and good-humoured company, and seemed pretty easy-going. Even if he were to have a further twelve years of karate training I could not imagine him breaking bricks with his forehead.

As a walker Philippe was labouring under several disadvantages. For one thing he had brought a mobile 'phone with him. Secondly, he had a girlfriend back at home in Belgium. And finally (maybe most fatal of all) he was unsure how far he intended to walk. I felt slightly uneasy as I sensed that the combination of these factors was already weakening his resolve to continue with his expedition.

After coffee and a further beer I returned to my *gite d'etape* and crawled into my sleeping bag. It had been a good evening, for it was a blessing to have enjoyable conversation with a stranger and to be able to speak easily in English. Philippe and I had agreed that we would meet again for breakfast and attempt the walk to St.Jean-Pied-de-Port together. During the night I could hear rain outside the window and occasionally a car swished past on the road a few metres away.

In the morning I was vaguely aware of Laurent and Fabian moving around as they prepared to depart. When I got up at

6am Pierre was also preparing to move. He thought that with an early start he might press on beyond St.Jean and use his tent for the first time that night. I packed my kit and walked down into the centre of the village with him. It was already raining a little and the low cloud and humid air held the prospect of plenty more precipitation to come. I wished Pierre *"bon voyage et bon chance"* knowing that I was unlikely to see him again, for by the time I had made my intended diversion to Roncesvalles he would be ahead of me by two or three days.

Philippe and I ate a pleasant breakfast and got going at 8 o'clock. It was not a good morning for walking, and we were soon dripping in a mixture of sweat, rain and general humidity as we worked our way uphill through the woods on a series of sandy and stony tracks.

"What do you call these plants in English?" Philippe asked at one point.

"We call them ferns."

Philippe grunted. The vegetation was chest-high and we were getting soaked by it. "This is awful," he said.

"I know," I replied. "We call *these* wet ferns."

For the second day in a row there seemed little point in heading up into the clouds, so we left the GR10 and cut east across lower ground, following country lanes. The hamlet of Guermette was a ghost-town with three dogs that couldn't be bothered to bark and not a human in sight. We stood under a tree in the rain eating a couple of apricot-flavoured turnovers which I'd bought in a supermarket back in St.Etienne. Hot coffee would have been most welcome. The village of Anhaux was larger, but not large enough to sustain a café, so we were disappointed again. As we plodded on my feet were desperately painful, though I thought they were marginally better than the day before. Eventually we struggled into St.Jean and collapsed onto the plastic chairs on the pavement outside the first bar. Here we consumed two large *cafes au lait*, soaked

90

in perspiration and wondering whether we smelled as bad as we felt.

The coffee had made us slightly stronger but no cleaner. We continued into the town and located a moderately-priced hotel, where we managed to book into a room with two single beds and an *en suite* bathroom. The room also had a balcony which might, in theory, have been an asset for drying our kit, but its value was compromised by the fact it faced north. Of course the sun was not shining and there was no wind either, so our kit was destined to remain damp. Having cleaned ourselves up we headed through the drizzle to a bar above the Nive at the Pont Neuf. Here we attacked the *plat du jour*, which was a massive side of pork ribs served with *pommes frites*. Until I met Philippe I had associated Belgians with beer and chocolate: I had not known that they were so fond of mayonnaise. At any rate, he devoured large quantities of it on his two portions of chips.

Philippe was a friendly and encouraging companion, but I felt unsettled walking with somebody who was already losing the determination to carry on. Over lunch he admitted that he was toying with the idea of giving up, right here in St.Jean. He had set off from Hendaye, hoping to get to Cauterets in about three weeks, but it seemed he had already had enough. The tricky descent on the path to Bidarray had really frightened him and broken his spirit. As I said to him, he might have been scared of heights but I admired his courage in admitting it. I didn't want to persuade him to give up, nor to encourage him to carry on. It would have to be his decision.

Eventually Philippe resolved that he would head for home the following day, which would be a Friday. We discovered that a train from St.Jean would get him to Bayonne, from which he could reach Bordeaux. From Bordeaux it would be a fast train to Paris and then on to Lille. If his girlfriend was able to collect him from the railway station in Lille he'd be home by ten o'clock in the evening.

I did not blame Philippe at all for his decision. Meanwhile I was as determined as ever to persist with my own project. Nevertheless, Philippe's state of mind had some effect on my own, and I weighed up various possibilities, wondering whether I should abandon my intended detour to Roncesvalles and thus save a couple of days. Even at this early stage in the expedition I was worried about my progress, or rather the lack of it. The first five days of walking had barely moved me a fraction of the distance across France, and with less than six weeks to go I knew that time was not on my side. I considered going to Roncesvalles and then striking east, to pick up the GR10 further on, but I could not buy anything like a decent map for the Spanish side of the frontier.

Eventually I came to a decision. Friday would be a rest day in St.Jean, so that I could soak up the medieval atmosphere and allow my feet to toughen up a bit. Then I would head for Roncesvalles on the Saturday, and retrace my steps the following day, aiming for the hamlet of Esterencuby just to the east of St.Jean.

I slept reasonably well, though my mattress was soft and I woke with some slight pain in my lower back. Philippe reported that his bed had been pretty firm, and suggested that I switch to that one for the following night. He would not be needing it, of course, because by then he ought to be at home in Belgium. His advice sounded sensible but alas, when I tried to book a further night in the Hotel Itzalpea I found it was not possible. I had feared that the hotel might be booked up, but this was not the case. On the contrary the staff were going to be away for the weekend and so the hotel was closing that afternoon. I was bemused: it was a Friday in late June and my hotel was closing. This information reinforced the somewhat whimsical impression I had built up of this charming town when we had arrived the previous day. It had been noon and it was the middle of the summer, so the Tourist Office had a notice up saying that it was closed for lunch until 2pm. I had then tried to take money out of a dispensing machine, and that hadn't worked either. The second machine I tried was also out of order, but I eventually scored a success with the third.

After breakfast I strolled down to the railway station with Philippe and bade him farewell. If the French railway network was as efficient as it was rumoured to be then by nightfall he would be reunited with his girlfriend halfway across Europe. I wished him all the best, but I knew that if I had been in his position I would rapidly have been regretting the decision to quit the walk - probably before the weekend was over. Philippe wished me luck for the remainder of my odyssey. He reckoned I would make it to the Mediterranean because I had the right attitude, and I promised that I would send him a postcard when I got there.

After Philippe's departure I headed back to my hotel and packed my kit. The Hotel Itzalpea had suggested I try the Hotel Central, so I lugged the great rucksack down the hill in a thin drizzle. The people at the Central were keen to help but they had no vacancies. After a couple of 'phone calls they told me I could have a room at the Hotel Continental. So I carried the rucksack back up the hill and installed myself at the Continental, which was just round the corner from the Itzalpea. I was now about fifty metres away from the room where I had spent the previous night, and moreover I was in one of the more expensive hotels in town. So be it; at least I had secured a base from which I could spend a relaxing day exploring St.Jean.

For an hour or so I wandered aimlessly, soaking up the pseudo-medieval atmosphere and revelling in the fact that there was no weight on my back and that my feet felt relatively comfortable in their training shoes. I bought seventeen or eighteen postcards and sat for another hour in a café, scribbling messages to relatives and friends and giving odd snippets of information about my current location. For example: "St.Jean-Pied-de-Port is the capital of northern Navarre, and owes its name to its position at the foot of several Pyrenean passes, the most notable of which is the Pass of Roncesvalles. It is something of a crossroads where routes from Pamplona, Biarritz, Bayonne and Lourdes all converge at a natural bridging point on the Nive. Its location was obviously a strategic one in both the economic and the military senses." And so on.

Having finished my coffee and posted my cards I headed first for the citadel, which dominates the town from a crag to the north-east. It originally dated from the early 17th century, having been built by a knight called Deville, but around 1680 it had been given a thorough facelift by Vauban, who was Louis XIV's great commissioner for fortifications. Vauban's work can be seen all over France of course: his genius for military architecture basically consisted of aligning walls in elaborate patterns so that attackers would be channelled into killing-zones where they could be cut down by crossfire.

From the citadel I worked my way down the hillside to the ancient gateway of the Porte St.Jacques. Several of the medieval pilgrimage routes converged at a village called Ostabat, just north of St.Jean, and then the pilgrims would enter the town through this gate. Indeed they still do. A few yards inside the gate, and heading down the steep Rue de la Citadel, I came to the office where contemporary pilgrims were getting their papers stamped. It seemed that those carrying the correct cards could prove that they were genuine pilgrims, and this would help to secure them accommodation along the route. Moreover when they reached Compostella, which meant another month of hard walking along the Cantabrians, the ecclesiastical authorities would exchange their fully-stamped cards for certificates, thus giving them proof of their achievement. The scallop shell, symbol of St.James, was ubiquitous, and many of the pilgrims had one dangling from the outsides of their rucksacks.

Further down the cobbled street were a smattering of the inevitable souvenir shops, all playing on the historical theme, and at the bottom of the hill I entered the church of Notre-Dame-du-Bort-du-Pont ("Our Lady at the end of the bridge"). Like much of the rest of the town it was constructed out of sandstone with an attractive purple tinge to it. This was obviously a traditional place of worship for pilgrims heading for Compostella. For many of them the ultimate hope would have been to get a miracle of some sort from Saint James, but in the meantime they would have been aware that they were facing the daunting crossing of the Pyrenees. I was aware of it too, as I followed the Catholic custom of dabbing my fingers in the baptismal font and making the sign of the cross on my forehead, before settling down for a few minutes of quiet reflection. I wondered how many countless thousands of souls had sat in this building before me, before going outside, turning left through another medieval gateway and crossing the bridge over the Nive? Beyond the bridge the cobbled Rue d'Espagne ran uphill through the quarter south of the river, and then the next stop would be the monastery at Roncesvalles. I reminded myself that for most of our forebears the mountains were a fearful place and were to be avoided if at all possible. The great ranges of the Alps and Pyrenees were the abode of dragons and goblins, and this realm was only entered by the foolhardy or the truly desperate. Even today it is barely two centuries since the first ascent of Mont Blanc, and mountaineering as a recreation is largely a British invention of the 19th century.

Of course it would be foolish to enter the mountains today with anything less than the greatest respect for them. I was apprehensive about the weekend's detour to Roncesvalles, and after consuming another *plat du jour* for lunch I bought up supplies of food and mineral water. I was unsure about my chances of getting accommodation at Roncesvalles, and did not particularly fancy the prospect of sleeping rough on a Spanish hillside on the Saturday night. But I would take my chances: at least for a day I could enjoy the illusion that I was a medieval pilgrim.

If I was expecting the walk to Roncesvalles to be tough then I was not disappointed. It eventually took over eight hours to get there. Most of the way was relentlessly uphill, and my feet hurt horribly as they discovered new pressure-points where they could develop blisters.

I had settled my bill at the Continental the previous evening, so that I could leave at the crack of dawn. As usual I woke a couple of times in the night, and at one stage I could hear thunder, though it seemed to be some distance away. Breakfast, consumed quickly in my room, was an apricot-flavoured pastry and a banana. I slipped out of the hotel before 7am and entered the old town through the French gate, going past the restaurant where, the previous evening, I had enjoyed a decent meal of chicken and rice for 13 euros. At the Rue de la Citadel I turned right and headed down past the church and out over the old bridge, following where countless Christian feet had trodden before me. As I continued up the Rue d'Espagne I fancied myself surrounded by these thousands of ghosts, and wondered what effect their presence and spirituality might have had on the atmosphere and fabric of the town.

For the moment there were no other souls in sight. If there were any other contemporary pilgrims heading for Roncesvalles that day they had either left even earlier or they were still in bed. Outside St.Jean the road rose steeply and steadily and the route continued along a winding lane. I overtook two middle-aged Frenchmen who were walking slowly, and we continued to leap-frog each other for the next

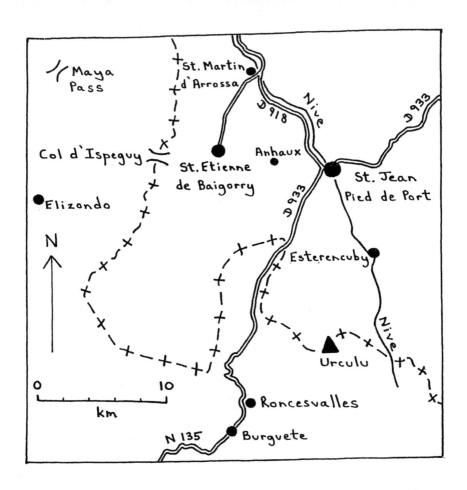

St. Jean-Pied-de-Port to Esterencuby.

few hours. It was a good temperature for walking, but far too humid, and as I ascended through the clouds I was hampered by my glasses misting up over and over again. It was another exercise in serious sweating, pausing regularly to gulp down more water or eat the occasional snack. I tried to walk as much as possible on the grass verges beside the road, hoping to grant my feet some relief from the asphalt and passing enormous thistles in the process, as well as beautiful purple and yellow flowers and butterflies with fantastic colourings. The road was only wide enough for a single vehicle, and the few that passed in the course of the morning were almost exclusively little white vans driven by Basque shepherds. As the angle of ascent levelled off the sun finally managed to break through the mist and I emerged onto more open hillside. The road continued south over bleak and featureless terrain, with the moorland inhabited only by loose flocks of sheep and goats.

Five hours into my day's walk I was overtaken by a young German. He was moving quickly and easily and had a scallop shell dangling from his light rucksack. A little further and I ran into a kindly old man who was dispensing drinking-water from containers which he had driven up there in his car. This was the point where the pilgrim route (marked intermittently with blue and yellow paint) left the road and headed off across the hillside. I had found that these painted waymarks alternated with the more familiar red and white, with the latter designating not the GR10 but its smaller cousin the GR65. The pilgrim route, now marked with little sticks, continued across open hillside, and with growing anticipation I sensed that I was approaching the frontier. I passed a stone cross surrounded by a rusty railing which was itself festooned with smaller wooden crosses and other tokens – clearly it functioned as some sort of wayside shrine. Around a couple of corners and I was walking alongside a wire fence with a wood on the other side: I reckoned I was now following the border itself. I passed a large slab of stone with a scallop shell inscribed on it, plus the words "St.Jacques de Compostella" and, in large digits, "765 km." "Lord, have mercy," I thought. I had been aware that Spain was a large country, but it was nevertheless a shock to be told so bluntly that at this point a pilgrim was still the best part of 500 miles from Compostella. I continued past a little resting-place at a fountain, and suddenly there it was: an imposing slab of pink rock with another depiction of the scallop shell and the single word "Navarre." This was the point where France became Spain, and in a couple of strides I moved off the *Chemin de St.Jacques* and onto the *Camino de Santiago*. Was it not part of the legend that Santiago Matamouros – "Saint James, slayer of the Moors" – would return to save Spain in its hour of greatest peril? I raised my hand, clutching at the hilt of an imaginary sword. "For Santiago and for Spain!" I roared stupidly. I had not noticed the young couple snogging in the grass a few metres away, and they scrambled to their feet with terror in their eyes.

Having apologised profusely for frightening these young lovers I beat a hasty retreat - or to be more accurate I continued my advance into Iberia. It was strange to think I had just crossed an international border, indeed a frontier which had been fought over by two substantial powers for centuries. Yet I had walked across it without encountering a fence or a gate, let alone a customs post or a policeman.

A short distance into Spain and I was overtaken by Roberto. He was an architect from Brazil who had just flown to Lisbon, Madrid and Pamplona before using a bus to reach St.Jean. It was the first day of his walk to Compostella. Like many modern pilgrims he was taking some time off work to reflect on where his life was going. We walked alongside each other, talking for about ten minutes and negotiating some patches of wet mud before he raced on ahead. My conversation with Roberto prompted me to think more about the motivation for pilgrimage. During the Middle Ages Compostella ranked third, behind only Jerusalem and Rome, as a place of pilgrimage for Christians. Indeed it was reckoned that Saint James came second only to the Virgin Mary herself in terms of the efficacy of prayers directed to him or through him. The first foreign pilgrimage to Compostella was organised during the 10th century by the Bishop of Puy, and the destination became particularly popular with English pilgrims. For the medieval pilgrim the journey to Compostella was probably about penance and paying for one's sins, and possibly about seeking a miracle from Saint James. For many of the modern pilgrims it is more an exercise in internal reflection, though I had heard that some people would carry a stone in their rucksacks to symbolise their burden of sin and guilt. On reaching Compostella these stones could be left on a large pile, to signify the completion of the penitential journey. Nevertheless, I was forming the impression that for many people these days the driving force behind their pilgrimage was less to do with finding God and more to do with finding themselves.

The whole concept of pilgrimage intrigued me. Superficially it looks like a counter-cultural thing which goes against the grain of much of our modern western lifestyle. But it occurred to me that in some ways it is actually very well suited to modern life. The pilgrims travelling to Compostella would each have their own reasons for making the journey, but it was possible that their walk, just like mine to the Mediterranean, was actually the ultimate in individual self-indulgence. It may well have been a hard path that they were treading, but ultimately each of them had chosen to follow it, presumably seeking pleasure and fulfilment at some level or other.

I wondered what I would find at the Roncesvalles monastery – whether there would be any sort of a community into which I could plug myself and which would act as a counterweight to what I perceived as the individualism of the pilgrimage. A

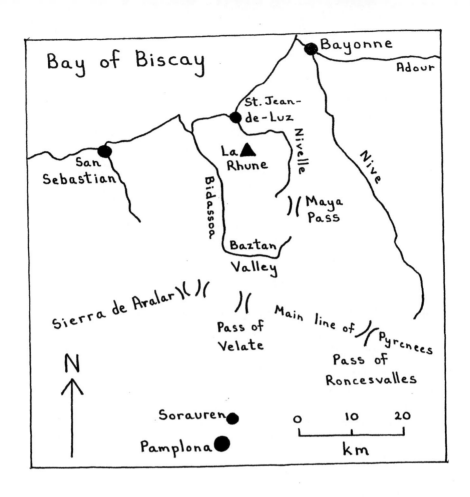

The Pyrenean Battlefield.

monastery has a communal dimension to its life, and once a person is involved in a community they have to make sacrifices and compromise to some extent. I had now reached the Col de Lepoeder and could make out the position of the monastery far below. I knew that a couple of miles away to the west – to my right as I looked down at the monastery – there had been some significant Napoleonic fighting in the Pass of Roncesvalles.

Following Wellington's crushing success at Vitoria on 21st June 1813 the French had been driven back over the Pyrenees, leaving their two fortresses of San Sebastian and Pamplona as besieged outposts. On 12th July Napoleon installed Marshal Soult as the new commander-in-chief, ordering him somewhat optimistically to "re-establish my affairs in Spain." In fact Soult did a remarkably good job of restoring discipline and morale to the shattered remnants of the forces previously under Joseph Bonaparte and Marshal Jourdan. Within a fortnight he had assembled a useful army of over 70,000 men and by the end of the month he had hit back at Wellington and caused some serious discomfort to his opponent.

Wellington's front ran from the coast, at the point where the River Bidassoa empties into the Bay of Biscay, along the line of the Pyrenees to the pass at Roncesvalles, which is over thirty miles inland to the south-east. He could not advance further, or even feel totally secure, as long as San Sebastian and Pamplona were holding out to his rear. Having only a single siege train Wellington deployed it against San Sebastian, hoping to capture the strategic port, and he left the blockade of Pamplona to Spanish troops. This left the remainder of his forces, just over 60,000 British and Allies, spread across a huge swathe of rough country as they covered the frontier and protected the two sieges from any French interference. The headaches were compounded by the Sierra de Avalar, the rugged range which connects the Cantabrians of northern Spain to the Pyrenees, because these hills bisected Wellington's forces and provided a formidable obstacle to lateral movement. So the danger was that if Soult brought overwhelming pressure to bear at a single point Wellington would not be able to move his reserves quickly enough to counter the threat, and this is more or less what happened on 25th July.

Wellington had been expecting Soult to make a thrust on the coast in an attempt to relieve San Sebastian. The port-city looked ready for capture and Thomas Graham, the general commanding the First Division, was in fact planning to storm it on the 25th. However, Wellington had guessed wrongly. Soult was intending to march on Pamplona, and he had scraped together enough rations to feed his men for four days. Wellington was at his headquarters at Lesaca, just west of the Bidassoa, when he received news that Graham's assault had failed, and he set off in a state of some anxiety to ride to San Sebastian.

As soon as Wellington left all hell broke loose on the Allied right. One French corps, commanded by D'Erlon, attacked the Maya Pass with the intention of advancing to seize the Col de Velate which was the main pass over the Sierra de Avalar. The loss of this pass would have made it much harder for Wellington to feed reinforcements across to his right and to counter the main French thrust, which consisted of two corps under Reille and Clausel coming through Roncesvalles. At Maya the British defence was mishandled and Rowland Hill's Second Division was forced to fall back on the village of Elizondo in the Baztan Valley. Meanwhile over at Roncesvalles Lowry Cole was coming under increasing pressure.

Cole was commanding 11,000 men, consisting of his own Fourth Division plus a single brigade of the Second Division and General Morillo's Spaniards. To describe the fighting as a battle in a pass may conjure up a misleading impression: it suggests a narrow defile between vertical cliffs where the topography enables a small force of defenders to block the advance of a more numerous host. (The classic example of this sort of scenario would be the 300 Spartans who obstructed a quarter of a million Persians in the pass at Thermopylae). However, in the Pyrenees this was not exactly the case. Both Maya and Roncesvalles were strong positions but the passes, seen in profile, were fairly shallow. In this rolling countryside small groups of French infantry could cross the frontier with ease at any number of points: provided they were not opposed all they had to do was what I had just done – walk up to the crest and down the other side. However, roads were necessary for bringing up the artillery, the cavalry, the baggage and for the orderly movement of larger bodies of infantry: hence the significance of the passes. So the fighting was not simply in the bottom of the Roncesvalles pass but involved the high ground on both sides, and in places the French were easily obstructed because the ridges were so narrow that they could only advance in single file.

Cole was able to hold his ground all day against greatly superior numbers. However, in the late afternoon a thick mist descended and Cole lost his nerve, imagining that the French were creeping through the murk to surround him. That evening he began to disengage and retreat. Wellington, who had only received one message from Cole during the 25th, believed the Roncesvalles attack to be a feint and spent the early part of the 26th halting D'Erlon's advance in the Baztan Valley. With no fresh news from Roncesvalles Wellington decided to ride over and see Cole, taking the Sixth Division with him.

Near the top of the Col de Velate a letter was delivered to Wellington, and it made alarming reading. Cole had written it from a position ten miles below the Roncesvalles Pass, and its tone was defeatist. Although retreating down a valley with abundant defensive positions Cole was talking about falling back on Pamplona or even Vittoria. If that happened it was conceivable that the British could yet be pushed all the way back to Portugal.

By now Cole had been joined by General Picton with his "fighting Third Division." Picton was an eccentric and fiery Welshman who had played a heroic role at Vittoria, amongst other places. He was destined to be wounded at Quatre Bras on 16th June 1815 and, concealing the extent of his injuries, he would fall at Waterloo two days later when a musket-ball went through the front of his top hat. He was senior to Cole but the latter's depression seemed to affect his judgement and he ordered their combined force of 17,000 to continue the retreat. By the time Wellington reached them on the 27th they had halted on a steep ridge above the village of Sorauren, just outside Pamplona.

The defensive position at Sorauren was immensely strong, but had one serious drawback. The road by which reinforcements might arrive came out at a junction in front of the left end of the British ridge. So Wellington needed to divert his reinforcements by a more roundabout route, and sat on the parapet of the bridge at Sorauren to dictate orders to his military secretary, Lord Fitzroy Somerset. The latter galloped off to the west: later in life he would achieve fame as Lord Raglan, the British commander in the Crimea. Wellington rode out of the south end of the village just as French cavalry entered it from the north. There followed one of the most dramatic moments of the entire Peninsular War as the lone horseman galloped up the flank of the hill to the Allied ridge. One of the Portuguese battalions recognised him first, and the cry went up of "*Douro! Douro!*" – this being the name they had bestowed on Wellington following his audacious storming of Porto back in 1809. The chanting spread along the line as the British joined in with "*Nosey! Nosey!*" Wellington was not given to flamboyant gestures and normally he would not allow the troops to cheer him, but on this occasion he made an exception: he wanted both sides to know he was there. The effect was immediate, not only on Allied morale but on Marshall Soult who postponed his attack and waited for his own reinforcements to come up.

Wellington's theatrical entrance had bought some time. That night a tremendous thunderstorm soaked the troops, but the British were coming to regard these downpours as a portent of victory on the morrow. The same thing had happened the night before Salamanca and the pattern would recur, up to and including the night before Waterloo. The next day the fighting was grim and bloody. Wellington described it as "fair bludgeon work," but by the end of the day it was Soult who was organising a retreat.

By 2nd August Soult was back in France. His foray into Spain had inflicted 7,000 casualties on the Allies but cost him twice that number. Morale in his army plummeted. Soult made one or two further attempts to take the initiative, and was still trying to relieve San Sebastian on the day it eventually fell at the end of August. The French garrison in Pamplona held out until the end of October, but that factor failed to deter Wellington from resuming the offensive. By then he had crossed the Bidassoa and taken La Rhune: the next stage would be the Petite Rhune and the Battle of the Nivelle. The Peninsular War was moving inexorably towards a conclusion.

I needed to move on too. Feeling refreshed by my break I continued along the pilgrim path. It took me a further hour or so to descend 1500 feet, though the route was well marked as it wound down through attractive woods of beech. At last I emerged just behind the monastery and worked my way round to the front. The young German was sitting on a bench in the sunshine, deep in conversation with another man who sounded Teutonic but in fact came from Rome. For a while we discussed the concept of pilgrimage and whether it had become more popular over the last twenty years or so, maybe as an escape from the pressures of modern life. The German and the Italian both reckoned that the facilities and organisation along the Camino had improved greatly during that time. At least, they had improved for genuine pilgrims. In my case, not being bound for Compostella and not having the requisite cards, I would be unable to get a bed in the pilgrims' dormitory.

This was what I had been expecting, but I had heard that there was some sort of hostel or "*auberge*" at the back of the monastery which would cater for people such as myself. I made my way through the complex of buildings to the northern courtyard, where a notice on a locked door declared that the auberge would open at 4pm. That gave me thirty minutes to wait, so I sat on a fragment of stone pillar which was in a shady corner of the yard. An elderly woman emerged from one of the buildings and proceeded to pace up and down the courtyard along a marked path and with the precision of a metronome. Slowly and deliberately she plodded back and forward, seemingly counting the paces in each direction in what was, I presumed, a daily discipline of exercise. She made no attempt to acknowledge my presence, which suited me well as I was covered in sweat, dust and grime and perfectly content to remain invisible, wallowing in my weakness and exhaustion.

After a few minutes my peace was disturbed. A group of middle-aged visitors entered the courtyard, possibly looking for admittance to the *auberge*. Their party consisted of a man, who appeared to be some sort of guide, and four women. I struggled to exchange a few words with them, but in my fatigue my brain was struggling to dredge up much in the way of foreign vocabulary. For a minute or two they stood around me in a semicircle, a few feet away, saying little and staring at me as though I was an animal in a cage. It seemed to me that this was the sort of sullen hostility with which civilians might examine an enemy pilot that had been captured, and I wondered what I had done to merit their contempt. It was probably a good thing that I could remember little French and spoke next to no Spanish, as I might have been tempted to tell them where to go. In the event they arrived at some silent concensus themselves, and skulked off to examine another part of the monastery or its grounds.

At the appointed hour the *auberge* opened for business, but it did not open to me. Although I was the first potential customer the woman behind the reception desk was not very welcoming. I had no booking; I was not a genuine pilgrim; the place was fully booked, and so on. Any and all of these reasons may have formed part of her torrent of Spanish or Basque, to which I sought to respond in my broken French. I knew that there was a hotel just down the road, and when I told her that I would seek accommodation there her face betrayed relief all too quickly.

At the hotel I was soon experiencing the ecstacy of a bath followed by a shower. Dressed in clean and dry clothing I made for a small bar and consumed a couple of glasses of sangria. The drink contained less orange juice than I had expected, because the barman seemed to have his own recipe in which this ingredient was substituted by vermouth. I had no complaints, and was now in a much more positive frame of mind for exploring the village. I had felt slightly vulnerable in the bar, owing to my lack of knowledge of the Spanish language. Once I had said *"buenos dias"* and *"cafe con leche, por favor"* I had pretty much exhausted my stock of vocabulary. It did not take me long to look around the village, as the entire place consisted of a mere handful of buildings clustered along a hundred metres or so of curving road, just where it came up from Pamplona and began its steep ascent to the pass.

It was no accident that a Napoleonic battle had taken place here, because the pass was one of those geographical features which would be of strategic and tactical importance in any age. There was testimony of this not a hundred metres away down the road, where the building next door to my hotel purported to be the tomb of Roland. Following the collapse of the Roman Empire western Europe had experienced varying degrees of chaos until Charlemagne became sole ruler of the Frankish kingdom towards the end of the 8th century. His campaigns included an invasion of Spain in the year 778, when he was invited by Ibn al Arubi, the governor of Barcelona, to come and help counter the Muslim forces of Umayyed the Caliph of Cordova. The first resistance to Charlemagne came from the Christian Basques of Pamplona, and Charlemagne duly besieged and captured their town. A lucrative campaign through Saragossa followed. Defeating the Caliph of Cordova was an event of some long-term significance, as it constituted the first step in the long process of Reconquista which would culminate in the decisive victory over the Moors at Las Navas de Tolosa in 1212.

However, disaster struck as Charlemagne withdrew through the Pyrenees. His narrow columns, weighed down with their plunder, were winding their way slowly through the pass at Roncesvalles. It was the perfect spot for an ambush and the aggrieved Basques closed in. The Frankish rearguard was being commanded by Roland, who was governor of the frontier marches of Brittany and was also Charlemagne's nephew. Roland and his companions were cut off, forced back downhill into a meadow, surrounded and slaughtered to a man. The whole event was written up as an epic poem, the "*Chanson de Roland,*" which became a medieval classic. In the poem Roland tries to summon help from his uncle by blowing into his great horn Olifant, but he blows so hard that blood bursts out of his mouth and ears, all to no avail. The poem clearly reflects the date of its composition in the 12th century, for its author transposes the Basques into Saracens so that the saga can serve as propaganda supporting the First Crusade to the Holy Land.

I made my way back into the monastery complex, which appeared to be extensive and well maintained. In fact it looked more like some sort of conference centre than a monastery, and the impression that substantial money was being invested in it was reinforced by a giant green crane which was anchored somewhere behind the buildings. I slipped into the chapel just in time for the Mass. The elderly priest spoke quickly and in Spanish, and the acoustics did not make it any easier to follow. The only words I could pick out were Pedro, (for the gospel text had been about Saint Peter), and "*peregrino*" which is the Spanish for "pilgrim." The congregation eventually built to about eighty. There were no hymns, and I was surprised to see the collection basket being handed around by an acolyte during the prayer of consecration.

I did not take the sacrament: I would have liked to but I knew that the Pope would not approve and I did not wish to abuse the hospitality of the Roman Church. However it was moving to sense something of the size of the global ecclesiastical monolith – to think about being one out of a thousand million people, all of whom are in communion with the Bishop of Rome and thereby in communion with each other. The end of the service reinforced this and provided a touching moment as the priest read out a list of countries. Several dozen pilgrims made their way to the altar rail for a special prayer of blessing: clearly the list consisted of the nations from which tonight's batch of *peregrinos* had come.

Dinner at the hotel consisted of a massive salad, followed by large chunks of lamb in a delicious sauce but without vegetables. I asked for a glass of wine and received a full bottle of the local Navarre red, so I drank just less than half of it. I woke at 3am and moved quickly into the bathroom as I was overtaken by an attack of diahorrea. I felt weak, with the familiar sensation of slight nausea which I had noticed several times during the first week of the walk. I put it down to hard exercise in a warm climate, combined with not enough food, or at least not enough of the right sort of food at the right times. I kept hoping that I would come upon an Italian restaurant where I could stoke up on pasta, but this seemed unlikely for the foreseeable future. I scrambled back into bed, determined to snatch a little more sleep. In the morning I would have to face the daunting ascent back up to the Col de Lepoeder, which meant about 1500 feet of climbing.

In fact the following morning proved to be enjoyable. The hotel's breakfast was substantial and raised both my energy level and my morale. I was tempted to sign up for a guided tour of the monastery, but that would have meant delaying my departure until about noon which would have destroyed any chance of reaching civilised accommodation later in the day. As it was I set out rather late, at 9.30am, and the clear sky suggested that I would be facing hot sunny conditions. The ascent back to the col was quite pleasant, for the path up through the beech woods was easy to follow and well shaded, and a breeze was freshening the air. My feet hurt, but compared to the agony of a few days previously the pain was nothing, and this fact in itself served to give me confidence. I could also sense that some fitness was beginning to come through. I had been walking for a whole week now, and I was starting to get the benefit of the training effect. It is a simple fact that our modern sedentary life prevents most of us from getting seriously fit, unless one happens to be a professional athlete, a soldier or a Basque shepherd. For most people it is impossible to exercise all day long, and our lifestyle has softened us in comparison with our ancestors.

After ninety minutes of ascent I was back at the col. The wind was stronger at this height and I could see clouds blowing in from the south and west – possibly a portent of changing weather. But I was not unduly worried. In fact I felt stronger, physically and mentally, than I had at any point during the

111

previous week. Psychologically it was good to know that my detour to Roncesvalles was over. I was now heading north and east to rejoin the GR10 and to continue in what was, for me, the correct direction, towards the Mediterranean. An added inspiration was the fact that Crane had passed this way.

Nicholas Crane's epic walk from Cape Finisterre, near Compostella, to Istanbul had taken him along the mountain backbone of Europe. Having followed the Cantabrians he had joined the Pyrenees at Roncesvalles, heading east along the High Level Route more than the GR10 until he reached Mount Canigou in Roussillon. From there he had struck north, crossing the Cevennes to reach the Alps. By the time he got to Vienna he was still only half way to his goal, the former Constantinople, and he still had a couple of great loops through the Carpathians and Balkans ahead of him. The whole journey was something like 10,000 kilometres or 6,000 miles, and it took him 506 days or roughly seventeen months. It was a phenomenal achievement, and beautifully documented in his 1996 book *"Clear Waters Rising."* My own walk, even if I made it to the Mediterranean, would be dwarfed by Crane's: measured in terms of time or distance my peregrination would not be a tenth as long as his multi-marathon effort.

If I was inspired by Nicholas Crane it was clear from his book that he in turn had been a disciple of Patrick Leigh-Fermor. The latter's book, *"A Time of Gifts"*, was and is a classic of the walking and travelling genre. Leigh-Fermor had set out in December 1933 at the age of eighteen, determined to walk to Constantinople. So his journey took him across Germany in the year after Hitler had become Chancellor. In the end he would be away for more than three years, wandering down through pre-war Europe and sleeping in castles and haystacks.

In fact *"A Time of Gifts"* only described the first half of Leigh-Fermor's walk, from the Hook of Holland to the border of Hungary. I had read it and thoroughly enjoyed it, but I found the sequel *"Between the Woods and the Water"* less enthralling, as I felt the author got bogged down in being clever about languages. Clearly he was an outstanding linguist and he had learned several languages during the course of his walk. There can be no doubt that Leigh-Fermor was a remarkable character. At the outbreak of war in 1939 he joined the Irish Guards and fought in Albania, Greece and Crete. He subsequently returned to occupied Crete several times, and spent a couple of years living in the mountains there. Disguised as a shepherd he sought to ferment further resistance, and his activities culminated in the kidnapping and evacuation of the German commander on the island, General Kreipe.

So now I was walking in the footsteps of Crane and approaching the frontier, about to cross from Spain to France in a reversal of the previous day. This fact reminded me of the curious switching of sanctuary which had taken place across the Pyrenees around the year 1940. During the Spanish Civil War the Republicans had used the high passes of the Pyrenees to flee in droves from Franco's forces and escape into the haven provided by France. It is difficult to imagine the desperation with which these wretched people, mostly civilians, had fled their own homeland with their lives hurriedly stuffed into suitcases. Then, with Spain neutral during the Second World War, the direction of flow had reversed and the Pyrenees were crossed by Jews and others who had fallen foul of the German or Vichy authorities. It is estimated that 35,000 people escaped into Spain during the 1939-45 War. Many were Allied airmen and escaped prisoners-of-war who were spirited along escape routes by the sophisticated *"Maurice"* organisation, presumably making their way on to Gibraltar or Lisbon and contacting the British authorities.

I had a passing interest in the Spanish Civil War which dated from the Fourth Form in school. Compelled to write a dissertation on a twentieth-century author I had chosen Hemingway, attracted principally by the fact I had read and enjoyed *"For Whom the Bell Tolls."* It no doubt said something about my adolescent psychology that I called my essay "To Whom the Bell Told" and added a subtitle – "How Ernest Hemingway's life and work were affected by an interest in death." I had little difficulty assembling plenty of material relevant to my topic, and much of it came from Hemingway's time in Spain. His book *"The Sun Also Rises"* featured Pamplona, now just a few miles away behind me and scene of the famous bull-run which was, of course, the sort of stupidly masculine showing-off in which the great man revelled. Hemingway's bullfighting book, *"Death in the Afternoon,"* was another obvious source of material, and so was his involvement in the Civil War. I had always had serious problems with this particular conflict because the more I learned about it the more confusing it seemed to become. Given the bewildering array of political parties, groupings and acronyms involved in the struggle it is quite an achievement just to remember who was on which side. An added complication was that, it seemed to me, both sides were as unpleasant and repulsive as each other. I had tragic visions of people being sucked into the struggle from all over Europe: on one side naïve idealists fighting for some imaginary Brotherhood of Man and on the other side young fools who had been intoxicated with the glory of fascism. Nevertheless Hemingway's rugged literature stirred something in my formative and impressionable mind, and by the time I had reached the Sixth Form I was attempting to write a novel. The result was a crude and immature piece of literature in which the Spanish Civil War provided the background for a psychologically-tortured mountaineer (a former anarchist) who

114

was engineering an elaborate suicide for himself by attempting to conquer an unclimbed Alpine peak. Enough said.

I had always enjoyed writing and being creative myself. My Sixth Form novel may have been a flop, written during an adolescence in which I had softened my brain with regular overdoses of *Abba* and Tchaikovsky, but I had achieved modest success elsewhere. During the 1970s there had been a spate of pornographic books and films with titles such as *"Confessions of a Window Cleaner"*. I decided I would cash in on my status as a House Chess Captain and was pleased when my short story *"Confessions of a King's Bishop's Pawn"* was reproduced in the school magazine.

If I had drawn inspiration from Nicholas Crane's walk I was also inspired by his book, and it helped to crystallise an idea which had occurred to me back in St.Jean-de-Luz. Maybe, in addition to completing my own walk, I too could write an account of my adventures – a sort of cathartic autobiography? It would certainly add an extra dimension to my journey.

The idea had been on the back burner for a few years. Every so often I would give it a gentle stir and adjust the heat under it. At times my writing could border on a compulsion: when I started being creative I could not stop. Something inside me had to express itself. As I thought about the idea it seemed to me that my book, if that is what it would eventually be, already existed. It was there even now, buried in my subconscious. A few parts were already in the conscious part of my mind – a few outcrops of rock jutting out above the surface and already visible – but the rest was hidden deep in the geological substrata. I just needed the chance to do a bit of mining and bring material to the surface, and it was possible that this very walk might provide me with the opportunity.

I was already keeping a diary or journal, and writing up a few notes each evening as I reflected on the day just gone. I knew that even if I could write them up as something worth reading the odds would still be stacked against getting the book published. But no matter: I would write it for my own satisfaction in the first instance. If it ever reached the shelves in Waterstones so much the better. Having said that it occurred to me that it would be pleasant if my book sold plenty of copies and the royalties were sufficient to put me on Easy Street. I decided that to achieve the latter my book would need a catchy title – preferably something akin to those lurid tabloid headlines that link clergymen with sex.

By now I was drawing close to the frontier. My diversion into Spain had been a bit disappointing, and I was looking forward to crossing back into France where at least I could speak a little of the language. I wondered how Marshall Soult's men must have felt, straggling back from their various abortive attempts to relieve Pamplona and San Sebastian, knowing that they had been defeated yet again but clinging to the prospect of reaching safety on their home soil. No doubt many of them would have empathised with the old idea that "Europe ends at the Pyrenees." Of course this sentiment is a cultural comment, but it is reinforced by the physical geography of the mountains. The French side of the range receives far higher precipitation and the topography is generally steeper. Besides providing gushing torrents and waterfalls this makes hydro-electric power and a degree of light industry possible. The French slopes are rich in beech and pine, whilst the Spanish hillsides are generally barren, sunscorched and shadeless. The entire Pyrenees have undergone rural depopulation over recent centuries, but it is more marked on the Spanish side of the frontier where entire villages can stand abandoned, some of them miles from the nearest roadhead. In recent years parts of the mountains have experienced a slight reversal of the trend, with wealthy urban dwellers building or renovating properties in the hills, but of course this is not on a scale which is likely to restore the population to the levels of the medieval or early modern periods.

By 11.15 I had been walking for less than two hours, but it was at this point that I met the first pilgrim heading in the opposite direction. He must have set out from St.Jean at about 5am. From that point my walk to the frontier took me forty-five minutes, and during that time two or three dozen walkers shot past, mostly in ones and twos but with the occasional foursome. They were a mixture of young and middle-aged people with one or two who were quite elderly. They came in all shapes and sizes, but most of them looked pretty fit. Clearly I was moving against the current. Was this the race to secure a bed for the next night about which Philippe had warned me?

I passed the stone marking the border, and fifty metres further on I stopped at the fountain of St.Jacques to replenish my water and to eat a snack. A few people were already sitting there, resting from their exertions. Pilgrims continued to go past, but one in particular attracted our attention. He was an immensely tall youth and it looked as though his body had been constructed from pipe-cleaners. He could barely have weighed seven stones. Without saying a word, or indeed acknowledging anyone's presence, he proceeded to entertain us with a series of stretching exercises, bending his body into a variety of impossible shapes. After a few minutes of this he shouldered his pack and continued into Spain, walking barefoot. I noticed that he had a pair of sandals with him, for they were dangling from the outside of his rucksack along with the inevitable scallop shell. Maybe they were a concession to comfort and would be brought into play when he encountered sharp stones.

A few metres beyond the fountain I passed the large grey stone again: it was still 765 km to Compostella. Or in my case 765 km from Compostella. The stone reinforced an odd point which had been troubling me. With each of the thirty or so

117

pilgrims I had passed I had exchanged greetings, which in most cases meant a quick nod and a *"bonjour"* or *"buenos dias."* In a few cases I had had a brief conversation, and had been asked why I was going in the wrong direction. I had tried to explain, in my broken French, that I was really on an expedition along the Pyrenees and I had only gone to Roncesvalles on a brief detour. But I could equally well have said that in the Middle Ages you would have seen plenty of pilgrims going "the wrong way." When the medieval pilgrim reached Compostella, or for that matter Rome or Canterbury, the job was only half done. They still had to get home, and there was no bus or train to whisk them off to an airport. They simply had to walk – back across Spain to Roncesvalles and then to St.Jean and on to wherever their homes were in France or Germany.

I now left the pilgrim trail for good. Up to this point I had been retracing my steps from the previous day, but now I struck east across the hillside to pick up a country road. Indeed it was a continuation of the same metalled track I had followed up from St.Jean just twenty-four hours earlier. I followed it east and north as it contoured around a huge basin below the peak of Urculu, and a few miles further on I descended on long zig-zags through the Forest of Orion. It was tedious work and hard on the feet, but I knew that a few hours of solid marching would bring me to Esterencuby and put me back on the GR10 a whole day east of St.Jean-Pied-de-Port. So from St.Jean to this point would have taken me two days instead of one: the diversion to Roncesvalles had in effect taken me around the two long sides of an isosceles triangle rather than letting me cover the shorter third side.

In this way I justified the journey to the monastery, telling myself that it had not jeopardised the overall expedition because it had only really cost me one day. However, it had also cost me considerable wear and tear on my feet, which were now suffering on the tarmac even as the rest of my body was tormented by horseflies. It was an increasingly hot afternoon. The clouds which I had seen blowing in a few hours earlier continued to do so, but they broke up into smaller formations and remained high. At one point I had stopped to rest when a young French couple drew up in a car. They were searching for the source of the Nive, and I was able to put them right by using my map. They offered to give me a lift down to the valley. I thanked them for their kindness but dismissed the offer with a laugh, saying that I was walking all the way to the Mediterranean. The laughter was directed at myself and at the absurdity of my project. For the moment I was suffering badly and the Med was an unimaginably great distance away.

I got down to Beherobie where dozens of people were enjoying a blazing Sunday afternoon at a pleasant spot on the river. Pausing to strip off my boots and socks I submerged my feet in the freezing water, seeking to draw some of the heat from my skin and taking the opportunity to examine some enormous blisters. The two largest were on the insides of my feet near the heels. After this cold water treatment it was a little easier to continue, and I followed the road north alongside the Nive. This water would in time become part of the Adour and would empty into the Atlantic at Bayonne. After eight-and-a-half hours of effort it was a relief to reach Esterencuby and get booked into the Hotel Larrymendi.

This was my fourth different hotel in four nights. My room numbers had been 4, 17, 29 and now number 1. I had discovered that I really liked staying in hotels, having a shower to myself, wallowing in the luxury of clean towels and clean sheets, and especially having a double bed where I could stretch my aching limbs. For some reason my legs felt they were recovering faster when I could spread my feet wide apart in the bed. The other tactic was the old cyclist's trick - whilst awake I would lie on my back on the bed with my feet high up the wall, as this enables the lactic acid and the other waste products of exercise to drain back out of the leg muscles.

The evening meal was enormous. It began with a massive bowl of soup containing vegetables, potatoes and pork. Along with its accompanying bread and water it added up to a decent dinner in itself. However, it was followed by a second course of fish and a third course of *jambon* (bacon) with *ratatouille* and salad. I had lubricated all this with half a bottle of the local white wine, even before the ice-cream and coffee arrived. My food was served by a pleasant waitress with blond hair and prominent cheekbones. I failed to finish all of every course, but it had been magnificent, and I knew I was fuelling my body ready for the marathon effort I would have to put in the following day.

Back in my room the television was showing football. France were playing Cameroon and I gleaned from the commentary that there had been some sort of tragedy: it sounded like one of the Cameroon players had collapsed and died during a game a few days earlier. The actual football looked tedious, so I decided this was the time to deal with my largest blisters. Maybe the half bottle of white wine had given me courage. In the bathroom I assembled the various equipment for the operation, namely a box of matches, some antiseptic cream and plasters and a pile of paper tissues. However, in my First Aid box I could not find any needles, and I remembered that I had thrown them away in Bidarray in one of my attempts to reduce weight. It might not matter: I still had my nail scissors and they would do the job. With a mixture of amusement and trepidation I lit a match and sterilised the sharp end of them. Then I chose the largest blister, picked my spot, and shoved the scissors into my skin. Fluid sprayed across the bathroom and struck the opposite wall. I went on to repeat the procedure on my other foot. There was no pain and after I had applied cream and plasters to the damaged areas I went to bed strangely satisfied.

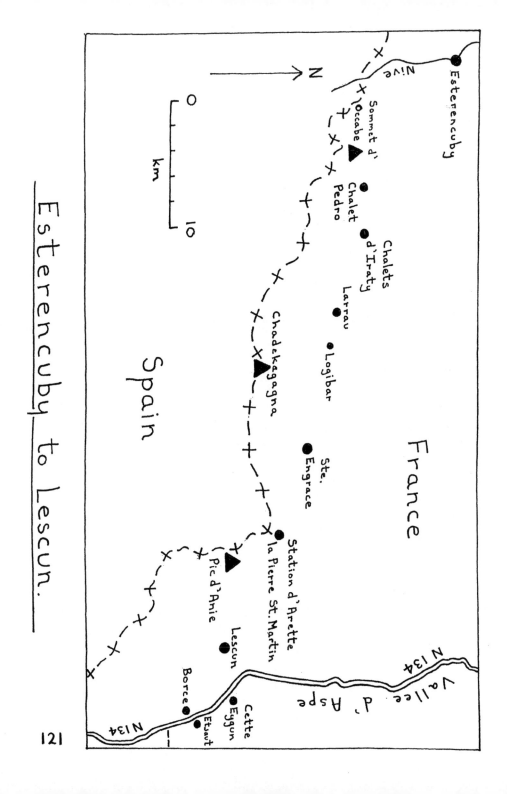

Esterencuby to Lescun.

121

Chapter 5.

In the footsteps of Crane.

Days earlier I had identified Monday's stage as a tough one: possibly the crux of the entire expedition. On the map it looked like a hideously great distance from Esterencuby across to Chalet d'Iraty, and there was no hint of any accommodation along the way which I might use to shorten the stage. I was anticipating a marathon of nine or ten hours, so it would be my third long day in a row.

The first part, from the church in Esterencuby, was horribly steep, but then the gradient slackened off as I followed country lanes. The conditions were warm and at this altitude I was still amongst cultivated fields and woodlands, so there was no breeze and the humidity was high. For my first rest I perched on a fallen tree trunk and dripped perspiration everywhere. It was difficult to see how a man could sweat so much without melting away completely. After an hour or so I had emerged onto more open hillside where it was a little fresher, and I followed the lanes across the plateau of Phagalcette and up to a col. The next hour or so was disappointing. Through my efforts so far I had gained 2000 feet in altitude, but I now had to sacrifice 600 of these as I followed a rough vehicle track down the side of a valley.

At the end of the valley the track swung back, traversing a couple of streams and bringing me to the bottom of a frightfully steep hillside. My progress on the ascent was painfully slow. The angle was not steep enough to warrant scrambling on all fours, but nevertheless I was measuring each stride in inches. I was well aware that I did not want to strain anything, particularly in my knees, so I stuck to my snail's pace. But even a snail's rate of progress is still progress, and provided you can keep a steady rhythm going it is always surprising how rapidly you gain height. Moreover the Basque hillsides tend to have a convex profile, so the steepest section of the ascent comes first and then the gradient eases slightly. I fought on, panting heavily. I was determined to resist the temptation to keep stopping and looking down in the hope of seeing significant progress. As long as there is more hill left to climb you are better off attacking it, and then when you are forced to rest you can look back down the slope with that much greater encouragement. Gradually the angle eased and the path traversed off across the hillside through deep grass, still ascending but not quite so steeply. A few horses watched me as I continued upwards, scrambling over a couple of rocky sections before I came out at the next col. The ascent had taken one hour of continuous exertion.

At the col a small farmhouse advertised the sale of cheese and honey. Here I had a brief conversation with an Irishman called Brendan. He was a short but resilient-looking character in his fifties, and I had seen him previously in the hotel back in Esterencuby. It seemed that he had left the hotel about twenty minutes before me that morning, and he had been resting at the col for twenty minutes, so on that basis we were moving at much the same speed. He pressed on whilst I sat down to consume my lunch - a large cheese sandwich made from half a baguette.

After lunch the next section ran across open grassland. It reminded me a little of the hillsides above the Amman Valley in South Wales. This was where my mother had grown up and as a child I had been taken there every summer for a couple of days with my grandparents. I had always loved this Carmarthenshire hillside, with the bareness of the grass blowing in the wind and a few sheep scattered around. The narrow lanes followed stone walls and telegraph poles until, at a greater height, they struck out across the bleak moorland. Wandering along them I felt that I was in spirit connected to the High Plains of the United States, or maybe to the Pampas in Patagonia, the High Veldt in South Africa or the sheep country in New Zealand: areas to which Europeans (including a few Welshmen) had spread during the 19th century in an era of adventure and enterprise, opening up challenging landscapes.

These romanticised memories did not last long, for I came once more to a steeper section of grassy hillside. The route was marked with paint on odd rocks and little wooden poles, but these were spaced well apart and it was obvious that I would have to use my compass. At first the bearing was 120 degrees, then I switched to 150 degrees as I swung south towards the summit of Occabe. The main difficulty was provided by the wind. It had been rising steadily throughout the day, and now it seemed determined to scour me off the hillside. I fought my way upwards, bending into the howling gale as I was buffeted sideways and backwards on every other stride. Numerous clouds had blown up during the morning, and I had assumed these would bring rain, but it never materialised. Instead the clouds remained high and scudded across a blue sky, with their shadows racing each other across the grass. On the skyline above I could see the tiny figure of Brendan, who was moving resolutely and appeared to be covering the ground at some speed, which was remarkable as he was going uphill and more or less directly into the wind. At least the wind was granting me one pleasure as, for once, I could feel totally free of sweat. As I advanced into the screaming gale any semblance of perspiration was evaporated instantly.

Just below the Occabe peak the trail turned east, and immediately I was more sheltered from the wind. An hour of descent, much of it on badly eroded tracks, brought me through woodland to the Chalet Pedro complex, where I bought and guzzled an ice-cream, a chocolate bar and two glasses of sangria. I had been walking for seven hours. From Chalet Pedro it was another couple of hours over to Chalet d'Iraty, and it was a hard and tedious grind. This brought me to the place where Douglas and I had been soaked in a night of rain back in 1987, but I didn't really recognise the place. Extra ski chalets and odd facilities had sprung up, and I had the impression that some of the forest had been cut back. There seemed to be a few people wandering around but not in vast numbers. I located a small Tourist Office and booked a bed in their *refuge*, finding that I had been put in the same room as Brendan. He seemed to be well settled in the place and had obviously been there for a couple of hours. It's possible that I had more or less matched his time for the morning's walk, but during the afternoon battle against the wind his strength and stamina had served him well whilst I had been struggling.

I headed downstairs and into the bathroom. This was a slightly odd arrangement as to get any water from the shower you had to feed it with tokens bought from the Tourist Office. As I was drying myself I was disturbed by a French couple who burst in. They did not seem perturbed by my nakedness. Indeed they were heading into the shower together, presumably to save tokens.

In the bathroom I had opened my toilet bag and discovered that I had lost my shampoo. I must have left it in the hotel in Esterencuby, and I was not going to walk back twenty miles to collect it. I realised that through tiredness I was beginning to make careless mistakes. At Chalet Pedro I had allowed my rucksack to topple off a chair and smash to the ground. Fortunately neither my compass nor my camera seemed to be damaged, but it was still a stupid error and it annoyed me for an hour or two afterwards. I was also aware that I needed to guard myself against getting overtired, which could make me

125

vulnerable to colds and infections. I had a history of being prone to mouth ulcers when generally run down. Many of these had been pretty harmless, but some had been excruciatingly painful. I could still remember an occasion years earlier when my tongue had been suffering badly. I was trying to chew a slice of Battenburg cake and I was in agony. At the clinic I had stared at the ceiling whilst the doctor probed around my mouth with a wooden spatula.

"I think you've got Hector's infection," she announced.

That did not sound good. I had only ever heard of two Hectors. One had been a hero in the siege of Troy, and the other was a cartoon dog in a children's television programme. I wondered which of the two was responsible for my current plight.

I never found out. A merciful prescription of antibiotics put paid to Hector and his germs within a few days. But I did not want to experience similar problems on my current trip, miles from any possibility of medical help. I had now had three long and punishing days in a row, and I was relishing the prospect of a softer day on the Tuesday, for it should be a mere six miles or so downhill to Larrau. After that I would have to negotiate the tricky set of gorges which would bring me to the notorious (and in my case historic) ascent to Station d'Arette-La Pierre-St.Martin.

Mouth ulcers were not necessarily the greatest of my medical sufferings. Before travelling to India I had undergone a series of injections which included cholera and typhoid (administered simultaneously, one in each arm) plus a rabies vaccination. All of them were unpleasant, but the worst was the gammaglobulin injection, supposedly a precaution against hepatitis. As the nurse was preparing her equipment my instinctive fear of the needle was multiplied by the sight of the syringe. It was large, and the contents appeared to be a glutinous orange substance with a consistency somewhat similar to sweet-and-sour sauce.

Worst of all, the injection was to be administered into my backside. It went in slowly, and it hurt. Yes – it really hurt. I emerged from the experience with a pair of sweaty armpits and a grudging respect for the gay Christians.

Moreover, once the procedure had been completed the nurse explained that there are actually six different strains of hepatitis, and my injection would only protect me against two of them. I cleared out of there fast: I wasn't going to hang around to hear about her antidote for the other four strains.

Later in the evening I ate dinner with Brendan in a small restaurant near our accommodation hut. In the corner a television was showing the tennis from Wimbledon. Ferrero of Spain, the third seed, was struggling in the first set against Grosjean of France – a curious match-up given our current position so close to the Pyrenean frontier. I told Brendan about my detour to Roncesvalles. He was not too surprised to hear of my rather rough reception there, for it bore out what he had heard previously from friends who had done the journey to Compostella.

Much of my kit was either damp or outright wet, so I tied it to the frame of a children's swing and retreated to bed, trusting that the wind would dry it out overnight. The following day, a Tuesday, would herald a new month: it was the first of July. At breakfast we watched eagles circling, for here at Iraty we were at 4000 feet and the great wingspan on these enormous birds enabled them to soar up effortlessly on the mountain thermals before dipping their wings and swooping down in great arcs. Brendan set off shortly after, determined to make further substantial progress that day. I got going at a more leisurely pace, knowing that it should take only three hours or so to get down to Larrau. Nevertheless I managed to make a slight navigational error leaving Iraty and ended up walking through a herd of cattle. These massive bovines, each with its own giant bell around its neck, eyed me as I passed but continued to

127

munch their grass impassively. Descending through ferns and scrub I regained the road and followed it for a while. On the way down numerous cyclists went past in the opposite direction. There were maybe thirty of them in total, all decked out in serious cycling kit and all suffering on the steep climb. Two had dismounted to push their bikes. Possibly they belonged to some sort of club which was pursuing its own punishing training regime. Closer to Larrau a tractor passed me, and it in turn was overtaken by a convoy of eleven motorcycles which were clearly travelling in a group. I barely saw a car all morning.

The Hotel Etchemaita had two stars and was excellent. The only room available required the payment of a single supplement, so I swallowed hard and agreed to it. It turned out to be good value. For one thing the shower showed evidence that it had been designed by an architect who occasionally used one: it had simple controls, a shelf for the soap and even a "clothes line" which could be extended from one side of the cubicle and attached, under tension, to the opposite side.

The television in my bedroom did not have a lot to offer, with just three or four French terrestrial channels. On one side there was a ghastly "reality TV" offering called *The Nice People*." It seemed to consist of a dozen vacuous non-entities from different countries locked in a villa together. On another channel George Clooney and his hospital colleagues had been dubbed into French. With nothing to distract me I began to think more seriously about my schedule for the walk, and I became increasingly concerned. I had no desire to end up walking against the clock in order to complete my project, but it looked likely that I would be forced into doing precisely that. As I studied my maps I made various calculations, and however cleverly I tried to rework the figures they always led back to the same conclusion. The five weeks remaining for the expedition would be the barest minimum of time in which it was possible to reach the Mediterranean. There would be little margin for error. For that matter there would be precious little margin for illness, injury, bad weather or bad luck.

The following morning I got away from the hotel in good time, but immediately I had a problem because a large dog latched onto me and would not go away. It had no collar, and wagging its tail it proceeded to follow me down the road towards Logibar. This was disconcerting. A couple of times I told it clearly that it could not stay with me all day, and it certainly could not accompany me all the way to the Mediterranean, so it ought to return to Larrau where it belonged. But it did no good, and the animal continued to lope along, sometimes thirty metres behind me and in the middle of the road. There was not a lot of traffic, but I was still worried that it might get run over. I was equally concerned that it might cause an accident for which I would then get the blame. I shouted at the animal to go back but again it refused. Eventually, after about a mile and just approaching Logibar, a couple of cars drove past in the opposite direction. The second one pulled up with a screech and reversed slowly back towards me. I thought that the driver was going to remonstrate with me for not having the dog on a lead, and I was about to start explaining that I didn't own the wretched thing when he jumped out with a grin and began to coax the animal into his vehicle.

"Is it your dog?" I asked.

"No. It lives at the hotel in Larrau where I work. I'll soon get it back there."

"Thanks. It's good to see you. I was beginning to wonder what I was going to do with the poor animal."

"Oh, don't worry about it." The man gestured towards the dog, which was now climbing into the back of his car. "He runs off regularly like this. This is the third or fourth time I have caught him. The owners are used to it."

The young man shoved the dog's hind-quarters into the car and clambered in himself. It was a blessing when he drove off and I was relieved of any sense of responsibility for the sad creature.

At Logibar I entered the bottom of the Gorge d'Holzarte and began to ascend on a narrow, rocky trail. Signposts warned that the actual watercourse was dangerous: the river was controlled as part of a hydro-electric scheme so its level could rise suddenly even in good weather. I climbed steadily, dripping in the humidity of the surrounding forest, and after an hour I had turned into the Gorge d'Olhadubi and its suspension bridge had come into sight. This bridge was thrown across a gorge so deep that you could barely see the bottom of the abyss amongst the trees, and it was not for the faint-hearted. As I crossed it the whole structure swayed and bounced with every stride. Several of the timber planks on the walkway were clearly due for replacement, and the suspension cables themselves had their own coating of rust. I proceeded as rapidly as I could, trying to concentrate on minimising the sway and bounce by treading only on the centre-line of the walkway. When I reached solid ground again I decided to celebrate my survival, and thus my continuing existence on the planet, by eating a half-melted chocolate bar.

Beyond the bridge the path wound up a steep hillside before it traversed along a contour to the head of the gorge. It crossed the stream again on a smaller bridge and gained height on the opposite bank, now heading north-west which was virtually the direct opposite of my desired line of travel. In fact I'd been following a variant of the GR10 in order to explore the gorges. At a grassy col I rejoined the main trail and had a talk with a pleasant French couple in their late forties. They were the first people I had seen since I had entered the bottom of the gorges at Logibar three hours earlier. I had found the gorges mentally taxing, as their forested sides gave them a somewhat claustrophobic atmosphere and the ascent out of them was on a narrow path across steep grassy hillside. An unfortunate walker who tripped and landed awkwardly might quickly assume enough momentum to go bouncing down to the bottom.

Lunch was not a problem because I didn't have any, other than a few biscuits. I then made rapid progress to the south-east along a level but rough vehicle track, with good views of the bulky peak of Chardekagagna on the frontier to my right. Passing through a flock of several hundred sheep I ascended to yet another col and spoke to a Belgian man who had walked up from St.Engrace in five hours. After a few minutes he moved on, heading for the gorges and Logibar. From my point of view the correct route down from the col was not immediately obvious, and as I was studying my map I noticed a gangling youth with long hair and a yellow jacket coming up the track towards me. He was moving quickly but something in his body language conveyed the impression that he did not really know where he was. The only equipment he was carrying was a blue water bottle. He asked the way to Logibar and I pointed him in the right direction, but I would not have had the confidence to bet a lot of money on him finding it before nightfall.

Further down the track I passed a French girl who was sitting beside the path eating a snack. She looked well equipped and said she was camping out, using a small tent. A little further on I came upon a man and two women who I had previously seen from a distance at the Chalet d'Iraty. The women were probably in their late thirties, and the man maybe slightly older. He was a great bear of a character, and as I walked past them he bawled something incomprehensible at me in a rather aggressive tone. He seemed to be warning me about the true path being across the valley. Indeed it was, in as much as there were two alternative lines of descent on opposite sides of the

Gorge de Kakoueta. I replied that I was perfectly happy with the route I was following.

During the course of the afternoon I gradually became entangled with these characters as a long downhill track gave way to a path descending overgrown sunken lanes. First I got talking to the French girl, Danielle, who told me that she was actually German and came from Frankfurt. In fact one of her parents was French and the other German, which accounted for her Gallic name. She had just finished telling me this when we came round a corner and ran into the bear-man, who was standing still and scanning the hillsides above. He began to complain about the GR10 being poorly marked at this point, which was true enough. He seemed to be talking French but I could not follow much of it owing to his accent, which was possibly Spanish and which, combined with his tone of voice, had the unfortunate effect of making him sound aggressive. Suddenly he broke off the conversation and shouted something up the hillside to where his two female companions had just appeared on the skyline.

Danielle and I continued down the hill. She told me that she had talked to this odd trio earlier in the day. The man had told her that his two companions were his "gazelles" and that they were useful as route-finders. Indeed, my brief meeting with them had left me with the impression that if navigation was ever problematic the bear would simply stop whilst the two gazelles fanned out across the hills scouting for the correct trail.

It was spotting with rain as we reached the valley and began to trudge up the main road. Danielle was aiming for the hamlet of Senta, where she intended to pitch her tent at a campsite. My plan was to halt a kilometre earlier, at a place called Calla, for I understood that there was some sort of *gite* or possibly a small hotel there. However, as we slogged up the road we never noticed a sign for Calla, and we certainly never saw a hotel or anything resembling one. The road narrowed and went on interminably, as it does so easily at the end of a fatiguing day. It became obvious from the map that we had missed Calla and its hotel, if it had ever existed, for we had now reached another hamlet with a couple of small *gites* opposite an 11th century Romanesque church.

There was no sign of life in either *gite*, nor in the bar between them, but as I turned a corner I walked straight into Brendan. He had arrived a few minutes earlier and had already installed himself in a dormitory, so I figured I would do likewise. I stripped off my sweaty clothing and grabbed my soap and towel to head across a few yards of open ground to the outhouse which contained the shower. At that moment Danielle came round the corner with a young blonde woman who seemed to be part of the management of the place. *"Puis j'avoir une nuit dans votre gite, s'il vous plait?"* I asked in my best French. The blonde grunted and said something in reply: I didn't catch all the words but the meaning was clearly "it looks like you're pretty well established here already." I completed my ablutions quickly – with no hot water there was little incentive to spend too long under the shower – and having got dressed I went to search for the blonde so that I could register my presence formally.

Having found her behind the bar I signed in for the night. "Is there a restaurant somewhere near here?" I asked, remembering that a couple of hundred metres back down the road I had seen a billboard advertising one. "Yes," she replied icily; "you're standing in it. Dinner will be at 8 o'clock."

I gave a weak smile and retreated to the dormitory, cursing myself for my stupidity. Of all the crazy things I could have done in the Pyrenees I had succeeded in booking myself, full board, into the very place that had poisoned me back in the 1980s.

In the event the dinner was fine, though I didn't eat very much for personal psychological reasons. When the desserts appeared I gracefully declined the offer of *gateau basque* and settled for two peaches instead. Brendan and I shared a table: fortunately both of us were sufficiently easy-going to let the management describe us as *"les deux anglais"* even though one of us was Irish and the other Welsh. Danielle, who had set up her tent behind the *gite*, joined us for dinner. It was a good humoured business as we downed a large bottle of the local red wine. Danielle had travelled in Africa, and spent several weeks in Rwanda. Brendan, who was a maths teacher, had taken a year off work and had travelled extensively in Latin America and India. We compared notes on the subcontinent, for I had been there for two months at one stage, albeit half-my-lifetime ago. In fact I had travelled there as an undergraduate geography student who needed to produce a dissertation as part of his degree studies.

My plan had been to spend one month in the town of Madurai, three hundred miles south of Madras, and I had my accommodation booked in the local theological seminary. The intention was to write a thesis on poverty and economic development in rural India, and to do so via a case-study looking at the history of electrification in Madurai District. The electricity was a strategic thing in several respects, principally because it powered small pumps which in turn irrigated the fields.

I spent a couple of days as a tourist, visiting Madurai's massive Hindu temple complex and climbing up the insides of the highly ornate towers. Then it was down to work. My attempts to collect data were soon being frustrated. The original intention had been to visit the State and District Electricity Boards, study their records and interview their personnel, but in this I was obstructed by the all-pervasive bureaucracy. I fared no better with the local Economic

Development agencies and my situation was beginning to look desperate. I had a back-up plan which involved visiting villages and electricity sub-stations, but as Madurai District had over one thousand villages in several thousand square miles of countryside it was not a practical or attractive prospect. There simply would not be enough time.

Feeling somewhat disheartened I was wandering along the busy West Masi Street. It was hot and dusty and awash with people, and in addition to the pedestrians I had to dodge the rickshaws, the taxis and the odd sacred cow. Passing one particular shop I felt an overwhelming urge to stop and go inside. In fact I soon realised that it was not a shop as such; it had a sign saying "Government Literature Centre" over the door and the inside appeared to consist of some sort of public reading room with the day's newspapers spread across large desks. I wandered around, and noticed that in the shadows at the back of the room there was a mass of shelving supporting files and folders. Out of curiosity I pulled down one or two boxes of papers and began to browse.

Within an hour I had found exactly the data I required for my thesis, and there were even maps to go with it. The following day I returned with my notebook and spent the morning scribbling furiously. The only problem lay with the maps. There were eight or nine which were pertinent to my thesis and there was no way to copy them.

That evening I solved the problem. Concerned about the standards of health and hygiene I might encounter on my journey I had travelled to India with several packs of Izal's medicated toilet paper in the bottom of my rucksack. It was tracing paper in all but name. Of course the individual sheets were not large enough for my purpose but it did not take long to lay out numbers of them on the floor and to tape them together. Back at the archives I spent a couple of days doing some painstaking tracing and the job was done. Within a week

135

of embarking on the research I had accumulated enough material to write an interesting essay when I returned to England, and in the meantime I was free to be a tourist again.

In the course of time I received a pleasant letter from my tutor at Cambridge. My final overall degree was an Upper Second but the examiners had awarded my dissertation a "First." Indeed they had been so impressed by it that they wanted a copy for the University Library. For all I know it is still there.

I did not want to bore Brendan and Danielle with all these details, and as we were at the dining table I decided not to recite the saga of how I had turned toilet paper into maps. By this stage we were eating our main course, and we had been joined by the bear and the two gazelles, who were eating at a table on the other side of the room. In fact they weren't eating much at this point, for the bear seemed to be giving the other two some sort of pep-talk in preparation for the following day. On our table we speculated in low tones about the nature of this bizarre *ménage a trois*, but failed to reach any solid conclusions. We let the subject drop. As Brendan wisely observed, the three of them were no doubt holding a similar conversation about the three of us.

Back in the dormitory I unrolled my sleeping bag on a mattress in the corner. I was a few mattresses away from one of the gazelles, who slipped into her bag wearing a fetching white tee-shirt and pants. Outside the window Danielle's tent had been joined by a second one belonging to a young couple from the Midlands who were studying medicine in Cardiff. I slept like a log.

In the morning Danielle was away first; her tent disappeared whilst Brendan and I were consuming breakfast. In deceptive early sunshine the strange threesome set off in a new formation, with gazelles to front and rear. Maybe this was the fruit of their team-talk the previous evening. Then Brendan got underway and I followed a few minutes later, just after 9am. I was expecting a tough climb, for it would be roughly 3000 feet of ascent to reach La Pierre-St.Martin. I also knew that I had not eaten enough the previous day, and I had no snacks to carry with me. However, I was not unduly worried. In fact I felt thankful, for I was getting out of this particular valley with my health intact, and compared to the 1987 debacle that was a hugely significant improvement.

The ascent was hard work. The first part was through woodland which gave way to something reminiscent of a tropical rainforest, confined in the darkness of what appeared to be a narrow offshoot of the Ehujarre gorge. Above that it was interminable forest, all at a steep angle. I moved upwards desperately slowly, but in spite of that I found I was overhauling each of the people who had set out before me. After two hours I came to a cattle trough which had a distinctively-carved human head on it, and shortly after this I caught up with Danielle who had set out with forty minutes start on me. At this point the woods were petering out and giving way to open grassy hillside, and as we talked Brendan reappeared from below, moving strongly and steadily. By now the bear and gazelles were some distance behind us, and were being overtaken by the young medical students.

Brendan, Danielle and I plodded on through the mist and cloud, taking a further hour and a half to reach the col. This is the actual location of "St.Martin's Stone" and the site of a bizarre annual ritual. The ritual can be traced back to a 14th century dispute over grazing rights between the inhabitants of the Baretous valley on the French side of the frontier and the people in the Roncal valley on the Spanish side. The better pastures were on the Roncalese side of the col. It was a classic case of competition for scarce resources leading to conflict, and after a series of violent encounters a settlement was reached in 1375. This involved the "Tribute of the Three Cows." Every year the Baretous villagers had to hand over three heifers in return for the right to use their neighbours' pasture. The ritual is still enacted every year on July 13th, so we were ten days too early to see it for ourselves, but I had heard that in recent years the event has attracted crowds of hundreds. Possibly it is the oldest treaty remaining in force anywhere in Europe.

My two companions stopped at the col to eat a snack but I decided to continue as I felt suddenly chilled. We were now above 5000 feet and the clouds were blowing across in a freshening wind. I followed the main road towards la Pierre-St.Martin, noting how the vegetation had changed over the last few miles. I was clearly into limestone country here, and the trees consisted of conifers dotted across the bleak hillsides. I left the road and cut across the grass towards a low ridge. Coming over the ridge the sudden sight of the ski resort was a shock, for an almost surreal scene lay before me. I remembered the resort as an ugly place from the 1980s expedition, but in the intervening years its size and ugliness seemed to have multiplied. The high-rise concrete blocks were square and functional; the car parks had expanded and masses of new chalets were dotted across the bleak lunar landscape leading towards the Pic d'Anie.

Keen to find some accommodation I wandered into the centre of the resort. It was the most depressing dump I could remember seeing anywhere. "If God had any taste at all he'd have left here long ago," I thought. Maybe he had. The place had the forlorn decay of a ghost-town. Nothing seemed to be open and there was hardly anybody to be seen. I eventually got into a building which appeared to be some sort of centre for the resort. On the ground floor the food shop was shut. A notice on the door proclaimed that it had closed in April and would reopen on July 5th. As it was currently Thursday 3rd that meant I had forty-eight hours to wait. I found a cash dispensing machine but it was out of order. Cautiously I began to explore the building, checking each room and working my way up through the floors. The sinister atmosphere was heightened by some ghastly rock music which was blaring from somewhere out of sight on the upper floors. It was like being the first sailor to board the Marie Celeste after she was found. For a moment I wished that I had the comfort of a weapon to hand – preferably a revolver or a machine-pistol. I eased open a door and thirty yards away down a corridor I could see a figure working in an office. She had her back to me and, deafened by the music, she remained oblivious of my presence.

Softly I closed the door and retreated down a staircase, wondering whether I had somehow wandered onto the set of the latest Stanley Kubrick film. I knew Kubrick had died but I figured that, with his powerful imagination, he would not allow that small nuisance to deter him from making further films. Down on the second floor I turned a couple of corners and pushed open another door, which granted me access to a café with a tiny bar. Four or five people were sitting around a table smoking. Their expressions suggested that I had interrupted a meeting - or possibly a séance.

I asked whether the place was open, and one of the women got up. She had little to offer in the way of food or drink, but I managed to buy two crunchy fruit bars and a beer flavoured with tequila. For the latter the waitress gave me an empty glass and presented me with a bottle: she had removed the top and jammed a slice of lemon into the neck of the bottle as though this would convince me that I was now on some exotic Caribbean island. I consumed it quickly and left the premises. Outside everything was closed, and the only hotel I could locate looked boarded-up and derelict. I speculated on whether the resort had fallen victim to global warming. Maybe the climate had changed, and possibly the place was at too low an altitude and no longer got sufficient snow.

Briefly I considered pressing on to Lescun, but that was another six hours away and I was tired already. I could not possibly reach it before 8pm and I had no food with me. The last hope was to investigate a *refuge* which I had spotted perched on a rock near to where the GR10 had entered this godforsaken settlement. If I could not find food there then I would be in trouble. I would be forced to continue walking, simply because there would be nothing to gain by stopping, and it might well lead to a hungry night huddled under a rock somewhere out on the hills.

I struggled up to the *refuge* and found Danielle and the medical couple pitching their tents outside. We entered the hut, where Brendan was eating a sandwich and dispensing Irish Whiskey to everybody from a plastic bottle. I got the impression that he had been holding this resource in reserve until his journey became particularly desperate. Clearly his judgement was telling him that he had reached that point now. I gave the group a short report on my reconnaissance to the centre of the village, and without a word Brendan offered the whiskey around again.

The five of us discussed our situation, and reasoned that it could have been a lot worse. For one thing the couple who were running this *refuge* were warm and welcoming. Indeed, their hut seemed to be the only warm and welcoming establishment for miles in any direction. It had one or two drawbacks, notably water shortages caused by the limestone geology, but it had a friendly atmosphere. Owing to the water situation the shower was limited to three minutes per person, but once cleansed we regrouped around a crackling fire in the main room. Later in the afternoon clouds rolled across and rain fell intensely. It came down in sheets for thirty minutes, and after a brief interlude there was a second burst nearly as long. Of the bear and the two gazelles there was no sign, and we became increasingly concerned. We could only speculate about their fate. The two medical students had been the last to overtake them, and reported that the trio seemed to be moving slowly and stopping frequently. We had all noticed that it was cold around the col, and none of us relished the thought of being caught on the open hillside in such torrential rain. However, it was clear that there was nothing we could do to help them. Even with all five of us searching we would have had no chance of finding them in the mist and rain, and would probably have got lost and hypothermic ourselves. With no hard evidence that they were even in trouble we resolved to stay put and be thankful for the roof over our own heads.

The evening meal was a splendid mixture of soup, spaghetti and meat prepared by our host, Jean. He and his wife had built up the hut as a personal thing and were keen to cultivate a convivial atmosphere. They seemed to be succeeding admirably, taking good care of their guests without becoming too fussy. When we had completed our meal Jean produced a bottle of eau-de-vie-de-pomme and proceeded to pour measures into a series of tiny glasses, warning us that it was at least fifty-per-cent alcohol. The atmosphere became yet more convivial. It emerged that Jean had been a serious mountaineer, and in 1985 he had been part of a team that had scaled the fearsome vertical face of El Capitan in the Yosemite Valley of California. On one wall of the hut there was a large poster, which showed Jean working at the end of a six-inch-wide ledge, tethered by a rope fed through a series of metal pitons. We asked him about the ascent, which had taken five days. His expression suggested that it had been desperately hard. This type of big-wall climbing, using masses of artificial aids, is clearly a world of its own. It takes a special sort of nerve to spend days on end dangling over a drop of thousands of feet. Having retired from such serious climbing he had set up his Refuge to create a special atmosphere catering for walkers and climbers. I reckoned that if I had been in Jean's position I would not have chosen this spot for my hut – with its views across the tarmac expanses of the car parks to the square tower-blocks of the resort and with a dodgy water supply to boot – but I was very thankful that *he* had chosen to locate himself here.

I slept well, at least for the first part of the night. When I woke I found I was worrying. The failure of the cash dispenser in the resort had landed me with a fresh set of problems, as I had been relying on the idea of replenishing my supply of banknotes at this stage in the journey. By the time I had settled my account with Jean I would have barely forty euros left. In theory I could keep going by staying in hotels and using my VISA card, but this created problems in turn. Not only was it more expensive to stay in hotels than in the cash-only *gites*, it would mean that my progress across the country would be dictated by the locations of the hotels. If they were spaced five or six hours apart they would undermine my long-term effort, because I really needed to be putting in days of eight or nine hours at this stage in the trip. Moreover, the hotels might well be full, not least over the coming weekend. I could always camp out rough, using my sleeping bag and bivouac sack, but if I resorted to that tactic I would have to buy food and my meagre cash would soon run out.

Turning these thoughts over in my mind I dozed until dawn. On the more positive side of the equation the new day appeared to be confounding the weather forecast by dawning brightly. Danielle and the medical pair had been cold in their tents, whilst Brendan and I had been too warm inside the hut. The medical students were making a slow start to the day and when the other three of us got moving it took a few minutes to locate the correct path amongst the wilderness of ski lifts on the hillside. Soon we were heading south and east and we were greatly heartened to run into the bear and the gazelles, who had now been joined by a third woman. It seemed that they had reached the resort just in time to shelter from the first massive cloudburst the previous afternoon, and they had then spent the night in some accommodation belonging to a friend of the bear.

A couple of days previously I had been sitting on a rock beside the path, chewing my biscuit-lunch and meditating on the futility of the human condition. (Excessive and morose introspection is the curse of the Welshman travelling abroad). I had also been wondering whether the number two exists. Of course I was familiar with the adage that "two plus two equals four," but I was unsure whether "two" has any objective reality in the universe or whether it is actually just a human invention which we have projected onto the world around us. I knew I was pretty ignorant about mathematics, but Brendan was a maths teacher and in the refuge the previous evening I had seen him reading a book about Fermat's last theorem. So I took the opportunity to pick his brains on this topic. Brendan's account began with Pythagoras' famous triangle, in which the squares of the short sides add up to the square of the hypotenuse. (For example, $(3\times3) + (4\times4) = 5\times5$). Apparently Fermat claimed to have proved that for powers higher than two, such an equation could have no whole-number solutions. In other words, if X-cubed plus Y-cubed equals Z-cubed, you can invent no end of solutions in which X, Y and Z involve fractions, but there are no solutions in which X, Y and Z are whole numbers.

Intriguingly Fermat hinted that he had found an elegant proof of this theory, but he neglected to tell anybody what it was. In reality he could not have proved it, for when a proof was eventually found it involved whole fields of mathematics which were simply not available in Fermat's day. Refuting Fermat's claim had been problematic, because as Brendan said it is always going to be difficult to prove that something cannot exist. I commented that I found the whole thing fascinating, though of course it went way beyond anything I could understand. Indeed, as a layman I had picked up the impression that when it came to mathematics and physics the most advanced work had less to do with logic and deduction and more to do with imagination. Brendan agreed that my comment was probably true, though he added that even as a secondary school maths teacher he couldn't really judge. He modestly admitted that when the theory reached the level of the Fermat resolution he would never understand it, nor even understand "the theories behind the theory," so to speak.

As we were discussing all of this we had begun to pick our way across a distinctive limestone environment, and this scenery continued for a couple of hours. For much of the time we were ambling along as a threesome, and every so often we would find ourselves with the bear and his team in a loose group of seven. The leader was whoever happened to be in front at the time, and as luck would have it I was in this position when the path, which had been running along the base of a cliff, suddenly twisted back on itself and presented us with a few feet of scrambling to get up to a col. This short rock pitch was nothing like El Capitan but it was almost steep enough to warrant a rope. I grunted my way up it, finding abundant holds but feeling that I was being pulled off balance by the unnatural weight of the rucksack on my back. I knew that a fall was unlikely to end in death but it could have led to serious and inconvenient injury. After a couple of minutes I was able to haul myself over the top. I had reached the Pas de l'Osque.

My companions scrambled up behind me and we continued across a relatively small basin towards the Pas d'Azuns. I had strained a muscle in the front of my thigh at some point crossing the limestone pavements. It was not too painful but I was increasingly aware of it as the day wore on. It was a Friday, and the thirteenth day of my walk, so maybe it was appropriate that something had gone wrong.

In the next valley Brendan, Danielle and I stopped for a sandwich lunch just below a shepherds' cabin. I remembered this spot clearly from 1987, for Douglas and I had spent a night on the bare hillside just a few hundred metres away. We had sat there watching the shepherds selling their *brebis* – cheese made from ewe's milk – to a passer-by. I had been in a pensive mood that evening, for it was the first one since the significant and sobering *gateau basque* incident. I actually remembered how I had looked up at the mountains and sought courage by reading from my favourite psalm:

"I lift up my eyes to the hills,
From whence does my help come?
My help comes from the Lord,
Who made heaven and earth."

This psalm, the 121st, goes on to say that "the sun shall not smite you by day," which was ironic when I got badly sunburnt ten days later. I smiled ruefully to myself. However serious the 1987 problems had seemed at the time they could not have been too bad: I had survived and now I was back here after sixteen years.

I suppose the psalm is appropriate for hillwalkers, and for anybody travelling in the mountains and aware of how tiny they are in such an environment. In fact it is described in the Old Testament as one of the "Songs of Ascent" which were probably sung by Hebrew pilgrims as they approached Jerusalem to attend the annual religious festivals. I felt that "to lift up your eyes to the hills" is a refreshing and encouraging thing in itself. It can be relaxing to look at a horizon several miles away, or just to stare into the distance, especially in the modern world where so much of life is up close and "in your face." Metaphorically speaking it is healthy in other ways to lift one's gaze for a while: if you constantly walk around with your head down, focussed on the immediate and the urgent, it is harder to keep trivial problems in their true proportion. With the "worms-eye" perspective on life even blades of grass can appear to be insuperable obstacles.

After lunch we continued east, descending gradually as we passed beneath the towering ramparts of the Orgues de Camplong. As we trudged down towards Lescun I felt a vague but real sense of depression and loss. Danielle and Brendan were planning to stop at a campsite just beyond the village. I had contemplated pressing on, using a road to descend three miles into the Valley of the Aspe and then following a main road, the N134, five miles along the other side to Etsaut. In this way I could effectively steal a day by completing two sections of the GR10 in one go. The forced march on the roads would not be much fun, but it would be easy from the navigational point-of-view. My sadness stemmed from the thought of parting company with the two of them at Lescun. I had only known the German girl and the Irish teacher for a few days but they had been good company: they were easy-going and cheerful and what is more we all seemed to walk at much the same speed.

Just outside Lescun we lost the path in a field and ended up slipping and falling down a steep bank of long grass to get back onto a country lane. Laughing from this incident I resolved that if I could find accommodation in Lescun I would stay there for the night, and we could have a decent evening meal together. There might well come a point when I would have to undertake some ridiculous forced marches to make up time on my schedule, but I had not reached that stage quite yet. If I was going to end up attempting marathon stages and epic feats of endurance I could do so later on, when such activity would also serve to mask any loneliness. For the moment I had found two good friends and it would be silly to walk away from them before I had to.

Lescun was an extremely compact village with grey slate roofs. After we had enjoyed a cold beer I managed to book into the Hotel du Pic d'Anie. It was a quaint but friendly place, and moreover it would permit me to pay for my room and our three dinners using my debit card. My two companions disappeared to seek out the campsite, and I set about the various chores which had so quickly become second nature. After a shave and shower I washed the day's kit and tried to arrange the rest of my clothing to best advantage to get it dry.

When Danielle and Brendan reappeared we entered the hotel's excellent restaurant and attacked one of its major set menus. This included *pate de foie gras, confit du canard* with *pommes frites,* and cheese followed by dessert. It was a pleasant binge, and our bottle of red wine was even supplemented by some extra supplied by the bear and gazelles at the next table. They seemed to have built up a measure of affection for the three of us: maybe they recognised that we too were a curious but harmless trio.

After dinner I bade farewell to all of them. The following day Brendan would follow the GR10 to Etsaut and pick up a rail connection which would ultimately take him to visit friends on the Riviera. Danielle would follow the GR10 as well, but only as far as Borce, which was slightly short of Etsaut but had a good campsite. As I said to her, I could not do what she was doing, which was simply walking for six weeks without a definite target. For me the simple act of walking did not confer a vast amount of pleasure in itself. I was driven onwards by the feeling that I was making progress towards my goal.

Indeed, that was my plan for the morrow. The roads which I had identified should enable me to reach Etsaut two or three hours before Brendan, who would get there by means of the official route along the GR10. That would leave me several hours to push on, getting well above the significant landmark of the *Chemin de la Mature* and finding a *refuge* or even sleeping out on the hillside on the Saturday.

That night I had a curious dream. I was being appointed as chaplain to a regiment called the Queen's Irish Rifles. I have no idea whether such a regiment exists in real life. But in my

147

dream the colonel of the regiment was showing me around their barracks and spelling out his expectations. He seemed to be in a grim mood, and it was apparent that my predecessor had departed under some sort of cloud. It was not clear exactly what had happened, but I recognised the predecessor's name as a clergyman who had been in a nearby parish in one of my previous dioceses. The colonel was telling me that he had been relieved when the predecessor left.

So too, apparently, was the regimental goat.

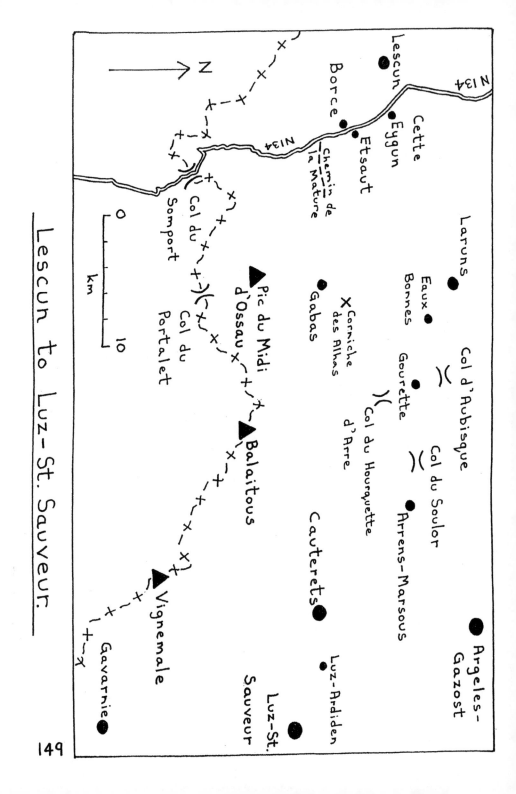

Lescun to Luz-St. Sauveur.

149

Chapter 6.

Adventures beyond the oxygen debt.

I made a good start and was clear of the hotel by 8.45am. The first three miles were downhill all the way and on tarmac, but I was pleased with how my feet had toughened up: the bottoms of them already felt like leather. As I descended into the valley I could feel the temperature rising. Indeed, the ascent forty-eight hours earlier had taken me from something akin to a tropical rainforest to scenery resembling the surface of the moon. The following day, descending to Lescun, had been almost the reverse. Brendan, who was a veteran of several serious walks such as the Inca trail in Peru, reckoned the descent was one of the most memorable days of hillwalking he had done anywhere, for the geology and vegetation had been changing throughout. We had started on a limestone pavement with odd conifers, and then come down through upland pasture and deciduous woods to emerge into fields. In the course of a few hours we had scrambled up steep rocks and tumbled down a grassy embankment.

After three miles I passed an ugly complex of electrical or chemical works and came to the main road, the Route National 134, slipping into some bushes for a few minutes to exchange my trousers for shorts. The sky was overcast and I was seeking relief from the oppressive heat and humidity. I could change back later in the day when the sun eventually broke through. Then I trudged several miles up the road. There was relatively little traffic at that time on a Saturday morning, though the odd truck came thundering down from the Spanish frontier at the

Col du Somport. Walking along the road was a lot more pleasant than I had anticipated. I stopped in Cette-Eygun and ate an apple, sitting at a picnic table next to the Aspe. The water was running playfully over the stones in the riverbed, whilst the vast heights of the Aspe gorge towered above.

Beyond Cette-Eygun I was walking for a while alongside the rusting remains of the old Pau to Saragossa railway. This had been built back in the 1920's and was a considerable feat of engineering, particularly the long Somport-Canfranc tunnel under the Pyrenees. In 1939 the line brought trainloads of Republicans into France, many of whom were interred in refugee camps at Gurs. The railway had stopped functioning during the 1970's after a train was derailed.

At Etsaut I bought a few provisions and a cup of coffee. A pack of half-a-dozen assorted dogs was roaming around harmlessly in the sunshine, and an equal number of walkers seemed to be milling around with no great sense of purpose. Another mile or so to the south and I began the ascent which would bring me to the bottom of the *Chemin de la Mature*. At this point the sun was at last breaking through, so I slipped my trousers back on and ran through the suncream drill before taking a few photographs of the Fort du Portalet perched on its crag in the valley below. I remembered from my previous experience here that the path I was about to negotiate received the full force of the sun's rays and reflected them back off the rock, cooking walkers from both sides at once.

The *Chemin de la Mature* ("The Way of the Masts") is like nothing on earth. At first sight it is difficult even to make out the line of a path across a cliff-face which is all but vertical. The path itself is broad enough – five or six feet in most places – but the drop of several hundred feet into the gorge makes it a dizzying experience. For a walker who tripped or stumbled and went over the edge there would be no way back. And the path continues like this for a good kilometre or more.

151

One might wonder how the path got to be there in the first place. The answer is that in the 18th century the French Navy needed masts for its ships. The forests of Bearn and the Upper Aspe contained trees of suitable size and quality, but there was no way to get them down from the mountains. The solution was this pathway, carved out of the cliff-face by convicts and completed in 1772. To construct the path was a mind-boggling achievement: I could not begin to imagine how they would have manoeuvred the giant logs down it. Goodness knows how many labourers were lost over the edge. No doubt they were expendable – another case of *"jetez le mouton!"*

As I worked my way up the *Chemin* I noticed how the uneven rocks of its surface had been smoothed by the passage of countless feet. Those on the inside of the track, next to the rockface, seemed to have been polished the most, reflecting the instinct of generations of walkers to shy away from the edge and the drop. Once clear of the top end of the *Chemin* I paused for some lunch and then pressed on through endless forest, always moving upwards and constantly under attack from horseflies and other insects. At least I was gaining height in the shade, but it was hot and humid work. Gradually the trees thinned out and then I continued for miles up a huge open valley, eventually zig-zagging up to the Col d'Ayous and reaching it at 5.30pm. During the last few minutes of the ascent I found the air freshening as the wind rose and clouds blew across, frustrating my plan to capture some decent photos of the massive valley which now lay to my north. Instead I pointed my camera to the east and got a couple of pictures of the imposing Pic-du-Midi-d'Ossau which was appearing briefly through and above the clouds. From this angle the mountain appeared to have a flat top but with a deep gash cut in it, and its local name of "Jean-Pierre" is probably a reference to the odd double-summit. I remembered how Nicholas Crane had climbed it during his traverse of the Pyrenees, scrambling up "cinnamon-coloured rocks", but he was clearly made of sterner stuff than I.

After a few minutes on the col I was feeling chilled, so I packed the camera away and began the descent towards the lakes at Ayous. On the way down I passed a strange spectacle, namely a dozen donkeys or mules, each heavily laden with camping equipment, and an equal or greater number of humans trying to coax these beasts of burden up the mountainside. The animals looked pretty unimpressed and most of them were standing still and stubbornly refusing to advance. Having just come down from the cloud and wind of the col myself I could not say I blamed them.

Below the lakes it was a long and tedious descent. I was tired and knew I had already done enough for one day. My plan was to get to the Refuge Pyrenea Sports which would mean that I could sleep with the satisfaction of having completed a substantial distance during the afternoon. The clouds were coming down, and combined with my fatigue I found depression closing in. The sight of the *refuge* did nothing to lift my spirits. The place appeared to be derelict – a miserable shell standing where I had hoped to find a vibrant café. A few yards away several dozen camper-vans were crammed into a car park from which their occupants had a view of a reservoir ponded up behind an ugly dam. A couple of people were fishing in the lake. For me there was no alternative but to plough on yet further, and hope that I could find something three or four kilometres down the road at Gabas.

By now my feet were hurting badly – they had not toughened up quite as much as I had thought. My legs were also hurting and by the time I reached Gabas I had been walking for nearly twelve hours. It had been a good day, all things considered, but far too long. I hoped desperately that I would find accommodation, fearing that because it was Saturday night everything might be fully booked. However, when I found a hotel the barman took pity on me and even offered to carry my rucksack upstairs. After the usual ablutions I staggered back down to the bar. By now I was too late for dinner in the dining room, which in any case had been closed off for a private party and was thumping to the rhythm of some kind of teenage disco. However, the barman recommended an *"assiette anglaise"* and disappeared into the kitchen to arrange it. I have no idea how this dish got its name, for I have never seen anything quite like it in England. It was a magnificent platter of ham, cheese, salad and melon, with various other bits and pieces, and for somebody in my state of exhaustion it was perfect. It was brought from the kitchen by another gentleman and served with the sort of smile that suggested he would not be taking much interest in the girls in the disco.

I knew that the Sunday was going to be hard, because the previous day had been far too long and in spite of demolishing the entire *assiette anglaise* I had not had anything like enough food or sleep to let my body recover. If this was my expectation then the day certainly lived up to it. As soon as I left the hotel I had pain in both feet, and in the case of the right foot it was intense. It was coming from under my heel, probably a result of the miles of descent on asphalt roads at the beginning and end of the previous day. The pain was bad, but there was nothing I could do about it.

I was soon traversing and climbing in thick woodland, having left the D934 road just outside Gabas. Eventually I reached a signpost where the path split. The right-hand route led to the *Corniche des Alhas*, which I remembered as the most dangerous part of the entire GR10 in the 1980s. The sign warned that it was a *"passage vertigineux."* Feeling tired already, and with painful feet and a heavy pack, I decided that on this occasion I would allow discretion to be the better part of valour. I took the left-hand fork, which led down to the Pont-du-Goua bridge. This meant sacrificing 500 feet of altitude which would have to be scraped back after the bridge, but as it increased the odds on being alive for the afternoon I decided it was worth it.

The ascent beyond the bridge was steep and interminable. It wound up and further up through the woods, much of it in short zig-zags over rocks and even, in places, over stones which had been deliberately arranged to make a sort of cobbled path. Predictably it was hot and humid in the trees: the usual experience of dripping with sweat. But this time I felt weaker, for the exertions of the previous day had taken their toll. Somewhere on this section of the track Douglas and I had tried to eat our unpalatable toasting bread. I remembered Douglas' battle-cry of "Banyuls and a bottle of wine!" In fact on this Sunday morning I was having fantasies about a heavenly sangria. It was a whole jug of ice cubes and red wine, with dashes of orange juice and vermouth and several slices of lemon floating on the surface. Never mind a bottle: when I reached Banyuls I was going to drink a bucketful of the stuff.

Eventually I had to pause through exhaustion and eat some lunch. I had not reached my intended lunch stop, which would have been at the top of the climb and out of the woods, but I needed the energy. I had been going for three hours and most of it had been uphill. Eating a cheese sandwich and a rather soft chocolate bar left me feeling marginally better. After lunch the path continued upwards for a short distance, eventually running out along the base of some cliffs, doubling back on itself a couple of times, and then heading east across open hillside.

At this point I decided that the following day would have to be a rest, come what may. I was now on my ninth straight day of walking, and seven of those had been long and tough ones. I needed real food and sleep. In the meantime my more immediate concern was water. I had carried only two litres from the hotel that morning, and it was running out. I could see from the map that there were springs on the mountainside a few miles to the east, and the path should go past them.

For the next hour or so it was a case of traversing the hillside, ascending at a gentle angle. As the ascent began to steepen again, swinging north to go up the side of a gully, I spotted a figure ahead. He was crouched over his rucksack, and from a distance he momentarily looked like Douglas. Immediately I realised that this was a ridiculous illusion, brought on by my exhaustion, for I was now fighting to grind out every yard. Before setting out from Gabas I had played the day's stage over in my mind, remembering it as a tough one but assuming that our struggle in 1987 was caused by weakness induced by the *gateau basque* sickness. Therefore, I reasoned, the actual terrain could not be too bad. But in reality I was discovering that the terrain *was* bad, and the next impending col was towering up before me. It made me realise that on the 1987 trip Douglas and I must have dug deep to get as far as we did. It was somewhere along this section of the track that I had sat on a rock, crying as I ate an apple.

In fact it might have been precisely where the figure ahead was now sitting. When I reached him I discovered that he was a young Frenchman called Cedric. He was originally from this region but was now working in Bordeaux. He said that he was too tired to go on: he had walked for eight hours the previous day. I questioned him and ascertained that he had a tent and some food in his pack. However, like me he was virtually out of water. Although he was holding a map he seemed unsure exactly where he was until I pointed it out to him.

Earlier in the day, struggling up through the woods in a state of fatigue, I had been thankful that I only had to think about myself. I was not in the position of the army officer who, whatever his own sufferings, has to think first about the wellbeing of his men. So I was less than thrilled to find that I was now partially responsible for the welfare of Cedric. I told him about the springs of water. I knew that they must be there because a fair-sized torrent was gushing down the steep gully several hundred feet below our position. If we followed the gully upstream, as the GR10 did, we must surely reach the source of the water wherever it issued from the hillside.

"How far is that?" asked Cedric.

"From the map, two or three kilometres," I said. I actually thought, and hoped, that the springs were closer than that, but I did not want to give an optimistic estimate only for Cedric to be disappointed later on, with the crushing effect that might have for his morale. Better to err on the side of caution and be boosted by a pleasant surprise if the water-source turned out to be closer than we thought. By now my mouth was dry and I was beginning to feel desperately thirsty.

We set off up the hill, with every stride a tough one. After a few minutes rain began to fall in large drops, though we were still ascending in sunshine. We came upon some sheep which were standing motionless, occupying a small plateau.

"This is where I will stop," said Cedric. His plan was actually to follow a path which went due east to the Col d'Auseilla, whereas I was following the GR10 proper and would go north-east to the Hourquette d'Arre from which I could swing north and continue down to Gourette. "I'll pitch my tent on this plateau."

"Okay," I said. "You should be alright here. Just make sure you go well upstream, above the sheep, to collect your water."

"I'll be fine," he said. "After a night's sleep I'll continue east. Good luck with your trip."

"You too," I replied. "*Bon voyage.*"

I shook hands with Cedric and we parted. It was a relief to be on my own again. However, I was getting increasingly thirsty. I crossed the stream and continued to work my way up the path on the far bank, at times sliding downhill as the stones and shale slipped beneath my boots. I wanted to get right to the source of the water before I risked drinking any, but the source never seemed to come. I was getting higher in altitude, but for all I knew sheep and cattle could be grazing out of sight on the mountainside above me. After another half mile, and with my tongue sticking to the inside of my mouth, I decided I was high enough. I had not actually reached a point where water was issuing from the rock, but there were no animals around and the stream could only have flowed for a couple of minutes after coming out of the ground.

I flung my rucksack down on the grass and scrambled inside for some water-purifying tablets. Three of these went into the empty two-litre "platypus" bag and I filled it from the stream. Giving it a good shake I resisted the temptation to drink immediately, and lay down on the grass. By now the few drops of rain had ceased and I was back in glorious sunshine. When I sipped at my water it was cold and refreshing. I drank deeply, getting slight cramps in the stomach but nothing worse than that.

Staggering uphill in search of the springs I had probably ascended half the height of the col. That was good, but there was still the other half to do. It was increasingly steep, and I paused every few yards to suck air into my lungs or to take a sip of water from the tube of the platypus. As I ascended a new factor was coming into play. I could hear thunder rumbling behind me, and as I glanced back I was alarmed to see a dirty mass of clouds boiling up from the south-west.

The last part of the ascent became a race against the weather. The previous afternoon, at about the same time, clouds had overtaken me just as I reached a col, spoiling my plans for photography but being no more dangerous than that. Today was looking much more serious, and the echoes of thunder were becoming increasingly frequent. Normally my strategy for ascending a col was to adopt first gear, switch my brain off and just keep plodding on slowly until I got there. In the current circumstances that was not going to be good enough. Ignoring my thumping heart I raced onwards. The grass of the hillside had now given way to shale – a nightmare collection of stones and pebbles with the odd larger rock thrown in. As I struggled upwards I seemed to slip and slide back on every other other stride. The only tactic available was to fix my attention on a large rock a few yards ahead and fight my way to it, preferably grabbing it to afford myself a couple of seconds of security before I chose my next target-rock and headed for that. I moved on swiftly, kicking my way across a patch of old and dirty snow to reach the final diagonal line to the col. By now the top was no more than a hundred metres away, but it was going to be a difficult hundred metres on such a loose surface. I was well beyond the oxygen debt with my lungs heaving and blood pounding in my head, and I was pausing every few strides to gulp in lungfuls of air before surging on, propelled by the ever-closer thunder and the clouds which were now overtaking me. I knew I was engaged in a desperate contest. The shale was a tricky surface, and the fact that I kept sliding back meant I was close to the critical angle at which upward movement would become really difficult or even impossible. If heavy rain arrived to lubricate the stones then that critical angle would suddenly be reduced: in the worst-case scenario I could be stranded just short of the col, unable to scramble up the last few feet to the top.

At 5.30pm, eight exhausting hours after leaving the hotel in Gabas, I found myself on the Col du Hourquette d'Arre. The yellow signpost said that the altitude was 2465 metres. As I was regaining my breath I did some quick mental arithmetic, multiplying the figure by three and adding an extra quarter of it to the total. If my sums were correct I was a shade over 8000 feet above sea level. This would be one of the highest points on my entire journey. I gulped at some water and immediately another crash of thunder broke around me, much closer than before.

The signpost pointed the way to Gourette, and indicated that it was still two-and-a-half hours away. I set off without further delay. Disconcertingly the first few steps of the "descent" were actually uphill, as the path twisted back up the side of a ridge before levelling off. More thunder rolled around me as the clouds closed in. Then the rain began to fall in large heavy drops. In seconds the visibility was reduced to no more than ten or fifteen metres, and I could barely make out the next cairn on the path ahead. Suddenly a wave of hailstones washed over me, stinging at the back of my head and neck. "Seven shades of shit!" I exclaimed; "I need to get out of here fast!" I whipped out my map and compass: the first part of the path from the col was tending north of north-east, so I set the compass quickly to thirty degrees and headed for the next cairn as fresh thunder echoed around me.

The rain and hail were heavy by now and I was soaked. It was not particularly cold, and I was more concerned about the rain making the stones on the path slippery. Fortunately the trail was discernible across both the rocks and the grass, for it was well marked with fresh daubs of red and white paint and also with small cairns constructed from piles of stones. However, it did not seem to be losing height at all. At 8000 feet and with lightning in the vicinity I was keen to get lower down as quickly as possible. The trail zig-zagged to and fro, but always more or less along the line of the compass bearing I had set. The thunder was persistent and I had mixed feelings about it: it sounded intimidating but I figured that every time I heard the thunder it meant the lightning had missed me. I hurried onwards, moving as swiftly as possible but wary of slipping and turning an ankle, and I was instinctively crouching as I literally tried to keep a low profile. Only once did I actually see a flash of lightning, and the accompanying thunder, six seconds later, indicated that it had struck the ground over a mile away. But that calculation brought no real comfort. In an electrical storm in the lowlands you can measure the interval between lightning and thunder and work out whether the storm is getting closer or moving away. But here in the mountains the storm was all around me, presumably caused by hot air from Spain rising over the entire range, and the next lightning strike could be anywhere. Nor was the direction of the thunder indicative of anything much: it was coming from all sides and I could never be sure what was an original splitting of the air and what was an echo bouncing back off the surrounding peaks.

I surged onwards, as fast as I judged to be at all prudent, and gradually the path began to descend as the rain lashed down. The critical thing was not to lose the pathway in the swirling cloud, for if I did so the compass alone would not be enough to get me down a steep mountainside in poor visibility. I would be spending a miserable night sheltering under a rock. At one point I came upon a small flock of sheep. They were pleased to see me. At any rate they seemed to take my advent as a sign that they should turn round and make for lower ground. With relief I found the path dropping more quickly, and then I was out below the clouds and saw that a lake had become visible, far below me and off to the left. The rain ceased and the map confirmed that the GR10 should descend towards the lake and then pass it on the right-hand side. Within a few minutes I was down beside the lake and pressing on towards the north on a clear path.

The thunder eased off, as though sensing that its prey had escaped. The odd detonation rumbled and echoed every few minutes for the next hour or so, but the storm had clearly moved on. Suddenly I felt very tired. Adrenaline had propelled me down from the col in a headlong flight lasting fifty minutes. During that time I had not thought once about my feet or legs. Now soreness and fatigue returned and took up residence with sullen obstinacy. I still had to face an hour-and-a-half of footslogging before I could expect to reach Station-de-Gourette. I was also suddenly aware that the shorts I was wearing under my tracksuit trousers had been chafing at my groin, and the tops of my thighs had areas which were red and raw.

This last part of the itiniery was tiring in itself. It made the day into a ten-hour marathon to add to the twelve hours of the previous day, and of course the fatigue had a cumulative effect. Bland descriptions of pathways and hillwalking might talk about "one hour to X" or "two miles to Y." But these statistics tell you nothing about the surface of the path or the difficulty of the terrain. If it were always a case of walking on a smooth surface (preferably of short grass) and at a steady gradient then most walkers would fly along. But normally it is not like that at all. A descent is likely to be a case of hopping downwards from one stone to another, always with the mentally taxing effort of concentrating to avoid injury to the ankles or knees. Even decent pathways are often eroded by rainwater into runnels with tricky edges, or there are patches of loose stones which can give the walker a nasty shock as his feet shoot out from under him. The simple act of having to look at where you are putting your feet makes walking more fatiguing: it is actually less tiring if you can look up and focus on a point some distance away.

At last Gourette came into view. It was a welcome sight at the end of a day which had come closer than any so far to breaking my spirit. Serious pain in my foot, exhaustion, thirst, danger from lightning: I had experienced all these and more besides in the ten hours since I had left Gabas. I staggered down past some tennis courts and into the centre of the village, and immediately I found the two-star Hotel Pene Blanque. It was virtually on the U-turn in the centre of the settlement where the main road goes around a roundabout and ascends towards the Col d'Aubisque.

I booked myself in for two nights and made for my room with my legs in considerable pain. Remembering how Miles Morland had adopted a "dead beetle position" I tried to emulate his tactics by lying on my back on the floor and clutching my knees to my chest. After several minutes of gently moaning in this position I accepted that it was not easing the agony in my feet, so I rolled over and crawled across the room and around the corner into my en-suite shower.

Having cleaned myself up I descended to the bar and ordered a beer. To my surprise and delight I learned that the hotel restaurant was still serving food, so I was able to consume an excellent dish of veal with half a bottle of dry white Jurancon wine. As I ate I stared out of the window, across the roundabout to the Intersport shop, and as I watched low cloud billowed through the resort. I knew I had been suffering, but I was one third of the way across France and I had covered the distance in one third of the time available for my expedition. Tomorrow I would not need to rush to get up: it would be a day of rest. I ordered a vast bowl of profiteroles and a coffee, and when I had eaten my fill I went upstairs and collapsed into bed. I felt I had arrived in heaven.

In fact I had arrived in Gourette. It was another ski station out of season, but I actually quite liked the place. Compared to the ghost-town of Arette-la Pierre-St.Martin it seemed to have some life about it. Its position, just four kilometres below the Col d'Aubisque, meant that it had probably been a settlement in its own right before it became a ski station. It was not the totally artificial monstrosity which La Pierre-St.Martin seemed to be. Gourette was large enough to have hotels plus cafes and a shop or two, and although the local branch of the Credit Agricole Bank had closed it had a cash-dispensing machine outside which actually worked. For the first time in days I felt solvent again.

At the Tourist Information Office I enquired about a launderette, and was told that the closest one was five miles away down in Eaux Bonnes. This news sealed the fate of my two "walking" tee shirts. I had been using a white one and a pale blue one, wearing them on alternating days, and both were beginning to develop some sort of yellowish mould. So both were consigned to a dustbin, along with their fungus, and I bought two new shirts in Intersport. It felt a bit extravagant, but by wearing one of my new shirts for the remainder of the day I would be able to wash my khaki tee-shirt, which was the one I was using to look vaguely respectable in the hotels.

With my wallet full of fresh banknotes I headed into a bar and ordered a large lunch, washing it down with a beer and a liqueur. Back in my hotelroom I checked my wet kit, which I had left on the balcony to dry in the sun. Everything seemed to be drying well, but in my clumsiness I nudged my swimming trunks off the balcony rail and they fell two floors into what appeared to be a private garden owned by the family that ran the hotel. I had no choice other than to go downstairs and retrieve them. Outside the front door of the hotel there was nobody in sight so I hopped up onto the flat top of a metal fence and walked along it. The surface was only a few inches wide but it was no problem until I reached a large pile of twisted metal and other junk which the owners had dumped under my balcony. At this point I remembered, or became aware of, the alcohol which I had consumed with my lunch. Jumping down onto the grass I grabbed the offending trunks, clambered back onto the fence and somehow repeated the precarious balancing act so that I could get back round the corner and in through the front door. I seemed to have a knack of making things difficult for myself.

Back in my room I lazed on the bed with my legs up and my feet exposed to the fresh air. The television in my room had quite a good selection of channels. I quickly located Eurosport and was rewarded by a commentary in English. It was the second proper stage of the *Tour de France* and the riders were heading across a flat landscape towards Sedan. It seemed that the previous day had ended with a pile-up just before the finish, and the resulting injuries had forced several competitors to retire from the event. Of the survivors Tyler Hamilton, one of the pre-race favourites, was continuing to ride but with a cracked collarbone. A Frenchman called Jimmy Casper was also soldiering on, but with his neck in a brace. Even the hot favourite Lance Armstrong had been on the floor in the midst of the carnage.

Armstrong had come to the Tour seeking a record-equalling fifth victory. If he achieved the feat he would ascend into an exclusive club alongside the legendary names of Jacques Anquetil, Eddy Merckx, Bernard Hinault and Miguel Indurain. However, even before the Tour began it was clear that Armstrong's path to glory would not be a smooth one. Franco-American relations were at an even lower ebb than normal owing to the recent war in Iraq. Armstrong's victories in the Tours of the previous four years had made him the embodiment of all-conquering American power, and if that was not enough he also hailed from Texas and was a personal friend of President George W. Bush.

The antipathy between France and America is no doubt a multi-layered phenomenon, and an interesting one granted that they are both great republics which emerged through revolution at roughly the same time. Both were born amidst a conscious desire to reject monarchy and the divine right of kings, and both had a ferocious determination to separate Church and State. Maybe it is the very similarity which fuels the rivalry. The French certainly crave "liberty" and detest the idea that the

"American way" is the only or best path to progress. On the other side some Americans resent France's failure to appreciate that it was the power of the United States which liberated their country from the Nazis and then defended it against the Soviets.

So the bitter differences over Iraq were merely the latest episode in a saga of mutual loathing between two proud cultures. In Armstrong's case there were other personal factors which had not helped him to be well received in France. The suspicion lingered that his recovery from testicular cancer and subsequent return to sport (seemingly endowed with superhuman strength) were a bit too good to be true. Accusations of drug abuse had been voiced by spectators in the past. Having said that, some of the French fans were so blinkered that they remained convinced of the innocence of their hero Richard Virenque even after conclusive evidence had emerged proving Virenque's involvement in doping. To add to Armstrong's woes, Texans tend to be notoriously insular, even by American standards, and some of his previous comments had been undiplomatic: he had once said that it was a pity that the world's greatest bicycle race had to take place in France. Over the last couple of years he seemed to have tempered his tone and opened up more to French culture, though his employment of bodyguards had not helped in a sport which traditionally allows the public to get incredibly close to its heroes. Nevertheless, Armstrong's concern that he might make an easy target for some sort of terrorist attack was a reasonable and legitimate one.

So the Centenary Tour was starting against a political backdrop dominated by disagreements over Iraq. In a sense this was oddly appropriate, for the Tour's origins back in 1903 were located in the murky and unsavoury politics of the notorious Dreyfus case. A French industrialist called Comte Dion was running a bicycle factory and he was advertising his products on the green pages of a sporting journal called "Le Velo" which was owned by a certain Pierre Giffard. The fate of Dreyfus – an Alsatian Jew convicted of spying for the Germans – split the country and left Dion and Giffard in opposing camps. Giffard was with the Dreyfusards, who were republican, socialist and anti-clerical. Dion was on the other side – anti-semitic, Catholic and imperialist. So Dion withdrew his advertisements and set up a rival journal which became "L'Auto" and which was printed on yellow paper by one Henri Desgrange. Desgrange, a former cyclist who had held the world hour record, conceived the original 1903 Tour as a publicity stunt. It was a cracking success: circulation of "L'Auto" shot up and "Le Velo" went out of business. The famous yellow jersey, imitating the pages of L'Auto, was introduced in 1919.

Henri Desgrange was the real father of the Tour, and his personality dominated it. He had a brutal desire to watch the cyclists suffer, and he resisted any technical innovations which might serve to make their task easier. Indeed he once declared that the perfect Tour course would be one which only a single competitor could survive. His rules were of Byzantine complexity and he was a stickler for enforcing them. One example concerned a rider called Eugene Christophe, and took place in the Pyrenees in 1913. Christophe was holding the overall lead when his bike was damaged during the descent from the Tourmalet pass. The rider spent two hours carrying his stricken machine down the mountain to Ste.Marie-de-Campan, where he begged some metal from a blacksmith and spent a further two hours heating and welding it. Throughout the ordeal officials, including the tyrannical Desgrange, stood over him to ensure that he received no assistance. In fact Christophe's task was impossible with only two hands, and he had to ask a bystander to pump the forge bellows for him. By this stage his chances of victory had evaporated, but Desgrange fined him a further ten minutes nevertheless.

The Tour is a formidable ordeal today, but conditions during the early years almost surpass imagination. As Christophe's example shows, the cyclists were expected to carry out their own repairs. In fact they had to carry their own repair kits and spare tyres, in addition to their food and water, clothing and lights. And all this was on heavy bikes with primitive gears. Added to this was the fact that the roads were poorer. The Pyrenees were first included on the itinerary for the fourth Tour, in 1906, but in those days most of the "roads" in the mountains were little more than mule tracks and would readily dissolve into mud during bad weather. And if all that was not bad enough, the stages were longer. The first ever Pyrenean stage left Luchon for Bayonne at 3.30am, and even the man who won it turned on a couple of officials at one point screaming "you are all murderers!"

The early Tours were also greater in terms of overall length. The 1926 course ran to nearly 6000 kilometers, whereas the equivalent in 2003 was "only" 3434 km. One champion of the 1920's, Henri Pelissier, described the experience as "a Calvary of the road." Asked how it was possible for a man to endure the Tour Pelissier implied that answer was drugs. Even in those early days the riders were using chemicals including cocaine, chloroform, strychnine and ether to blank out the pain and enhance their performance.

Drugs are the dark underbelly of cycling, and indeed of much professional sport. In the case of the Tour drug abuse, and the suspicion of it, has been there right from the outset, and it has always been bubbling away just under the surface. The whole business was blown wide open by the events of 1998. Three days before the Tour was due to kick off French customs officers searched a car driven by Willy Voet, an official on the Festina team. They found it packed to the gunwales with syringes, steroids, human growth hormones, masking agents and EPO, (in effect a sort of artificial haemoglobin which boosts the blood's ability to carry oxygen). Over the course of the following days and weeks an enormous amount of dirty linen was washed in public. The entire Festina team and its management were rapidly implicated and had to admit that a controlled doping programme had been going on. In fact it eventually emerged that the Festina riders had been required to pay subscriptions into a fund to buy drugs for the team. Festina was removed from the Tour but further investigations spread rapidly to other teams, and allegedly-rough police raids led to the whole field threatening to quit the Tour. Voet himself, having lost his job and embittered by the feeling that he had been made the scapegoat, went on to write a shocking book, *"Massacre a la Chaine,"* which catalogued years of systematic doping and cheating. Voet described grotesque scenes of intravenous drips rigged up in cyclists' hotelrooms, and even of injections administered during races. In one case a syringe was administered through a cyclist's shorts to pump him up for a sprint finish. One can imagine that the scene has potential for comedy - the doctor hanging out through the team-car's window, the syringe slipping as they go over a bump, and suddenly the car's driver has been injected with enough hormones and adrenaline to kill a horse.

Joking aside, the logic of drugs is frightening. If everybody knows that everybody is taking them, then an individual competitor faces a stark choice: either he goes along with the practice or he looks for another job. (Why kill yourself with exertion only to lose to an opponent of equal or lesser talent, simply because the opponent has been using some illicit substance?) Of course if the rider is seeking to earn a livelihood to support a family then the whole dilemma can become even more acute. In 1998 the Tour riders stuck together in a touching display of solidarity and they were strengthened by public support. They felt that they were being made to carry the can for mistakes and evils which were an embedded part of the sport's structure, and to an extent they were no doubt correct. The scale and systematic nature of the drug abuse meant that the cycling authorities must have been aware of it, yet were turning a blind eye.

Of course money and vested interests come into play. The authorities have a duty, in theory, to enforce the rules and protect the health of the athletes. At the same time they are trying to promote the sport and its image, and they need to attract sponsors to it. Money is indeed found at the root of all sorts of evil. And of course it is money that fuels the entire circus, from commercial sponsors to pharmaceutical companies to the Tour organisation itself. The annual budget for the Tour is currently around thirty million pounds sterling. Running a top flight professional team could cost three or four million per year, but the rewards are potentially enormous if the team is successful. (Even the Festina company was able to sell more watches on the back of the 1998 scandal). Naturally everybody wants a slice of the lucrative pie which is the Tour. If there is a surprise it is not that the event involves such greed and cynicism, but that it can simultaneously be an object of beauty, courage and some of the nobler human virtues. Part of its unique appeal is that it holds a mirror to our human condition, reflecting aspects of life in microcosm.

Cycling is a strange sport, in which a man is married to a machine and must drive it relentlessly through his own effort, yet the machine knows no pain and never knows when it is time to stop. It is also an odd mixture of individual and team effort. Nobody could win the Tour if he was not a supremely gifted athlete, but at the same time it would be virtually impossible to win without the support of a powerful team. The team is organised on a hierarchical basis, with the purpose of propelling their leader to overall victory or, failing that, to at least snatch a few stage wins. Within the team *"domestiques"* toil for their superiors, fetching and carrying food and water and sometimes pacing team-mates back to the bunch after a puncture. The team may resemble a monastic order, with its own rituals of duty, loyalty and status. For that matter the entire field or *"peloton"* can have a sort of feudal or medieval structure to it. Eddy Merckx, the greatest rider of all, described the Tour as a quasi-religious experience, commenting on the paradox that whilst the champion is a hugely visible public celebrity, he is also condemned to live the life of a recluse for the duration of the Tour. The concept of monastic seclusion would no doubt have appealed to Desgrange, who advocated celibacy during the cycling season. His logic was simply that commitment to the cycling must be total, and as men need sex it follows that denying themselves is the best indication that they've got the willpower required to win.

The Tour clearly demands discipline and sacrifice from its participants, and in return it offers danger and the likelihood of injury. In a pile-up a rider can be flung into a heap of twisted metal and carbon-fibre wearing little more than his underpants for protection. Mountain descents at speeds touching sixty miles per hour are an obvious danger, where the slightest mistake can send a man somersaulting into a ravine. That is more or less what happened to Roger Riviere in 1960. He came to his first Tour as World Pursuit Champion and holder of the World Hour Record, but his bid for further glory ended when he plunged sixty feet and broke his back. Crippled, he died sixteen years later at the age of forty. And Fabio Casartelli was not the first person to die during the Tour itself: that dubious distinction had been claimed back in 1935 by a Spaniard called Cepeda. Equally poignant was the death of the British rider Tommy Simpson in 1967, as he expired in suffocating heat on the slopes of Mont Ventoux in Provence. Sadly Simpson's famous last words, "put me back on the bike," are apocryphal, for they were invented by a journalist.

Even if a rider avoids serious injury there is no guarantee that the activity is healthy in the long run. To be a champion cyclist a man has to be a champion eater too, and a Tour competitor will have a daily intake of around 8000 calories. If he does not eat enough there is the real danger that he might "bonk" - as the Americans call it in a curious example of how the two nations are separated by their common language. The equivalent expression in British English is "to hit the wall" which means that the blood-sugar level has dropped suddenly and the athlete is feeling weak and ravenously hungry. Exercising on such a vast food intake can hardly be healthy, and Jacques Anquetil was not the first or only cyclist to succumb to stomach cancer. Maybe there is an unnatural strain involved in digesting so much food whilst sitting in a cramped position with the legs pumping.

The Tour would never be the same spectacle without the mountains, and invariably it is the Alps and Pyrenees which provide the decisive stages where the contest is won and lost. The existence of the teams mean that an individual is unlikely to achieve a decisive lead on purely flat stages: a bold and well-timed breakaway may succeed but it is more likely that the main field (the "*peloton*") will chase the escapees and overhaul them. The peloton's advantage is not merely the psychological one of greater numbers. Its extra momentum derives from the laws of physics, for a cyclist riding in somebody else's slipstream will be facing up to a third less air resistance. So an individual or a small group which has broken clear will have to expend more energy to maintain the lead. Behind them, the chances are that the team of the yellow jersey will be at the front of the peloton, driving the chase along and gaining ground remorselessly.

In the mountains it is a different matter, for the steep climbs and descents make it inevitable that the peloton will break apart. On the flat, over 80% of the resistance to forward motion comes from the air, so it is hugely beneficial to ride in somebody's slipstream, especially in the approach to a finishing sprint. On a steep ascent the air resistance becomes negligible, and nearly 80% of the effort is expended in overcoming gravity. So in the mountains the natural "climbers" come to the fore; they tend to be lightly-built men who are blessed with the correct physiology. The classic example of a climber was Eduardo Bahamontes, the so-called "Eagle of Toledo" who was crowned "King of the Mountains" in six Tours during the ten years from 1954. However, Bahamontes only won the Tour outright once, for whilst a potential overall champion needs to be strong in the mountains he also needs to be a good all-round rider, capable of excelling on the flatter stages and in the individual time trials. Another case in point would be Robert Millar, who was King of the Mountains in 1984 and simultaneously achieved the highest-ever placing by a British rider in the overall classification by finishing fourth in Paris.

However, when it comes to ascending the giant passes of the Alps and Pyrenees it seems that physics and biomechanics are not an exact science. On an ascent it's possible that a big strong man is better off sitting on his saddle and turning a large gear at, say, 70 rotations per minute. Such an effort requires strength but every rotation will advance him further along the road. Conversely a smaller, lighter man may be better off out of the saddle and "dancing" on the pedals at 100 r.p.m, for this exertion will be harder on his lungs but easier on his legs. It's an interesting interface between physiology and mechanics. Some riders, such as Armstrong, will experiment with different gears and styles in their search for an optimum method.

Obviously Tour competitors train incredibly hard in preparation for the long steep ascents and mighty cols of the Alps and Pyrenees. But there is also a sense in which no amount of preparation can render a man ready to tackle the mountains. The prospect of these awesome ascents is a psychological business: the very sight of them can induce a paralysing fear which can only be overcome by simply going out and doing the job. To that extent there is an obvious and clear parallel with the hillwalking. The only hill that really counts for anything is the next one, and however large the brute appears you simply have to grind your way up until it is conquered.

Armstrong's comment – that it was a pity the Tour took place in France – was an unfortunate one. But he was also quite wrong, of course. The Tour could only happen in France. No other nation could have invented it, and to this day it remains unique. There is no other event anything like it anywhere in the world, and it embodies something of the essence of France and of the richness of French culture, character and geography. I had heard quotations variously ascribed to Louis XIV, Napoleon and General de Gaulle and all saying essentially the same thing: that France can only be France as long as it is engaged in the pursuit of glory. And there is something of that at the heart of the Tour: beneath the crass commercialism, the greed and the drugs there is a sporting event which is also a journey, and which for three weeks every July serves as a sort of pilgrimage.

If the Tour is about glory it is also about exhaustion, and the latter was a phenomenon with which I could readily identify on my current expedition. But by now things were looking more positive for me even here in Gourette. Twenty-four hours earlier I had been trying to use Miles Morland's "dead beetle" tactics to no avail, and had ended up having to crawl into the shower. But by the Monday evening I was feeling vastly stronger, and had no difficulty walking into the bathroom. I reclined on my bed, drawing satisfaction from this simple fact and grinning to myself as I recalled how I had escaped from the electrical storm the previous afternoon.

Maybe the Pyrenees have a special ability to attract eccentric travellers. They certainly seem to have done so in the past. One example would be Charles Packe, a Victorian barrister from Stretton Hall in Leicestershire. Packe was also a scholar, botanist, geologist and cartographer, and in 1862 he wrote his famous "Guide to the Pyrenees." He also made it his mission to conquer the Balaitous peak, which was nine miles due south of my current position in Gourette and right up on the frontier. In fact the area is so remote that on his first attempt Packe failed to even find the mountain. Returning with a local guide he eventually got to the summit, only to find evidence that a couple of military surveyors had been there forty years earlier.

An even more extraordinary character was Packe's contemporary and friend Henry Russell, or Count Henry Patrick Marie Russell-Killough to give him his full title. Russell had mixed French and Irish parentage, and he was a philosopher and violinist. More than that he was a traveller, and amongst other feats he toured through North America and lived with the Sioux Indians. He also travelled from Moscow to Peking before the Trans-Siberian Railway had been constructed, and got as far as Japan and Australia.

However, the end of all this journeying was to return and settle in the Pyrenees. In 1863, at the age of 29, Russell climbed the Pico d'Aneto which, at 3404 metres, is the highest mountain in the Pyrenees and lies entirely in Spain. He went on to make sixteen first ascents throughout the range, and his 1869 conquest of Vignemale was the first winter ascent of a major European peak. (The Vignemale is the highest peak in the French Pyrenees, being located on the frontier a few miles east of the Balaitous). Russell's subsequent obsession with

175

Vignemale, which he described as his wife, was a bizarre one. He climbed the mountain thirty-three times, making his last ascent at the age of seventy, and on one night in 1880 he got two guides to cover him with scree so that he could spend the night on the summit. He used various caves as summer homes and carved out others from the ice of the Ossoue glacier, and his eccentricity ran to throwing lavish parties in these locations. By 1888 he was renting both the summit of the mountain and the glacier on a ninety-nine year lease.

Meanwhile it was time for me to eat again, albeit in less flamboyant surroundings. I made my way down to the hotel restaurant and got the same table as the previous evening. Outside the window and across the roundabout the Intersport shop was again obscured as low clouds blew through the centre of Gourette. "In the Pyrenees," Russell had written, "God is a palpable presence."

Chapter 7.

Turbulent priests and a theology of football.

After my day of rest in Gourette I felt a bit unfocussed and out of sorts. It was a pattern I would come to notice, as it recurred after subsequent rest days. I took a long time to pack my kit, and when I left the Hotel Pene Blanque I tried and failed to find a short cut back up to the GR10. The upshot of the mistake was that I wasted nearly an hour thrashing around in the woods on a steep, boggy hillside, getting progressively more lost and more frustrated. When you are lost in a thick wood it gets tiring very quickly. It is impossible to walk in a straight line for any distance, and there is a tendency to drift downhill as you unconsciously take paths of lesser resistance. In this case I even found an old climbing rope which had been tied from tree to tree on a particularly steep section of the hillside. It seemed secure enough, so I used it to pull myself up hand-over-hand. It simply led to the foot of a small crag, and I accepted that my situation was ridiculous. This could not possibly be the correct path. I lowered myself back down the rope and eventually, via mud and bushes, I came out on the correct path and rejoined the GR10, heading for the Col de Tortes.

The path ascended steeply, twisting back and forth between rocks and heather on the hillside. I did not mind the steepness nor the exertion it required, because I was relieved to know that at last I was back on the correct trail and making progress. Somewhere on this hillside I had been staggering around sixteen summers earlier, having fantasies about a ham salad.

As an acknowledgement of this curious personal history I stopped to consume a chocolate bar, revelling in the fact that this time I was well-fed and even had food to hand. I washed it down with a few gulps of orange juice from a carton before taking photographs of the main road where it ran up to the pass at the Col d'Aubisque. The town of Eaux-Bonnes was also visible, five or six miles away down the valley.

Once over the Col de Tortes it was a fairly easy descent until I came out on a section of road running up to the Col du Soulor. It was a narrow carriageway which contoured along the mountainside, and it had a reasonable amount of traffic made up of tourists in cars, men on motorbikes and a number of cyclists testing themselves over terrain which had been used frequently in the *Tour de France*. I passed through a couple of dark tunnels and went past a signpost: I was moving from the *Pyrenees Atlantiques* to the *Hautes Pyrenees*. After a couple of miles on the road I was able to cut across the open hillside to the low Col de Saucede. From there it was a straightforward and pleasant descent into the village of Arrens Massous. By 3 o'clock in the afternoon I was booking into the *Gite Camelat* and being shown into a dormitory of six or seven bunks. There was no sign of any other walkers in residence. The adjoining shower was the cleanest one I have ever seen - it was so spotless it could have come directly from the factory that morning.

After cleansing myself I wandered into the village in search of a coffee, and to my surprise found I could buy copies of the previous day's British newspapers. Delighted with my purchases I made for a café and installed myself at a pavement table, eager to digest the newspapers' contents. Rapidly I learned that a young man who had graduated from my old college in Cambridge, and who had been trying to carve out a career for himself as a journalist, had been shot dead at a roundabout in Baghdad. Another young man, a parachutist, had plunged 13,000 feet to his death in Lincolnshire and foul play was suspected: it seemed that somebody had sabotaged his equipment. Meanwhile a Swiss called Roger Federer had won Wimbledon.

However, it had been the headline on the front page of The Times which had first caught my eye. It said "Church sacrifices gay bishop." Before I had left for France a debate had been brewing up over the appointment of the Reverend Doctor Jeffrey John, who was a theologian on the staff of Southwark Cathedral, as the next Bishop of Reading. In fact the day I had flown from Stansted I had been eating my breakfast in Essex and listening to the radio. The speaker on Radio 4's "Thought for the Day" had been Richard Harries, the Bishop of Oxford. It was Harries who had invited Dr John to become his suffragan – effectively an assistant bishop – because Reading was part of the Diocese of Oxford. Now Harries had got a difficult day ahead of him, for he was due to meet conservatives and evangelicals from within the diocese who were objecting to the appointment. The problem was that Dr John had been involved in a long-term homosexual relationship, though he had declared that he had been celibate for a number of years and had thus been conforming to the Church's official rules for clergy.

It seemed that over subsequent couple of weeks the dispute had been rumbling on – or rather escalating. What transpired from the newspapers was that it had come to a head the previous Saturday morning, with the Archbishop of Canterbury, Rowan Williams, summoning Dr John to an 8am meeting and telling him to withdraw his acceptance of the post. The meeting had gone on for six hours until they had come up with a statement of two paragraphs which Jeffrey John was willing to sign.

I read the articles and comments with a mixture of sadness and sickness, and wondered whether the Church of England would still be there in any recognisable form when I flew back to Stansted in four weeks time. The whole business raised any number of issues, and it was obvious that plenty of print had been expended in airing them over the previous fortnight. It illustrated more clearly than ever that the *ecclesia anglicana* was already, in effect, in a state of schism. It was split between two (or possibly more) factions whose ideologies and world-views were based on utterly different assumptions.

It seemed that the bare facts of the case were that the wealthy evangelical parishes in the Oxford Diocese had issued a number of threats, suggesting that if Dr John was consecrated they would refuse to recognise his authority and that they might seek alternative episcopal oversight from elsewhere. Their ultimate threat was to cease paying their "quotas" – in other words to withdraw their funding from the diocese. These threats had been echoed by like-minded parishes beyond the bounds of the Oxford Diocese, and some of these people had been enlisting the support of conservative bishops in Africa and the West Indies to bolster their position. The obvious conclusion to be drawn from all this was that money buys power, or at least that it could buy enough leverage to intimidate senior bishops including the Archbishop himself. The unfortunate implication of this incident was that if a party or faction was willing to donate enough money to the Church it could buy the right to dictate the Church's doctrine.

My first thought in all this was for Dr John. It sounded like his whole life had been subjected to the most appalling scrutiny and that his relatives had suffered too. I also wondered where it left the Bishop of Oxford, whose original invitation to Dr John had now been overruled by the Archbishop.

But surely the biggest loser in all this was the Archbishop himself. His primary concern and role was to maintain the unity of the Church of England and that of the worldwide Anglican Communion. It is a thankless and probably impossible task at the best of times, and clearly this was not the best of times. As is so often the case the Archbishop had found himself in an impossible position: whatever he did he was likely to lose. In this instance he had possibly contributed to his own problems. When Rowan Williams was appointed as Archbishop it was well known that his own theological instincts were liberal ones: indeed his own appointment had caused controversy in itself. Presumably he had also given a nod to the Bishop of Oxford indicating that there would be no problem with inviting Dr John to take up the post in Reading. But now he had been forced into persuading Dr John that persisting with the appointment would cause unacceptable damage to the Church's unity. So the Archbishop's own integrity and judgment would be called into question as a result. Whatever his own theological convictions might be, the bald reality appeared to be that he had been bullied into this course of action by a vigorous faction within the Church flexing its financial muscles.

When Rowan Williams had been appointed I had felt that he was the right man for the job, and I still did. It seemed clear that he had a depth of scholarship and spirituality which none of the other potential candidates could quite match, and whilst I did not necessarily agree with everything he said I thought that he was more likely than anyone else to get people thinking seriously about the Christian faith. What is more he came from Swansea, and I reckoned that was a good sign. Maybe part of his torment in the Reading saga was a consequence of his Welsh ecclesiastical background, in the sense that he was still grappling with the peculiarities of the Anglican scene in England. Of course there was also the fact – as I could have told him from my own experience – that any Welshman who gets ordained in the Church of England is likely to be perceived as some sort of noble savage.

181

Going back to the current debacle it was difficult to see how anybody could have won out of it. Certainly not Jeffrey John, Richard Harries or Rowan Williams, though Dr John seemed to have handled himself with dignity throughout. In his case he had accepted the job because the Bishop of Oxford had asked him to do it, and then he had withdrawn his acceptance because the Archbishop of Canterbury had asked him to do so, albeit taking six hours to submit to the archbishop's will. The liberal wing of the Church had suffered a defeat – there could be no doubt about that. But the evangelicals hardly came out of the affair smelling of roses either, as the whole business had the effect of making them appear bigoted, nasty and tiny-minded. Their arguments had come across as incomprehensible to many beyond the Church, though one suspected that some of the less scrupulous conservatives were adept at harnessing the latent hostility to homosexuality in the secular population and channelling it to their own ends. For that matter it seemed that the cultural gulf between much of the western world and some of the developing countries had been exploited in order to import allies into the debate. The Church as a whole obviously lost in every sense, not least from the increased perception that financial muscle could drive decisions and drive them a lot more forcefully than any serious theological considerations.

I could also see myself as a loser in all this, in the sense that if there were to be a formal schism I would have to decide which side to be on, and both sides looked seriously unattractive. I could only hope that I would end up on whichever side had control over the Church's Pension Fund. In the meantime maybe I should be thankful that this short day of walking into Arrens had been exceptional. The next four or five days would all be long ones as I aimed for Bagneres-de-Luchon. There would be no time or opportunity to buy newspapers, and that in itself might be a blessing and a mercy.

It had taken me a couple of hours, and several cups of *café au lait*, to work my way through the news reports. I got up and strolled lazily back towards the *gite*, my mind playing over the route for the next few days and feeling mildly worried. I was concerned that increasingly my journey was being driven by considerations of time, whether I liked it or not. I would have quite liked to have taken a diversion to the north and visited Lourdes. I suspected that I would not particularly like the place, but I thought it would be interesting. Equally I would have liked to strike south in order to go and see the great Cirque de Gavarnie. This massive amphitheatre of rock, with cliffs 4000 feet high and backed by a ring of 9000-foot peaks, is the most famous and most photographed sight in the Pyrenees. The central feature is the stupendous waterfall called the *Grande Cascade* which has a straight drop of nearly 1400 feet. It would have been good to see it, particularly as I had by-passed it on my previous expedition in the 1980s. Ideally I would have liked to get up to the Breche de Roland, the massive square gap in the ridge which looks like a tooth missing from a giant lower jaw. According to folklore the feature was cut by the tragic hero of Roncesvalles when, boxed in by the Saracens and about to perish, he repeatedly tried to smash his great sword Durendal into the ground to prevent it being captured by his enemies. Beyond the Breche lies Spain and the mighty Ordesa Canyon, which, by all accounts, is one of the most phenomenal natural features in Europe. Nicholas Crane had travelled across this awesome scenery on his journey, but he had not been labouring under quite such a tight schedule. Another option I drooled over was to go east from Luz-St.Sauveur and cross the legendary Tourmalet, highest road pass in the Pyrenees and steeped in the history of the *Tour de France*. It would have been an interesting exercise to walk up it and try to get some feel for what the cyclists have to face and overcome. From Luz it would be eleven miles of continuous ascent to the summit. Of course my assessment would be of limited value, as I would not be on a bicycle myself, but it would also be a pilgrimage of a sort.

The simple fact was that I wanted to go to all three places – Lourdes, Gavarnie and the Tourmalet – and that I did not have the time to get to any of them. So it would have to be the fourth option, which was simply to continue along the GR10 towards Luchon. The die was cast. Over the next few days I would be re-entering the arena of my greatest sufferings back in 1987.

Dinner was an odd affair, conducted in a sort of marquee which formed an extension on one side of the *gite*. I arrived a few minutes before the appointed hour of 7.30pm, and although other diners were already seated the waiter seemed unsure what to do with me. His problem seemed to be that I was actually staying in the *gite*, whilst all these other people had come in from outside to use the place as a restaurant. Eventually he directed me to a table in the corner which was laid for six people and had a handwritten notice on it saying "Espagnol, Lefebvre, Anglais, Paccard." The table already had some water and a couple of jugs of rough red wine standing on it.

I sat alone at the table and for a while nothing happened, except that a few more diners wandered in from the street. Most of them received their first course swiftly, but I was not served anything. Eventually a couple were ushered to my table. It seemed that they were the "Espagnols," though the young man wasted no time in telling me that he was Catalan rather than Spanish, and that he could not speak much French. For most of the time I could not really tell whether he was speaking Catalan, French or Spanish, but his meaning was clear enough and within a few minutes of meeting him I had heard three times over that he was a Catalan nationalist. His girlfriend spoke quite good French, so I was able to maintain a semblance of a conversation with her at least. She was friendly and well over six feet tall.

After a while two more people entered the dining area and they were shown to the seats at the far end of our little table, beyond the Catalans. They were an attractive young couple, and the girl in particular had the striking looks of a supermodel. Her legs went all the way up to the top and all the way back down again, and her torso was deliciously slim. These were the Paccards, and it emerged that they were from a French-speaking canton somewhere in Switzerland.

So there we were: an *anglais* who was really Welsh and was working in Scandinavia; two Spanish who were really Catalan; and a French-sounding couple who were really Swiss. Our problem now was Lefebvre. He, or she, had not appeared, which was a pity because the waiter was delaying serving us until this individual materialised and our table was complete. So that was the problem: everybody else in the restaurant was dining *a la carte* but the five or six of us were all inmates of the *gite* and we were going to be served a set-menu on a single, large platter. I glanced around the marquee, where by now several dozen people were tucking into salads of various descriptions. I was coming to realise that I had reached an age where I could go into a restaurant or café, look around, and get the strange feeling that I had seen everybody somewhere before. Maybe I was getting older or just getting tired. The sensation reminded me of Miles Morland's warning, that if you are not careful you reach a point where you suddenly grow old fast.

There was one person there who I had definitely not seen before. I could not help but notice her because she was sitting at the next table. Her skin was jet black and she had enough purple dye in her hair to make her the next Bishop of Reading.

Meanwhile my neighbour was rattling on about politics, and he was becoming increasingly boring. I was still not sure what language he was speaking, but I could tell that the gist of it was to do with the centralisation of power in Paris and Madrid. I decided I would have an easier evening if I played thick and pretended I could not understand him at all. This strategy was not entirely successful because every so often he would switch into a bit of broken English. I suppose, to be fair to him, he did not want me to feel left out of the conversation, but I had already guessed that like many politically-correct people he was likely to be seriously-challenged in the humour department. At one point I made an effort to join in, saying in my own stuttering French that I believed both England and Catalonia had George as their patron saint. He responded by stressing the close links between Catalonia and Scotland which had been forged, so I was told, through their common experience of oppression and suffering.

Meanwhile Lefebvre had still not appeared. In fact he never did: maybe he had known something that I had not. At last the waiter relented, accepting the fact of Lefebvre's absence and serving the rest of us a large platter of salad followed by an even larger one of pork and potatoes. The Paccard pair seemed to be a pleasant couple but from where I was sitting they were out of conversational range at the other end of the table. Indeed they spent most of the time staring into each other's eyes, and I could sense that they were not terribly interested in Catalan autonomy either. At my end of the table I interrupted the monologue at one point by mentioning my Welsh ancestry.

"Ah, yes." The Catalan thought for a moment. "Will Wales ever achieve independence?"

"No," I replied. "We are not large enough."

"I see." The young man surveyed me with a paternalistic sadness. "You have only got coal."

"And a bit of tourism," I added. I could not be bothered to explain that the mines in South Wales had all closed. "We've got sheep too, of course! *Jetez le mouton!*"

"Quoi?"

After cheese and apple tart I escaped from the marquee. I found that I still had my entire dormitory to myself, and an early night was in order. Tomorrow was another day and it was clear from the maps that it was going to be a long haul over to Cauterets.

The new day had an inauspicious start. When I awoke I could see immediately that the clouds were right down over the mountains. I did not fancy the prospect of ascending into the mist and getting lost somewhere on a col, but I judged correctly that the murk would lift and clear as the sun worked on it.

The *gite* still had an odd atmosphere: it was a pleasant place but it felt as though nobody was quite in charge of it. I ate breakfast alone, helping myself to some cereal and fruit juice which had been left out and making myself a coffee before leaving my dirty dishes in the kitchen. Eventually one of the staff appeared so I was able to pay my bill and depart a few minutes before 8am. I had a stiff climb up through an arboretum and after forty minutes I emerged into sunshine.

After that it was a long walk up the Vallee d'Estaing until I reached the lake of the same name. I took a detour along the lakeside to get to a campsite, where I was able to procure a cup of coffee and a slice of bilberry tart in a souvenir shop. Then it was back along the lakeside and time to attack the intimidating climb to the Col d'Ilheou. I managed the reach the col in less than three hours from the lake, which was pretty good going by any standards as this part of the route included three-and-a-half thousand feet of ascent. It was a tough job but I received a measure of assistance from some high clouds which blew across and granted me valuable protection from the sun.

For much of the morning my thoughts were dominated by the Jeffrey John affair, and the uncomfortable prospect of a schism in the Church of England. I feared that I might end up facing a choice between the Devil and the Deep Blue Sea. Following this figure of speech I regarded "the Devil" as synonymous with biblical fundamentalism, with its culture of anti-intellectual bullying, whilst the other extreme was the ultra-liberalism of the Sea of Faith network which, as far as I could tell, did not really believe anything at all. A "Deep Blue Sea of Faith," so to speak. I knew that it was unfair to characterise all the evangelicals as fundamentalists: some of them were far more intelligent than that and probably had more sophisticated hermaneutics for interpreting the Bible. Likewise it was equally untrue to suggest that the liberals had no respect for the Scriptures: many of them had a deep regard for the Judeo-Christian texts but were committed to seeking out truth in the widest possible sense. As the Bishop of Oxford had been saying on the radio, there were committed Christians on both sides who were holding sincere opinions with integrity.

On the conservative side the main plank in their argument was that the biblical texts unequivocally condemned homosexual behaviour. Indeed, many would say that there was nothing further to discuss, and that if anybody even suggested that a debate might be appropriate (as indeed Rowan Williams had done) that suggestion alone was sufficient evidence to suspect the person of heresy. The biblical argument might be reinforced or supplemented by some variation on the theme of natural law, emphasising the necessity of heterosexual coupling in order to reproduce life.

On the liberal side their cause obviously overlapped with a secular liberal agenda and the issue was cast in terms of justice, equality and human "rights." The specifically-Christian gay movement emphasised that they too were human beings created in the image of God, and that the experience of many of them was that their sexual orientation was a God-given thing. The argument would be that it is not possible or desirable to change this orientation, and that it could indeed be a source of blessing if sexual activity took place in the context

188

of a stable, faithful and committed relationship. (As far as I was aware no Christian was seriously advocating that relationships of any sort which were abusive, exploitative, violent or promiscuous could be a good thing).

These then were the contours of the debate, (or more often the shouting match), painted with a fairly broad brush. They reminded me of an old problem in philosophy which I vaguely recalled from my studies years earlier. In fact it might have been Douglas who had told me that in philosophical terms it is notoriously difficult to move from an "is" to an "ought." To which I had responded that it is probably even harder to get from an "ought" to an "is." It occurred to me now that this conundrum was pertinent to the issue at hand. Broadly speaking the conservative side was trying to get from "ought" to "is." In other words their basic ideology was that everybody ought to be heterosexual, and therefore (they posited) in fact everybody is heterosexual. Anybody who is not "straight" is an aberration, and has been perverted somewhere along the line by various possible influences, principal amongst which would be their own sinful choices and decisions. (Arguably this was the assumption which the original biblical authors were working from too). On the other side the liberals were trying to work from an "is" to an "ought." In other words they were starting from the fact that some people are actually gay or lesbian, and arguing that as *that* is the reality then society and the Church ought to recognise it by policies such as blessing gay partnerships and ordaining gays who are involved in sexually active relationships.

As I struggled up an increasingly steep hillside towards the Col d'Ilheou I was pleased with my little philosophical theory. I thought it had a certain elegance, but of course it suggested that there was less hope than ever that the two sides in the debate would find any common ground. My musings just seemed to underline the fact that they were working from totally different premises. Indeed, to push the logic in the direction of its theological conclusion it illustrated that the two sides had very different assumptions about God: about how God interacts with his world and about how God reveals himself. Tied to this, very obviously, are different ideas about the Bible: not just about how it should be interpreted but about how and in what sense it was "inspired" and about the nature of its authority within the community of faith. The strength of the conservative case, potentially at least, lay in the appeal to divine revelation. The weakness in the conservative case, as I saw it, was the tendency to be naïve in the attitude towards the scriptures. Constantly bleating "the Bible says" is not very convincing if there is no accompanying recognition that texts have to be interpreted, and that tradition and reason influence the interpretation at every stage. Quoting "proof texts" with no recognition of what type of literature they come from, let alone any awareness of the cultural context in which they were written, is unlikely to cut much ice with sceptics today. To use Brendan's mathematics as an analogy, the problems with the conservative case lay more with "the theory behind the theory" – ie in the realms of textual criticism or the lack of it.

So the two sides had very different world-views and were operating with very different conceptions of God. In a sense they were worshipping two different gods, whilst also hurling abuse back and forward at each other. Superficially the Jeffrey John business had been a conservative victory, but it seemed as clear as day to me that every time one side won a battle all it meant was that the other side would come back next time with even greater determination and bitterness. At the same time as the Reading saga was unfolding there had been the public blessing of a gay couple in a church in New Westminster Diocese in Canada, and it seemed that an actively gay man called Gene Robinson was going to be elected as a bishop in New Hampshire in the United States.

Clearly there was every likelihood that argument and rancour would continue for a long time to come. Schism at some level or other appeared inevitable: indeed maybe it was already *de facto* the case, with two or more distinct Churches operating in parallel under the same jurisdiction, each of course claiming to be the more authentic expression of Anglicanism. I could not see the fundamental debate being resolved in the foreseeable future, because even today we simply do not know enough about which factors determine or influence sexual orientation. But I also had a suspicion that the ultimate outcome of the whole issue had been predetermined before the debate began, at the point when the Church accepted contraception. Contraception of any sort is designed, by definition, to separate sexual activity from the reproduction of life. So as soon as it allowed, even within heterosexual marriages, there is an implicit recognition that sex serves purposes other than reproduction: it not only confers pleasure but reinforces a pair's bonding for one thing. More generally contraception affects society by weakening the links between sex, reproduction, marriage and love: it becomes easier to separate out the four elements in this package. If this is happening, or has happened, in the context of a society which is also democratic and which worships various totems such as tolerance and individual freedom, it leaves a situation where it is very difficult to argue that sexual pleasure should be restricted to some members of society and denied to others. In the long run the tide was probably flowing in favour of the Deep Blue Sea.

These tortuous contemplations had at least served to distract my mind whilst my body was battling its way up to the col. Once over the top I made for the Refuge d'Ilheou. This involved a slight detour but it enabled me to buy a tin of beer and rest for a few minutes before I continued the descent towards Cauterets. A section of narrow and stony vehicle track was followed by an ill-defined path across the hillside. I stumbled and fell a couple of times in the heather, and realised that I was getting tired. Eventually I came to a car park at the head of a genuine tarmac road, and I followed this downhill alongside a *telepherique* cableway which was mounted on some giant pylons of quite extraordinary ugliness. Leaving the road I was back onto the GR10 as it passed under the *telepherique* and twisted downwards, at last coming out beside a fast-flowing stream and depositing me in the centre of Cauterets.

A short search for accommodation brought me to a decent little hotel, and at dinner I was put on a table with an Austrian called Friedrich who was living near Nuremburg. He was attempting to do the whole GR10, covering half of it during the summer and returning in the autumn to finish it off. I was able to tell him that that was, more or less, how I had managed to complete it back in the 1980s. He seemed surprised when I told him that it was a German, my old friend Doctor Parrot, who had been the first to traverse the entire range. I learned that Friedrich's route for the following day was up the Lutour Valley towards the Cirque de Gavarnie, and I lamented that the constraints of time would not allow me to come and see this phenomenal natural feature myself. Friedrich questioned me about my own plans and schedule, and at first he was incredulous that I could have covered the distance from the Atlantic in the time I was claiming. He was a kindly middle-aged man, but the conversation was strained for both of us because we had to conduct it in French: neither of us could speak the other's first language.

I woke at 4am, disturbed by bad dreams and feeling generally anxious. Friedrich had been absolutely correct of course: the journey I was attempting was crazy. The daily stages were too long; my rucksack was too heavy; and I was rarely getting enough to eat in the middle of the day. I hoped that I had not damaged or enlarged my heart on this trip. Then again, if I had done so there was nothing I could do about it. Quite where this hypochondriac consideration came from I was not too sure, except that all sorts of concerns seemed to close in during the early hours when I was at my lowest ebb. I had no evidence that my heart was in trouble: on the contrary I would sometimes check my pulse when I woke up and was lying there dozing. At my fittest it was resting at 52 beats per minute.

I lay there for a while, trying to summon positive thoughts. It was, I told myself, only four or five more days to Luchon, and then I would be indisputably half way across France! However, my vague sense of melancholy persisted. I realised that whilst I was walking I never felt lonely, but nevertheless it was difficult doing the journey alone. It meant that, when all was said and done, I had got nobody with whom I could share the experiences, either good or bad, and that fact in turn was threatening to make my memories meaningless. Of course I was meeting different people each day, or at least on most days, but they were all strangers and it was not the same thing as real friendship. Indeed, I was finding it hard work when I was forced to share a dining table with strangers and we had to make conversation, especially if we did not have a language in common. A more extrovert person might have found it energising, but I was an introvert and I tended to just find it draining. I had no wish to appear unsociable, but on occasions I would have preferred to simply dine alone, using the peace and quiet to mull over the day's events. I realised that this was one reason why I had begun to keep a diary: it enabled me to record my thoughts and feelings in my own language. And if my scribblings ever got published I could share my impressions of the Pyrenees with everybody, or at least with anybody who was interested.

The climb from Cauterets to the Col de Riou went well, and compared with the monstrous ascent of the previous day it was almost easy. The initial paths up through the woods were a delight, with a good surface and a gentle gradient. Out on the open hillside the route zig-zagged enough to reduce the angle to something manageable. There was quite a procession of characters toiling upwards. I spoke to one young man who was a journalist from the next valley, and he said that he was heading for Luz-St.Sauveur to cover an impending jazz festival. His companion was another young man who was carrying a massive camera and stopping regularly to take pictures - apparently he worked as a professional photographer.

I reached the col at noon and was rewarded with a view down to Luz-St.Sauveur, still several miles away beyond the ski-lifts of the Luz-Ardiden resort. The subsequent descent seemed to go on for an eternity. It took hours to work my way down to Grust, and then on through Sazos to Sassis. And something was changing during the course of the day, namely the temperature. It seemed to be rising by the hour and it felt infinitely hotter than during my descent into Cauterets the previous afternoon. Having paused for a drink and an ice-cream next to a small open-air swimming pool I hurried on down, but ended up in a field which became somebody's back garden before I scrambled over a fence and out onto a road.

Even here the route into the town was not at all clear. Indeed there was a substantial river between my position and the town centre, and I had to head south for about a mile before I could cross a bridge. All this time the heat was having an effect. My original plan for the day had been to push on up the road to Bareges, but by 3.30pm I had been on my feet for seven hours and my energy felt sapped. Sometimes it takes courage to keep going towards the end of a long day. On other occasions it takes courage to know when to stop. I knew it was time to call it a day and find some accommodation.

This took a little effort in itself. The first *gite* I tried was full, and I was directed to a second one. Outside the latter a small group had gathered, including several people I recognised from earlier in the day. The photographer and the journalist were among them, and we had a further chat whilst we waited for *le Patron* to appear. When the man arrived he set about directing us into the various available rooms: he struck me as a slightly eccentric young character who was friendly but probably not brilliantly organised. At length I was directed to a bed in one of the dormitories of an adjoining *auberge*, from which I would have to walk around the outside of the buildings to reach the showers and toilets.

I made a brief foray into the centre of the town and bought an apple pastry and a glass of iced tea in a large café. Outside in the square and pointing up the road to the east there was a signpost with the legendary words on it – "Col du Tourmalet." By this stage in the afternoon the heat was intense. In another bar I purchased a beer and learned that the 13th "Jazz Festival de l'Altitude" would be kicking off in Luz later that evening. I doubted that I would have the energy to go out again after dinner and listen to any of it, which was a pity. The programme for the event extended over four days, but of course I would be leaving town first thing in the morning.

Back at the *gite* I ate my evening meal in the open air with two giant Swiss walkers. They were both gentle middle-aged men who taught children with learning difficulties. It seemed that they came from one of the German-speaking cantons, but one of them spoke good English and told me that he had a sister living in North Wales. The following day they would be coming to the end of their holiday and catching a train to go home, whilst I would be attempting a marathon stage in the hope of reaching the refuge at Lac d'Oredon.

The two Swiss giants would be sleeping in the same dormitory as me, and when we turned in for the night we found the room was also to be occupied by two women. I found it difficult to sleep in the heat, and lay awake for a while with my mind churning over various things. My meditations on the homosexuality controversy had reminded me of my time in theological college, where the course requirements demanded that I write a dissertation on some aspect of pastoral theology. At the time I was the captain of the college football team, so I decided I would devote my essay to a study of competitive sport. There were a number of issues I wanted to explore, and besides reading around the subject I interviewed half-a-dozen Christian sportsmen from a variety of cultures, four of whom had competed at international level in one sport or another. However, I ended up focussing on soccer, partly because it transcends virtually all cultural barriers and can truly claim to be a global game.

I began from a sociological angle, noting how people seek to achieve a sense of identity through ritualised behaviour, and I went on to draw parallels between sport and religion. In football the match is the ritual; the stadium is the temple and the players are the idols. For the committed worshippers in the stands the game is a symbolic struggle of good against evil; of light against darkness and of hope against despair. The commentators and journalists assume the roles of prophets and priests, interpreting reality to the rest of us and offering moral judgements. Football may not be a religion in the strict sense of acknowledging the supernatural or providing serious answers to the ultimate questions, but it scores highly on a list of quasi-religious phenomena such as ritual, worship, doctrine, myth and ethics.

Of course it can also provide a sense of social cohesion by conferring an identity and a set of shared cultural values, not least to individuals living otherwise atomised lives in the modern urban wilderness. It is no accident that the game really took off in the late 19th century when the Industrial Revolution had uprooted people and concentrated them in large and anonymous cities. The sport confers identity and a sense of belonging to players and spectators alike.

The next part of my thesis was to look at the instincts which football seeks to satisfy, and I argued that it offers a disguised portrayal of our instincts for self-preservation and procreation. Desmond Morris had written about sport in terms of a modified hunting behaviour, with a football match being a reciprocal hunt performed by two groups. I suspected that there was more to it than that. For a start it appeals to the instinct for self-preservation, in that the fear of death is transposed into the fear of defeat. Whether one considers the individual player, the team or even (on occasion) the nation, at every level identity and worth are reinforced by facing and overcoming the fear of defeat. Of course for professional players the symbolic urge to "survive" is augmented by the very real issue of financial survival. At the same time they no doubt crave the affirmation and respect of their teammates and supporters.

Up to this point I thought my essay was solid enough, but was not saying anything particularly original. For an interesting and eccentric twist I drew on Richard Dawkins' concept of the "selfish genes" to argue that, at a genetic level, self-preservation and procreation are simply the same thing: for our genes to survive we have to survive and reproduce. So football is not just a disguised hunting expedition or a ritualised bid for self-preservation: it is a portrayal of sexual conquest seen from the male perspective. In the game various obstacles, such as the opposition, have to be overcome before the desired female target (the goal) can be penetrated. During the game the fear of defeat and the exertion towards survival create excitement and tension for the players and spectators, and these are released in the climax of goal-scoring, which functions as a sort of social orgasm. The absurd celebrations which follow a goal, often including hugging and kissing, are not misconstrued as homosexual because the moment of climax has already passed;

the celebrations are merely acknowledging the fact. Of course in normal heterosexual intercourse the climax has a strong emotional impact and can serve to bind the partnership closer together by affirming the value, worth and identity of both participants. On the football pitch the identity which is affirmed is that of the player and team, and possibly that of the society and nation. If the sexual act is itself an affirmation of life and a denial of death then the social orgasm generated on the football pitch also appeals to our innate craving for immortality.

I decided that my theory would have pleased Freud, but I was not so confident that it would satisfy my examiners. There were one or two potential flaws in it. For a start, one fellow student confessed that he had spent his whole life supporting Scunthorpe in the English Third Division and he had never felt excited at all. I was also concerned that somebody might suggest that if my theory was true, then women who play football ought to derive greater pleasure from conceding goals rather than scoring them. Nevertheless, I felt that I had produced a plausible explanation of some widely-observable phenomena, albeit in a somewhat tongue-in-cheek form. If one wanted to assemble evidence to support the thesis then one did not have to look far for examples of tribes locked into a mutual loathing and hatred and expressing their antagonism through the support of football teams. The Celtic and Rangers clubs in Glasgow could provide an obvious starting point, with the former representing the Catholic tribe and the latter the Protestants. For that matter one only has to look at the bitter rivalry on the other side of the Pyrenees where Real Madrid (Franco's club) represents Castile and the centralisation of the Spanish state whilst Barcelona (the Republican power-base during the Civil War) stands for Catalan nationalism.

The last part of my Pastoral Theology dissertation was looking at how my theories on football squared with Christian theology. I was wrestling, of course, with the whole question of evolution and its theological implications. My suspicion was that the Church had never really come to terms with Darwin, and that large parts of the Church are still in a state of denial about Darwin's work even today. Of course the thrust of the evolutionary theory is at odds with the biblical accounts of creation in as much as it implies that selfishness, aggression and lust are not simply "sins" consequent on Man's historic fall from a previous state of grace: on the contrary they are part of the very process which God has allowed to operate in order to create us.

Finally I considered how Christian sportsmen might cope with the necessity for competitiveness and aggression, which in professional sport easily slip into hatred and de-humanising of the opposition. This was where the pastoral aspect came in. Several of the people I interviewed admitted that they had never really resolved the issues satisfactorily. The best solution I could offer was to say that as a Christian you should want to give your best to God and to everything you do, which means competing to the utmost within the rules. Indeed, if you don't try your hardest you are not really showing respect for your opponents. However, such a logic can look naïve, or at least inadequate, when a person is put in a situation where the choice is cheating or defeat. To go back to the cycling, what is the point of crucifying yourself in training so that you can lose to somebody else who has equal or less talent, but who has achieved the extra one or two per-cent edge through taking illicit drugs?

When I had finished assembling my bizarre and provocative ideas the essay circulated fast around the college, with most people seizing on the "social orgasm" as the most interesting bit. One friend handed the paper back to me. "Either you'll get ninety per cent for this or you'll get nothing," he said with a grin.

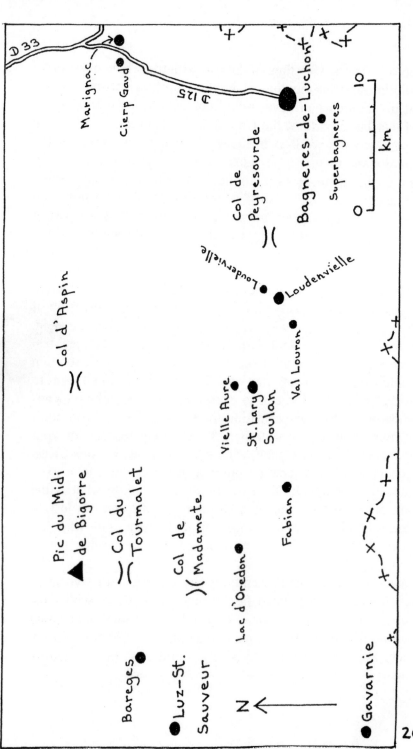

Luz-St. Sauveur to Bagneres-de Luchon.

200

In the end I got sixty-seven per cent, which was enough to secure a good grade. It seemed that I had assessed the odds correctly. In an evangelical theological college a little originality was worth its weight in gold.

Back on planet earth, at the point on its surface called Luz-St.Sauveur, the Friday dawned with a clear sky. There was every indication that it was going to be a very hot day indeed. I got away at 8.40am, determined to make rapid progress. In theory it should have taken me about four hours to follow the GR10 across country to Bareges, but I had decided to steal a march by using the road. Walking on a main road is never very pleasant, but it saves time by providing a good surface and a constant gradient, as well as a reasonably direct line to where you are going. On the outskirts of Luz I passed the first of a series of noticeboards which, I would soon realise, were set up every kilometre. The board proclaimed that there were 18 kilometres to go to the summit of the Tourmalet at 2114 metres. It also gave my current altitude (750 metres) plus the current angle of ascent in percentage terms along with a little logo depicting a cyclist going steeply uphill.

Although the *Tour de France* had started in 1903 it only passed through the Pyrenees for the first time in 1906. Henri Desgrange's friend Alphonse Steines had suggested that these mountains should be included in the itinerary, so Desgrange had sent him off on a reconnaissance. Steines managed to drive a car to within a couple of miles of the summit of the Tourmalet before abandoning the vehicle in the snow and fleeing downhill on foot, to arrive shivering and somewhat frightened in Bareges. The Tourmalet, which in those days was crossed by little more than mule-tracks, made its debut on the Tour schedule in 1910, which significantly was the year that also saw the introduction of a "broom wagon" – the vehicle which follows the cyclists and picks up any who are abandoning the race. The first rider to cross the Tourmalet in

1910 was a man called Garrigou. Since then the pass has been included virtually every year and has become one of the undisputed highlights of any Tour.

So I marched steadily up the D918, gaining altitude and reaching Bareges in two hours. It looked like a prosperous little tourist centre but I knew that the place had endured a difficult history. For years it was vulnerable to avalanches and even landslides owing to unstable soil on the steep slopes above the village. During the 19th century the problem became so serious that the village would be abandoned during the winter, and the villagers would return when the snows melted to start digging into the rubble of their homes. Eventually reforestation of the hillside served to stabilise the soil and remove the danger.

Arriving in Bareges I felt that my early halt the previous afternoon was vindicated: it had enabled me to tackle this substantial hill whilst I was fresh and in the relative cool of the morning. In fact I had even been in the shade much of the way up. Having said that, it was still uphill and it was never going to be easy. Numerous cyclists went past, decked out in the garish regalia of the top professional teams and breathing heavily as they fought their lonely war of attrition against the gradient. Some of them were young men no doubt dreaming of a ride in the Tour, but the majority appeared to be middle-aged specimens who were probably (like myself) trying to prove to themselves that they were still as good as they had never been in the first place. The spectacle saddened me a little, for every high road in the Pyrenees seemed to have this procession of humanity, all busy torturing themselves and to prove what? Equally depressing was the gutter alongside the road, for every few feet I saw yet another discarded packet or tube that had once contained some high-energy glucose-boosting substance or other.

I might have found the litter unsightly, but I was content to grab at opportunities to supplement my own energy when I got the chance. In Bareges I downed two large cups of *café au lait* with sugar and guzzled a chocolate bar. A few miles further up the road and I came to a small botanical garden at the Pont de la Gaubie, and I entered the bar opposite and ordered a beer. I knew that a cold drink could be a shock to the system on a hot day, but I was not too bothered and just thankful for any refreshment I could get. I was now at a point where the GR10 would leave the main road and strike south, whilst the road itself continued upwards and eastwards for another four miles or so to the Tourmalet pass. It was still not quite noon, so I was making good progress, but I knew that there was still a long way to go. In the event the afternoon turned into a real ordeal as I worked my way south and then east up a long valley to the little cabin at Aygues-Cluses. I suppose the scenery was attractive, but I was far more conscious of my fatigue. For much of the way the track led across boulders, rocks and stones of varying sizes, and all of these served to break up my rhythm and reduce my speed. Increasingly I found I was feeling weak and a little ill, which I took to be indicative of my body once again trying to burn fat in a quest to find energy. This expedition was reinforcing the lesson I had learned on the previous one, namely that you have to keep eating and drinking to give you the strength to eat and drink more.

Eventually, by about 3pm, I reached the little cabin and paused for a short rest. Then it was on towards the Col de Madamete, which was signposted as forty-five minutes away. It took me considerably longer as a strength-sapping scramble up a little crag was followed by two or three fields of large boulders. It is possible to cross these quite quickly, if they are dry and the walker is nimble, but it is dangerous work as a misjudged stride could lead to a broken leg. The concentration required is tiring in itself. After lying down to rest briefly near a small lake I at last came to the col at 2509 metres. I had been ascending constantly for eight hours and had risen nearly 6000 feet to reach what would be the highest altitude of my entire journey. If my mental arithmetic was accurate I was standing at 8154 feet above sea-level.

There were two French walkers already on the col, and we swapped cameras so that each of us could end up with a picture of himself in a stunning location. The view was good in both directions. To the north I could just make out a strange collection of buildings five or six miles away: it was the astronomical observatory on the summit of the Pic-du-Midi-de-Bigorre. Presumably it was a prime location for observing the stars, for the telescopes would have to contend with very little in the way of pollution or background light. To the south of the col the track wound down across yet more boulders into an area of lakes.

I felt exhausted. I reckoned that at my age standing on my hind legs for eight hours at a stretch was too long, let alone carrying a heavy rucksack up a mountain on a hot day. The descent to the lakes was long and painful. With a few miles still to go my water ran out, and increasingly I became obsessed with the thought of cold drinks. My dream was that when I reached the Refuge at Lake Oredon I would be able to buy three large orange juices and sink all of them at one go. Having come to a narrow asphalt lane I followed it down several long hairpins, feeling seriously weak and longing for the wretched day to end. At last I was rewarded with the sight of the Refuge, seemingly miles below me. However, I could make out the distinctive colours of umbrellas and tables on a terrace, and I was spurred on by the prospect of an open bar. For the last half-mile the road led me on a contour round a large wooded basin until, almost unable to believe I had made it, I staggered into the Refuge.

In the event I bought two large glasses of lemonade and consumed them on the terrace. The gas in the drinks seemed to settle my stomach, and the sugar renewed my strength. I returned to the bar and asked for accommodation. Christophe, who seemed to be barman, manager and mountain-guide all rolled into one, was quick to oblige. He was a tall athletic-looking man and when I went to haul my rucksack up the stairs he simply picked it up with one hand and did the job for me. He showed me to a dormitory with two long bunks: five people would sleep side-by-side on the bottom level and five more above them. The only space still unclaimed was on the top bunk, but after my 6000 feet of ascent during the day climbing the ladder to bed would not present me with a big problem.

Unfortunately there was something wrong with the plumbing in the building, so there was only one bathroom and shower functioning to serve several dormitories. However, my late arrival meant that I would not have to queue for long, because virtually everyone else had cleansed themselves already. As I entered the bathroom, carrying only my towel and toilet bag, a balding man with a beard was emerging from the shower and his wife – a blonde with a pleasant face – was about to take her turn in it. After a few minutes of splashing around she reappeared and joined us with her hair dripping and her body wrapped in a towel. She definitely made a more attractive sight than I did, and I knew that for sure because I could see myself in the bathroom mirror. My hair was a mess, as usual, and my glasses were streaked by the countless rivers of sweat which had dribbled down them since the morning. I was unshaven and suncream covered my face. There was a tan of sorts on my neck and arms, but the areas normally covered by my teeshirt were alabaster white and pockmarked with the bites of numerous insects. The woman grinned at her husband and laughed as she made some comment to me about the temperature of the water in the shower. She had probably never had sight of such a pitiful and unerotic example of masculinity before in her life.

In the dining-room I was placed with three French people – a man and two women of middle age. All of them were extremely pleasant and, like most of the people I met, they expressed incredulity that I had walked so far across France so quickly. I could not help glancing once or twice at the blonde woman. She was sitting on the other side of the dining-room and wearing the sort of shapeless tracksuit that would have been issued to East European sports teams during the 1970's. My encounter with her in the bathroom had not been romantic in any sense, but when you have seen a female dressed in only a towel it is natural to feel somehow deprived when you see her again fully clothed. I was also distracted by the *refuge*'s dog. He was called *"Pyrenee"* and he was a cheerful and good-natured character who scampered around under the tables and reappeared every few minutes with an appealing look, asking for crumbs.

That night I slept soundly and for once I was blessed with happier dreams. In one of them the balding man with the beard was speaking to me. "My wife and I have been discussing things," he said. "We have decided that in the interests of the *Entente Cordiale*, the European Union and the Single Currency it would be better if she spent the night with you."

"Well, that's jolly decent of you, old chap," I heard myself replying. "On that basis I am confident that a majority of my countrymen could be persuaded of the benefits of the single currency."

At that point his wife appeared, with her hair still dripping. She was saying something in that deep husky voice which women imagine to be seductive, and she was clearly about to divest herself of her towel. She fixed me with a pair of smouldering green eyes. "Give it to me now," she ordered.

I woke, sweating. Immediately I begged God to do the decent thing and let me fall back to sleep, so that I could dream further, but of course such prayers are never answered. It was just after three o'clock in the morning and all the other occupants of my dormitory, male and female, were breathing or snoring peacefully. I had been alarmed by the dream and began to worry about my health. It seemed that the blonde had raised my pulse to sixty-one.

Chapter 8.

A bicycle race to despair.

After the exertions of the previous day I had decided that for the Saturday I would make it easy on myself. I would simply walk down the road, six miles from Lake Oredon to the village of Fabian, and then another six miles along the valley of the Aure to St.Lary-Soulan. An early stop would give me a chance to catch up on washing my clothes, make a couple of phone calls and to write up my diary. And, of course, it would give me more time for eating. In spite of my sufferings the previous day I was in reasonable spirits: this weekend I would be half-way through the time available for the expedition, and if I made a big effort on the Sunday I might reach the geographical mid-point at Bagneres-de-Luchon.

As so often on the march I found myself humming tunes to myself. Nature abhors a vacuum and if my mind was not concentrating on anything it would tend to fill with music. More often than not these were irritating pop songs from yesteryear: for the first week of the expedition I had been tormented by an idiotic ditty called "*My baby takes the morning train.*" If the beat from any of these songs happened to match my rhythm of march it became almost impossible to cleanse my mind of it: the tune would return periodically throughout the day. In one of my hotel rooms I had been flicking through the TV channels and seen an old clip of the *Village People* performing their hit "*YMCA*". The film showed half a dozen young men with an excess of energy and a deficit of male hormones prancing around in outlandish costumes.

208

Now this wretched song was bouncing around inside my skull. Every so often I found it interspersed with the more tuneful strains of the *Horst Wessels Lied* – a curious juxtaposition of cultures to say the least.

When I arrived in St.Lary I discovered that the place had plenty of hotels but they were already fully occupied. For some reason there seemed to be a surplus of visitors. The Tourist Information Office thought there might be a room available about a mile down the road, and directed me to an establishment on the outskirts of the town. When I got there I found that it was a depressing, institutionalised sort of building, more akin to a block of apartments than a hotel. The staff were pleasant enough but the corridors were long and grim. The décor was brown throughout and included flowered wallpaper which had probably not been replaced since the 1960s. The apartments – at least the one I was in – were dark and functional. The whole place was like Butlin's without the fun and games: it reeked of some ancient Stalinist initiative to provide weekend breaks for the workers. I wondered whether, outside the summer season, it operated as some sort of nursing home or mental hospital. I am not sure where the idea of the mental hospital came from, but once it had occurred to me I could not rid myself of this conviction.

By 3pm I had carried out my various cleaning rituals and was retracing my steps to the centre of the town. Dark clouds were building up and thunder rolled ominously and continuously from the hills. Having visited a cash dispensing machine I ate a snack for tea and strolled around the shops. There were no evening meals available back at the "mental hospital" so I had a good excuse to end up in the restaurant of an expensive hotel, and ensconced there I proceeded to wolf down a substantial and exotic meal. As I ate I wondered vaguely where the blonde woman in the East European tracksuit would have got to by now. Presumably she would be sitting up half the night discussing existentialism with her husband - or whatever women do in France at the weekends.

The following morning there was some breakfast available in a dining-room in the place where I was staying, and I ate it staring at the brown wallpaper. It gave me the disturbing thought that this was the sort of institution where washed-out clergymen might be put to eke out their last days, and I hoped this was not a premonition. Determined to avoid this fate I packed my kit in a hurry and sped off north along the road to Bourisp. Here I turned right at a roundabout and after a few minutes came to a short sharp ascent up a lane between a couple of houses. At the top it opened out onto a green area with a few benches near to a church. I actually remembered this place from the 1987 expedition. By this stage of the previous expedition I had really "hit the wall," as marathon runners would put it, and was totally drained of energy. I had a vague recollection of stopping at one of the benches, eating a snack for lunch, then struggling to get my rucksack on my back and finding it almost impossible to progress the next ten strides up the slope. Somehow I must have managed to drive myself on. But it was odd to come back to the place now and recognise it. In fact I was being constantly surprised by how few places I really recognised from my previous expedition. I was not always following exactly the same route as in 1987, and the towns and villages had changed over the intervening years even if the shape of the mountains was still the same.

However, having arrived at this point I had more immediate concerns, namely an overwhelming desire to evacuate my bowels. They seemed to be churning away as a consequence of something I had eaten, and it was clear that action was imminent. It would be the first time on the entire walk that I had needed to perform this operation in the open air, and with natural anxiety I scurried into the cover of some bushes. There was a further problem: in my haste to escape from my quarters of the previous night I had not packed enough toilet paper. However, my arrival at St.Lary had moved me onto the fifth in my sequence of eleven maps, so the previous map would have to be sacrificed to the cause. It was a necessary evil, but nevertheless as a former geographer I felt it was a sad thing to do. There was also a certain irony involved. As a young man in India I had used toilet paper to make maps: now as a middle-aged cleric in the south of France I was tearing up maps to use them as toilet paper. I wondered whether this neat symmetry was some sort of parable, reflecting my rising and declining fortunes at different stages in life.

After the blow-out I felt a lot lighter and sailed up pleasant pathways to the hamlets of Estensan and Azet. I was thinking about the curiosities of time. It was a Sunday morning and therefore exactly three weeks since I had left the coast at St.Jean-de-Luz. A fortnight earlier I had been working my way up through the woods from Roncesvalles and over the frontier back into France. And the previous Sunday morning I had been embarking on the hellish day from Gabas to Gourette. Yet the memories from those three Sundays were equally vivid and equally fresh. Any one of them could just as easily have been yesterday. At the same time I found that I had to really concentrate to remember where I had been a couple of days previously.

"Does time really exist?" I wondered. "Or is it an illusion?" I knew that some scientists would say that it does not really exist. But if that is the case, then something else which we normally experience as time is operating. On my long walk I felt that, at one level, time had ceased. It did not matter much whether it was Monday, Tuesday or Friday. And looking back over the previous three weeks there were extremely vivid bits I could recall from different stages. It made me wonder how God looked at it: presumably if his perspective is from outside time then all times and events are equally immediate to him? He can see where I was a week ago, where I am now and where I will be after another week, and all are equally real for him.

Of course one thought tends to lead to another. If God can see the future, does that imply that the future is predetermined? I thought not, on the grounds that for God to know the future is not the same thing as God dictating the future. For various reasons I believed that humans are genuinely free agents: I did not regard predestination as a convincing description of the world we experience. As for God knowing the future, it was probably wiser to let him worry about that. As far as I was concerned, I had not stepped out of time completely. The fact remained that I could remember the past but could not remember the future.

Time intrigued me. When my late father had been a young man he had played a lot of cricket. In fact he had played for Wales at schoolboy level, and continued playing in West Africa during the Second World War whilst simultaneously fixing radio equipment in aircraft. Whatever talent he might have had for the game, I inherited precious little of it. Nevertheless, when I was in my school Sixth Form I ended up as an opening batsman for my House cricket team. This happened, not because I was any good at batting, but because most people were afraid to face the fast bowlers. I never managed to score many runs. However, I still remember the strange sensation of watching the ball approaching. From the point when it left the bowler's hand you had around half a second to choose and play your stroke. But I regularly found that during that half second my mind could have five or six separate and distinct thoughts, one after the other, before the ball struck my bat or whistled past.

I once heard a man describing a nasty experience he had had whilst driving his car. Whilst overtaking a lorry he realised, to his horror, that he was about to collide with an oncoming vehicle. It took him about a tenth of a second to react and jerk

212

the steering wheel to the left, swerving back onto the safe side of the road. But, he said, during that tenth of a second time stood completely still, and the whole story of his life had passed before his eyes in vivid detail. Presumably when the human brain is presented with such a dangerous crisis it goes into overdrive, working incredibly quickly and giving the illusion that time has slowed right down.

Beyond the church in Azet the route was poorly marked, but this was not a huge problem because it was following fairly obvious lines leading towards the Col de Peyrefite above the ugly concentration of buildings at Val Louron. The col was clearly a prime spot for paragliders, and in the course of my long descent to the lake at Loudenvielle I watched the colourful canopies as their pilots circled gracefully on the air currents and sank gently towards the valley. I was descending a road with numerous hairpins, and after a while I noticed that the same few vehicles kept shooting up and down. I realised that the paragliding people were working in small teams, taking it in turns to drive down and collect the fliers and their equipment from the bottom of the mountain.

After four hours of walking I had reached Genos and found a small café. My Sunday dinner was a large sandwich, two beers, a bar of chocolate and a tin of iced tea. Then I was off again. My plan for the afternoon was a desperate one, for it involved following the D618 road and crossing the mighty Col de Peyresourde. If the plan worked I should be in Bagneres and halfway across France by nightfall. However, it would mean covering a considerable distance and it would not be a straightforward exercise. The first part involved slightly tricky navigation because I had to cut across country to get to the tiny hamlet of Loude*r*vielle. This lay about a mile north-east of the larger village of Loude*n*vielle: absurdly this little valley had two settlements with almost identical names. Fortunately I guessed at the correct path and made rapid and sweaty progress uphill. I was struggling because I had not had enough time to digest my lunch, and I was conscious that with every minute that passed the air was becoming heavier. A mass of dark cloud was gathering over the peaks behind me.

Once into Loudervielle I refreshed myself with a wash and imbibed freely from a tap of drinking water. Then it was out onto the main road with three miles to go to the summit of the Peyresourde. By 2.45pm thunder was rumbling, and a few minutes later the rain began, turning rapidly into a heavy downpour. At first it was a refreshing sensation as the sweat which had been drenching my body and clothing was flushed out and replaced by clean water, whilst a light breeze added to the cooling effect. Then lightning began to play on the surrounding hills. "I should be safe enough on the road," I thought, for I was by no means the highest object around, but I was bemused as I noted that some of the telegraph poles I was passing were tall and thin and made of metal. Also I was still moving uphill, which one would assume to be a bad tactic in an electrical storm. I reasoned to myself that I was only heading for the col, and a col (by definition) must have higher ground on each side of it. As I approached the summit of the Peyresourde lightning was indeed breaking on the hills on both sides of the road, and a second and equally torrential downpour opened up just as I reached the col.

At the col a couple of dozen cars were parked and about fifty people were crammed into a café. I bought a lemonade and because the place was so full I sat outside under an awning where a handful of miserable souls were huddled around a plastic table. After a few minutes the awning began to sag and drip as the rain became yet more intense, and the wind was whipping up into something approaching a gale. We retreated into the café as the thunder grew even more intimidating, and there was a palpable nervousness in the air as the storm released a couple of massive detonations virtually overhead. It

214

was 4 o'clock on a Sunday afternoon. In exactly one week's time the Tour was due to pass this point with the riders 180 kilometres into a murderous stage from St.Girons to Loudenvielle. I hoped that the weather would treat them more kindly. For Tour purposes the Peyresourde, which they would be ascending from the east, was only rated as a "First Category" climb and was therefore reckoned to be easier than monsters such as the Tourmalet which were "*hors categorie*" or beyond categorisation. However, it would be the fourth first-category climb that the cyclists would tackle that day, to say nothing of two other second-category efforts.

I finished my lemonade and outside the café I put on my rain jacket. The shirt underneath was already soaked but I was beginning to feel chilled and wanted some protection from the breeze. Absurdly it occurred to me that this was the same goretex jacket which I had worn over my suit on the day that I had travelled to a reception in Oslo to meet Queen Elizabeth and Prince Philip. I made a mental note that I would have to get it washed properly before I went to visit them next time. For a few minutes I fiddled around with my rucksack under the awning, trying to delay the moment when I would have to step out into the full fury of the elements. There was a strange psychological security in being near to fifty or sixty people in the storm, and I was reluctant to abandon the illusory safety provided by their numbers. It was as though, at some subconscious level, I was making assumptions about the character of God: figuring that the Almighty would not be too bothered if a lone walker was struck by lightning but that he would think twice before wiping out a hut with fifty people in it. After a few more minutes the rain eased off slightly and I set out once more. If my study of the map was correct I had about nine miles to cover to reach Luchon, and it would be downhill all the way.

Three hours of hard marching sufficed to bring me to the town, but it was three hours which were increasingly tough on my feet. Towards the end they felt as though they were on fire. As I descended from the Peyresourde the temperature rose and I soon had to take my jacket off. The rain returned again, falling less intensely but more persistently. I was thoroughly soaked. It was touching that on the descent five or six drivers stopped and offered me lifts – something I doubted would have happened in Britain. Of course I declined the offers: even with my sore feet and aching legs I was not remotely tempted. Once or twice I had to be quite insistent because the motorists clearly had no concept of the overall exercise on which I was engaged. At one point a green van overtook me and pulled up, and a woman hopped out of the passenger door. The subsequent conversation was in French but it went something like:

"Can we offer you a lift?"

"No, thank you. It's very kind of you, but no thanks."

"But you are wet through."

"Yes," I laughed. "I am walking from the Atlantic to the Mediterranean."

"We could take you to Bagneres."

"No. I'm walking all the way. No vehicles allowed."

"Well couldn't we drive you as far as the next village?"

"No – that would spoil the point. Really, it's very kind of you, but no thanks."

She scrambled back into the van with a look of blank incomprehension. I hoped she had not thought I was rude or ungrateful. She should have been relieved actually: it looked like quite a clean van and it would not have benefited from having my sweating and steaming corpse deposited inside it.

I plodded on through the rain. A few yards further down the road and a woman in a white van pulled up. I declined her offer and waved her away with a smile and a grin. But I was beginning to get irritated. In fact every time somebody offered

216

me a lift I got more angry and more determined that I was going to walk to the Mediterranean whatever they thought. Of course I was soaking wet and I was dirty and my feet hurt appallingly, but I was basically at peace with what I was doing. It involved pain, to be sure, but at some deeper level there was pleasure too, for I knew that I was in the right place at the right time, doing exactly what I ought to be doing. I remembered Philippe and wondered whether I was a little like one of his Buddhist monks, wrapped in a wet towel at a freezing altitude but giving off steam as I drew closer to some state of enlightenment. And now these motorists – these well-intentioned idiots in their mechanical monstrosities – were trying to deprive me of my achievement. I had not travelled half-way across Europe and walked this far along the Pyrenees so that I could stand on a pavement in the rain arguing, and trying to justify myself, to these people.

Nevertheless it was basically a forced march to Bagneres. It was one of those occasions when the actual act of walking confers no pleasure: you just keep going because you want and need to get to somewhere else. The only real pleasure comes at the end of the day, when you look back and say "I'm half-way across France." When I eventually reached the outskirts of the town I came upon a sign saying *Luchon, Reine des Pyrenees.* It had a certain ring to it, "Queen of the Pyrenees." I was amused to see that Luchon seemed to be twinned with Harrogate which, according to the sign, had appointed itself as "Queen of Yorkshire."

I booked a room for two nights on the fourth floor of a hotel in the town centre, and set about patching up my feet. The hotel did not serve dinners but it had an arrangement with a local restaurant and I ate well there, relishing the prospect of a good night's sleep and a day of rest to follow. In fact the following day would be the fourteenth of July - Bastille Day. On the way back from the restaurant I ran into various parades. The streets of Bagneres were full of people in historical costumes along with jugglers, brass bands and *"Guides a Cheval"* who were twirling some sort of sticks around their heads and producing a sound like firecrackers. The horses under them were remarkably well-disciplined, standing still and impassive throughout this cacophony. However, when they came to move on they had left predictable deposits on the asphalt for somebody else to clean up. Horses do not use toilet paper or read maps.

Back in my hotel room I caught up with the Tour, via Eurosport. The day had seen Stage 8, the momentous climb to L'Alpe d'Huez and, as many had predicted, it had ended with Lance Armstrong in the yellow jersey. In fact he had only finished third: the stage had been won by a Basque called Iban Mayo and to my mind Armstrong did not look quite as commanding as in previous years. Be that as it may, he had done enough to assume an overall lead of about forty seconds.

Having watched the cycling highlights I would gladly have gone to sleep, but my feet and lower legs were throbbing painfully. So were my ears. Outside in the street, and four floors below my window, a mob was singing patriotic and revolutionary songs with a raucous gusto that was being fuelled by the capitalists running the local bars. I resisted any temptation to go down and investigate. Some of the singing was quite tuneful and the *Marseillaise* was moving, but it was also possible that they would be looking for some representative of the tyrant George III whom they could send to the guillotine. Besides, it was nearly midnight. I tried burying my head under a pillow but the racket was far too loud. For a moment I wished that I had command of one of Wellington's infantry regiments. A quick volley from the thin red line would soon shut these people up.

On Bastille Day itself I wandered lazily around the streets of Luchon, treating myself to a British newspaper and learning

218

that the Chelsea football club had been bought by a Russian tycoon. At lunchtime I found an Italian restaurant and entered it in search of pasta. The waiter who greeted me was a tall slim man with elegant hands, wearing a silk shirt and with his hair dyed bright pink. He was a caricature of a certain type of homosexual. "Serves me right for not eating French food on Bastille Day," I thought. "So this is what Paine's *"Rights of Man"* and Arnold's *"Dover Beach"* have led to." However, the lasagne was good, and it was a relief when the bill arrived without the waiter's 'phone number.

Back in my hotel I spent a lazy afternoon watching the Tour's last day in the Alps. The riders were heading for Gap, and four or five kilometres from the finish Vinokourov was holding a lead of ten or fifteen seconds, pursued by Beloki, Armstrong and a string of others. The shots from the helicopter showed the chasing group going downhill into a fairly harmless-looking right-hand bend, when suddenly Beloki's rear wheel slid out from under him. He slewed left and right and crashed heavily onto the tarmac. Armstrong avoided him, but only by riding off the road into a field. Subsequent pictures showed Beloki prostrate at the side of the road, sobbing in pain and despair until he was removed in an ambulance. Meanwhile Armstrong had ridden across the field and rejoined the road lower down the hillside. The commentators were gibbering with excitement. As far as I could tell they were discussing whether Armstrong should incur some sort of penalty for failing to fully cover the appointed course.

The next morning I set out from Bagneres with expectation but with a slightly heavy heart. I knew that I had done well to cross half of France as quickly as I had. The problem was that I needed to cross the other half even faster. The journey was turning into a forced march, walking against the clock whether I liked it or not. Time was clearly not on my side. In just three weeks I was due to board a flight from Perpignan back to

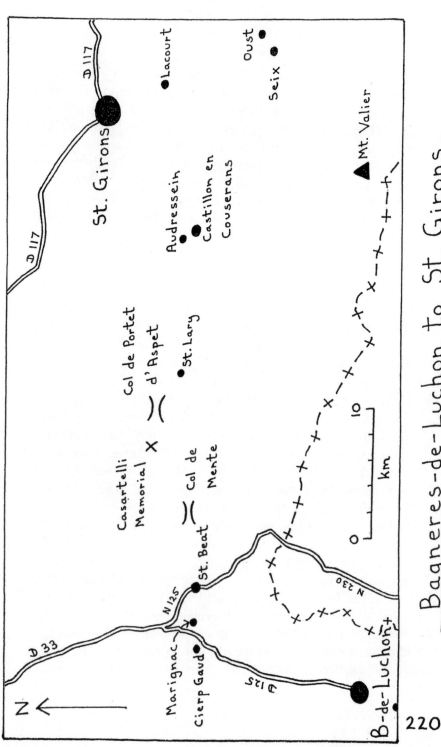

Bagneres-de-Luchon to St. Girons.

220

Stansted. I would have to get further east, and get there fast, if I was to have any time at all in the monastery at Mount Canigou. This was something I was looking forward to, anticipating that it might be a highlight of the entire trip, so I was keen to buy myself enough time to make my sojourn with the monks worthwhile.

At least I was moving. For four hours or so I headed north, down the valley from Bagneres and next to the main road. For some of the way I was also next to the railway – the self-same line which had evacuated me in 1987 and brought me back to the Pyrenees in 1988. As I walked I tried to imagine the Atlantic, an appallingly long way off to the left, and I told myself that I would soon be closer to the Mediterranean, which was equidistant off to the right. At length I came to Cierp-Gaud and, curving to the right, I continued through Marignac and came to St.Beat. Here I consumed two iced teas outside a bar, looking upwards at a curious crenellated church which was standing proudly on a crag above the Garonne.

When I crossed the river and began the ascent to Boutx the temperature seemed to rise several degrees. This was not something I had anticipated, for the weather forecast had suggested that rain was likely later in the afternoon. The rain never arrived, and the temperature went on rising. I pressed on. At Boutx I could estimate from the map that I had another six or seven kilometres to go to reach the Col de Mente. But I could not know how far I would have to go to find some accommodation for the night. At Bagneres I had left the GR10, which had been reasonably well supplied with hotels and *gites*, and I was now carving my own route across the countryside. The map suggested that there might be some sort of *refuge* near the col. Also it was possible that I could find a hotel open in the ski resort of Mourtis, but the latter was another couple of kilometres south of the col and even higher. It was quite likely that I would end up spending the night under a bush in my

221

bivouac sack without the benefits of a shower or a decent meal. It was not an enticing prospect, and it reminded me of an anecdote in Nicholas Crane's book where he mentioned two Pyrenean walkers who had crawled under a rock to shelter from a storm. By the time their bodies were discovered their faces had been eaten by vultures. Admittedly they had been at a higher altitude, somewhere on the bleak landscape between the Maladeta and the Pico d'Aneto, but their fate was hardly encouraging.

As I ground my way up the road it got hotter. I passed a couple of cyclists who were resting in the shade. A few minutes later they in turn passed me, but they were barely moving any faster than my walking pace. Indeed, when they reached the sanctuary of the next patch of shade they dismounted and rested again. They were a couple in their thirties who both spoke to me in French, though I suspected from their accents that they might be from Holland. Their bicycles did not appear to be designed for this sort of ascent and probably had the wrong arrangements of gears. The husband, a tall thin individual, looked a little like a circus clown in that the machine he was riding was forcing him to pedal at high revs but was only advancing him along the road at about one mile per hour. His wife was doing slightly better, in as much as she did not appear to be pedalling quite as hard yet she was achieving much the same speed. I left them resting in the shade, and they never overtook me again.

The last part of the ascent to the Col de Mente was up a neverending sequence of hairpin bends. The trees on each side of the road obscured any real view ahead, so you never knew whether you were about to come to the col or not. At each bend I crossed the road, which had no traffic, to reduce the distance I had to cover, and I noticed that the tar was melting in the centre of the carriageway. I did not count the hairpins, but I was beginning to wonder whether Alpe d'Huez had somehow been transplanted into the middle of the Pyrenees.

On one bend I noticed a stone plaque, set into the rock about ten feet above the road. Its inscription read: *"Lundi 12 Juillet 1971. Tragedie dans le Tour de France. Sur cette route transformee en torrent de boue par un orage d'apocalypse, Luis Ocana, maillot jaune, abandonnait tous ses espoirs contre ce rocher."* I had not realised that it was on this stretch of road that the Ocana incident had taken place, though I vaguely recalled seeing a grainy black and white film of it on television.

Luis Ocana was one of those great sportsmen whose career happened to coincide with somebody even greater. In Ocana's case his nemesis was Eddy Merckx, by common consent the greatest bike-racer of all time. Ocana's father had been a Republican refugee who had traipsed over the Col du Portillon above Bagneres-de-Luchon to escape the Falangists in 1936. On 12th July 1971 Luis was also heading for Luchon, wearing the fabled yellow jersey. He had come to the Tour as Spanish champion, surrounded by a strong team and in cracking form, and by this point in the Pyrenees he was holding the overall lead, some eight minutes up on Merckx. By the time the field had crossed the Col de Mente and begun to descend Merckx was at the front, with Ocana close behind. It was a cold, soaking wet day even before a torrential thunderstorm transformed the road into a river. Suddenly Merckx went aquaplaning off the road. Ocana tried to avoid him, slid and crashed – at these very rocks where I was now standing. In fact he survived the initial mishap almost unscathed, but his luck ran out as he was remounting his bike. The Dutchman Zoetemelk came hurtling down the hill out of control and ploughed into him. Ocana suffered injuries to his legs and shoulder, and that was his Tour over. For a minute he lay unconscious in the road, being struck by other bikes, until he could be rescued and removed to hospital. Arriving at Luchon

Merckx refused to don the yellow jersey; feeling that he had not earned it he would not put it on until the end of the following stage.

Obviously it was a sad end to Ocana's bid to win the Tour that year. But I thought that the plaque was rather overdone. No doubt it had been a bad storm, but to describe it as "apocalyptic" seemed a bit over the top in a region which gets almighty thunderstorms regularly during the summer months. And to call it a "tragedy" seemed out of proportion: Ocana may well have abandoned his hopes of victory but this was only four years after Tommy Simpson had abandoned his life on the boiling slopes of Mont Ventoux. (Ocana did eventually win the Tour, in Merckx's absence, in 1973. Sadly Ocana's life came to a tragic end, for he shot himself in 1994).

Eventually I came to the col, just five days before the 2003 Tour was due to cross it going in the opposite direction. To my delight there was a *gite* right on the col itself, and it turned out to be excellent. The place was run by a young man called Gilles who was a dog-racer: he had a pack of about a dozen huskies living in kennels under some trees. They were beautiful animals, and when he let a couple of them out of their compound and into the bar I could see for myself how large and good-natured these magnificent creatures were. The ten dogs still in the compound let out howls of protest but to no avail: the two in the bar had a good sniff at me and offered themselves for a cuddle. I remembered the old adage that "when a dog wants food it gives affection: when a human wants affection it gives food."

Gilles rounded up the two dogs and returned them to their compound, which gave me a chance to finish my glass of *kir* – a refreshing mixture of cold white wine and blackcurrant cassis. (The drink is named after the French Catholic priest who invented it). It was satisfying to sit in the sunshine on the Col de Mente, for in the eight hours from Bagneres-de-Luchon

I had covered a good twenty miles. Seeing the dogs reminded me of my own cat back at home, for I was missing him. He was the first and only pet I had ever had, and he was quite a character in his own right. I had never thought about having a cat. As a child I had always liked dogs but never had one, so I had assumed that if I ever had an animal of my own it would be a dog. However, when I moved to Norway I was prevailed upon to look after a kitten for a Scottish family who were going home for a week's holiday. The first twenty-four hours were fraught until the kitten and I got a little more used to each other and things settled down. After that he had a whale of a time, and in the course of the next few days he was in the shower and in the fridge and on the roof and into everything else. At the end of the week I felt sad handing him back. When the Scots were repatriated permanently I was given the first option on the kitten. Worried about the responsibility I decided to make my decision rationally. I took a sheet of paper and drew a line down the centre. On one side I wrote the plus points and on the other side I put the minuses. Within a few minutes I had got three good reasons for accepting the cat and eight good reasons for not taking him. On that basis I decided to take the cat, and so "Smokey" came into my life. Maybe it was not an entirely logical decision but love does not count the cost. Besides, it seemed I had found a being that wanted to be with me.

When dinner arrived I learned that Gilles was also a good cook. In between courses I read a couple of pamphlets which he had left lying around and which gave plenty of information on the bears of the Pyrenees. The bears had almost died out completely, but they were now staging a tentative comeback encouraged by various environmental groups.

These groups had joined forces to initiate a programme called "Pays-de-l'Ours." In 1982 President Mitterand had launched an appeal to save the Pyrenean bear population. Five years later a seminar on the Brown Bear, held at Seix in the Ariege, had proposed a project for reinforcing the population. It then took a few years to complete various feasibility studies, but in 1996 a seven-year-old Slovenian female bear called Ziva was released at Melles in the Haute Garonne. A few weeks later she was joined by another female called Melba: both weighed about 100 kilos. The following year a nine-year-old male called Pyros was let loose. Pyros was a more substantial citizen, weighing in at 235 kilos. The following winter Ziva produced two cubs and Melba three.

Unfortunately Melba was not destined to survive. After accusations of intimidation and sheep-worrying she was shot by a hunter. It went to show that the bears were not universally popular, especially amongst shepherds. For the next few days I would see odd bits of unsightly graffiti painted on rocks and walls saying *"non a l'ours."* In spite of this hostility Ziva was believed to be alive and well and might be producing further cubs.

During the night I awoke, startled, at about 2am. I was the only person in my dormitory and I had left the skylight in the sloping roof slightly ajar. Outside the window the night air was perfectly still and sound was carrying easily across the col. I was sure that I could hear something moving around, possibly a large animal. Every few seconds a branch or twig would snap, and the huskies, tethered in their enclosure thirty or forty metres away, sounded restless.

I lay in my bed in the dark, listening intently and wondering what the large animal might be. At nightfall I had seen a herd of about two dozen cows crossing the col, grazing as they went. Maybe one of them had returned? Or maybe it was a bear?

My situation reminded me of an occasion when I was camping in Norway with Graham and Douglas. It was mid-February and well below freezing. During the night we were convinced we could hear an animal of some sort prowling around in the trees outside our tent. We followed the sounds for several minutes, lying still in our sleeping bags and discussing in low tones what we should do. The concensus was to stay still and silent, rather than confronting the beast or trying to frighten it away. We were actually camping close to a frozen lake, and eventually we realised that what we could hear was the ice moving and splitting, possibly a couple of miles away and with the sound strangely distorted as it came to us.

Back on the Col de Mente curiosity got the better of me. I slipped out of bed and peered through the gap at the bottom of the open skylight. The col was awash with moonlight and all was still. Nor could I detect any movement amongst the trees where Gilles' dogs had their compound. I had wondered whether somebody could be trying to rustle a couple of the dogs but I decided it was impossible – the rest of the pack would make far too much noise.

In the morning I mentioned all this to Gilles, as best I could in French. He had heard nothing during the night, and suggested that if there had been an animal out there it was most likely a deer.

It had rained heavily during the latter part of the night, and as I ate my breakfast there was a substantial mist blowing across the col with further clouds above. I was encouraged by this weather: it would be a pleasant change to set out without hat or sunglasses, and without having to smear suncream across my face, neck and arms. As I chewed my bread and honey I looked across at the signpost on the col, which recorded an altitude of 1349 metres. I was about one thousand feet higher than the summit of the Col de Portet d'Aspet. However, I knew that in the course of the morning I would have to sacrifice roughly two-and-a-half thousand feet of altitude before climbing back up fifteen hundred of them to cross the Portet d'Aspet. It did not sound very efficient; but that is the reality of travel in a mountainous region. Either you are going up or you are going down, and routes tend to be dictated by the necessity of getting from one strategic col to the next.

I had enjoyed my night at the *refuge*. I was virtually the only guest, so the place was quiet. But in any case it had a sense of peace about it which probably emanated from the man in charge. I figured that anybody who ran a dog team and spent long hours in the wilderness training with his animals would have to have such a peace about him, otherwise neither he nor the dogs would be able to stand it. Of course in just four days Gilles' establishment would be anything but peaceful. When the Tour reached the Col de Mente the world and his wife would be going past the front door. Some of the cyclists would be battling their way to the col to secure points for the King of the Mountains competition, and others would be battling simply to survive. Countless customers would be thronging the bar, providing a windfall for the *refuge*.

I set off relatively late, but the cooler conditions seemed to imbue me with superhuman energy and I made rapid progress. Also I was going downhill, which was unusual at the start of a day. I flew down countless hairpin bends, wondering which side of the col would be the tougher ascent and, on balance, deciding I was thankful to have come up the western side. After a couple of hours I had reached a road junction at the foot of the Col de Portet d'Aspet. I was amused that the roadsign on one side of the junction had it as the Col *de* Portet d'Aspet, whereas the sign on the other side of the road said Col *du* Portet d'Aspet. "In that case the weaknesses in my own French spelling can't be all that important," I said to myself.

I knew from the map that it was about five kilometres to the summit of the col, and I knew that somewhere on the way I would pass the monument to Fabio Casartelli. I did not know how far the memorial would be from the summit. So I set off up the road, and rounding the first bend I spotted something white on a low wall about one hundred metres ahead. A few steps closer and I could make out what appeared to be a small wooden trestle supporting some flowers. Surely I could not be there yet? It was a shock to come upon the place so soon.

The white object was a plate inscribed in French and Italian, with a photograph of Casartelli in triumph at the 1992 Olympics. The flowers looked a little tired, but they had clearly been placed there fairly recently. I realised I was standing on the very spot where Casartelli had crashed, and almost involuntarily I found I was crossing myself and saying a short prayer. It was strange to stand precisely where a man had died. It had been right here: this definite place at one definite point in time. The sacrament of the present moment is transformed into the scandal of particularity. This happens supremely in Christianity with the stumbling block of the crucifixion. It is surely a fundamental issue in Christian theology: can the truth about the universe be focussed entirely onto one individual dying on a cross, at one specific place at one specific time? Is it credible? Put another way, if I could go to Jerusalem and travel back in time to see those three crosses on a rubbish tip outside the walls, what exactly would I see? And would I be able to draw the "correct" theological conclusions from what I was seeing?

I leaned my rucksack against the low wall and crossed the road to take a couple of photographs. The light was poor but they were a record of the place. Of course the wall was fairly new. The granite blocks which had been marking the verge of the road in 1995 had been removed. It was a bit like the way in which a dog that has mauled somebody will be put down, even though it was only acting in accordance with its nature. It occurred to me that it was a silly thing to be doing, taking photos of a bunch of flowers left here in memory of a man whom I had never met. In fact I had never even heard of him until he died, but then that is true of so many people whose personal tragedies catapult them into the headlines for a short season. And it is beside the point. The point, as I saw it, was contained in the words of John Donne – "any man's death diminishes me, for I am involved in mankind. And so, never send to know for whom the bell tolls; it tolls for thee."

Continuing up the road and around the bend I came to the monument. It was finely sculpted in white marble, and depicted a bicycle's disc wheel. The front of the wheel was swathed in a banner of stone, marked with the five Olympic rings in recognition of Casartelli's gold medal at Barcelona. The back of the wheel merged into two wings with a hint of feathers on them. It reminded me of the words of Marvell – "ever at my back I hear, time's winged chariot hurrying near." It seemed to be a morning for the metaphysical poets.

I took several pictures and left the monument behind me. Even in the few minutes I had been there, on this grey morning, a couple of cars had pulled up and people had got out to stare at the memorial in silence. It was an odd feeling to walk round the next couple of bends on the road. When Casartelli had negotiated these curves, going of course in the opposite direction, he had still been very much alive – a man not yet 25 years old and pursuing glory in the Tour – and yet unknown to him he had barely twenty seconds remaining of his life. Of course the same could be true for me. For all I knew there was even now some vehicle bowling down the road from the col and destined to run me over. But I did not know *that* for sure; whereas I did know for certain what had happened to Fabio a short distance back down the mountain.

I steamed on up the road, walking too fast and perspiring copiously in the humid air. I was glad to be putting distance between myself and that place of death. I noted the next few bends on the road. Some of them were, to my mind, tighter and steeper than the one on which Casartelli had come to grief. And, unlike his bend, they still had those dreadful square bollards marking the edge of the road. It occurred to me that in just a few days the current Tour, that glorious and absurd caravan of the not-yet-dead, would be sweeping down this very hill, and I hoped fervently that there would be no repeat of the tragedy of 1995.

I was still sweating heavily when I reached the col and left the road briefly to buy a bottle of orange juice in a small campsite. From the col it was fifty miles due east to the next dark place on the itinerary, namely the notorious Cathar castle of Montsegur. It was principally the desire to visit Casartelli's monument and the Cathar ruins which had driven me off the GR10 and onto a more northerly route, but it was possible that the detour might have the additional benefit of enabling me to make up time by crossing slightly flatter terrain.

After the Col de Portet d'Aspet it was an afternoon of small surprises. For a start the rain, which had been threatening all morning, never arrived. Instead I was able to benefit from the slightly cooler conditions as I raced downhill along the D618. I was further surprised to pass from "*Haute Garonne*" into "*Ariege*," which was welcome evidence that I was progressing to the east. And then, just around the next bend, I passed a small milestone – or rather a kilometre stone. It was marked "D618," and then it had an arrow pointing to the left and back up to the col from which I had come. Beneath the arrow it said "Hendaye, 276 km." Then there was another arrow, pointing along the road in the opposite direction and saying "Cerbere, 245 km." It was encouraging, on my twenty-fifth day out from St.Jean-de-Luz, to receive this unsolicited confirmation that I was now closer to the Mediterranean than to the Atlantic.

Also the vegetation was changing, even as I made progress down the Valley of the Bellongue through a string of villages, most of which began with the letter "A." In a surprisingly short distance it began to look more Mediterranean. At Orgibet I came round a corner and saw hills ahead of me. They struck me precisely because they were *hills*, not mountains: the

231

landscape was becoming gentler as the high Central Pyrenees receded behind my right shoulder. I surged on through Augistrou and Illartein to Aucazein. There was a further surprise in Argein where I rescued a man trapped in a telephone kiosk. A group of cyclists had just gone past, followed by a couple of vehicles with logos on them indicating that they were some sort of "cyclotourists." All the cyclists were wearing the same kit. One of them had been left behind when he stopped to make a 'phone call and found he could not open the door of the transparent perspex kiosk from the inside. By the time I reached him the cyclist was gibbering and gesticulating down the road to where his companions had disappeared around the next bend without a backward glance. His torrent of French was muffled behind the thick perspex, but there was no mistaking the look of panic in his eyes. The door was jammed tightly, and in the confined interior of the kiosk the man could not apply any real leverage to it. Moreover the sun had broken through and was already cooking him on a slow heat. The cyclotourist had realised he was likely to end the day's stage looking less like the King of the Mountains and more like a microwaved chicken. I applied all my weight and strength to the doorhandle and three or four violent tugs were sufficient to release him.

And so to Audressein, where I was relieved to be able to book into the *auberge*. Once again I had been walking for eight hours and had covered a good twenty miles. My latest room had a view south towards Castillon-en-Couserans, where there appeared to be some sort of castle, chateau or church on a prominent crag: I could not make out exactly what it was from that distance. Beneath my window the river ran over flat stones and below the terrace of the *auberge*, where there was a profusion of flowers in tubs and hanging baskets, before flowing under a picturesque bridge. In the dining room I found that the most exotic set-menu ran to seven courses and cost 53

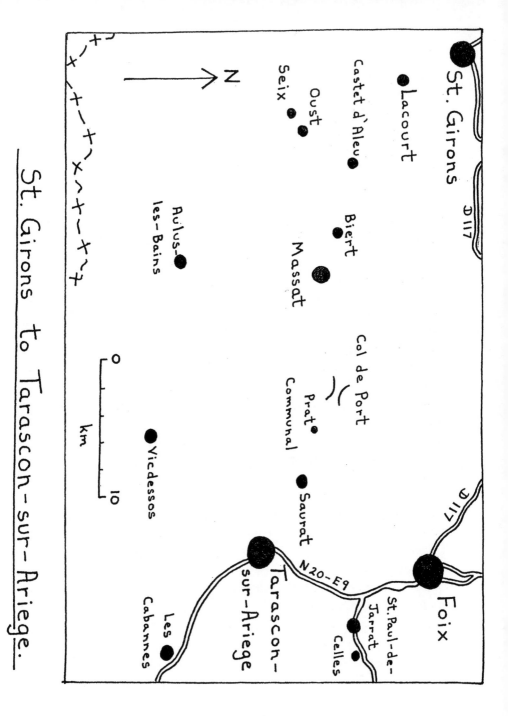

St. Girons to Tarascon-sur-Ariege.

euros. I chose the cheapest one - three courses for 18 euros - and found it tasty but not massively substantial. After dinner I went to bed and slept for over nine hours.

On the Thursday I could have headed south-east to Seix and rejoined the GR10, but I decided to go north-east in the belief that it would give me a slightly shorter and flatter route. It turned into a miserable day. By the end of it I had been walking for nearly ten hours. All of it was along roads – alongside the D618 in fact – and when I was not on the actual surface of the road I was on a pavement or a grass verge. I passed through the grimy industrial town of St.Girons and out past some kind of paper mill on the road through Eycheil. As I slogged onwards through Lacourt and Castet d'Aleu my feet simply hurt more and more, and there was nothing much I could do about it. I hoped that the village of Biert would have accommodation and thus grant me relief from my sufferings, but the place seemed to be fully booked-up. I was condemned to a further few kilometres with my feet on fire, until I eventually reached Massat and found salvation in the form of a room in an outhouse behind a hotel.

During the day I had covered 39 km or nearly 25 miles. None of it had been particularly interesting. It was simply a case of slogging on to get the job done and put the distance behind me. I was anticipating that some of the places further east, such as Montsegur, Montaillou and the monastery at Canigou, would be more interesting. But if I was going to have enough time to investigate them then I needed to claw back something from the clock.

The dinner in the hotel was not particularly appetising and I picked at my food, too tired to eat much of it. France felt like a very big country. I had walked hard for three days from Luchon and covered roughly 65 miles. It would take another two massive days to reach either Montsegur or Ax-les-Thermes. I had been hoping to reach Ax by the Saturday afternoon to see the Tour passing through, but I realised that I was not going to make it. However much I played with the map, and however often I redid the calculations of time and distance, the fact was that I would be half-a-day or so too late.

I chewed at my dinner without enthusiasm. I felt tired and depressed and hoped that the waitress would not notice that tears were coming to my eyes. In emotional terms it was the lowest point of the journey so far.

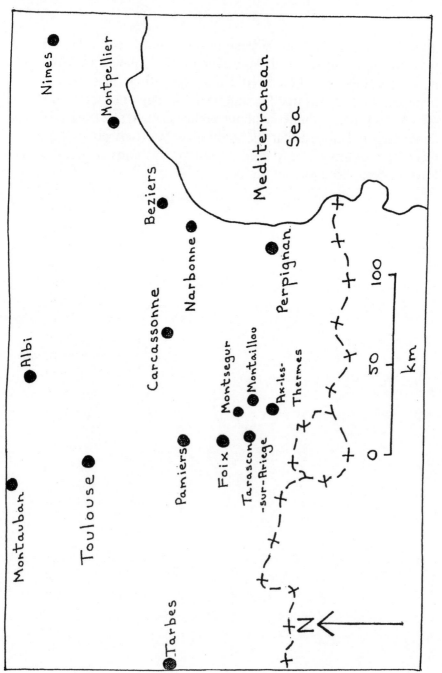

Cathar Country.

Chapter 9.

Chanting behind battering rams.

I remember distinctly the moment when I got interested in the Cathars. It happened in a bookshop in Durham. Browsing in the history section I decided that I was in a medieval sort of mood, and then Stephen O'Shea's book *"The Perfect Heresy"* caught my eye. I began to skim through the introduction and found a description of the horrors of the Albigensian Crusades, including mention of "the chanting of monks behind battering rams." That delicious phrase did it for me. I bought the book, and subsequently several others, in a voracious quest to learn more. And now here I was, entering Cathar Country myself, trudging up the road from Massat towards the Col de Port and heading virtually due east towards the notorious castle of Montsegur. If I came across any battering rams I would be happy to chant behind them.

The origins of the Cathar beliefs are obscure but probably lie in the Manichaen heresy, which was essentially a dualism which posited a primeval conflict between light and darkness. Any dualist philosophy can be seen as an attempt to resolve the conundrum posed by the existence of evil in opposition to a God who is all-powerful and all-good. The dualist answer may take various forms but it usually suggests that there are two gods, equal and opposite in power, with this world being the creation of the evil deity. The resulting rejection of the material world recurs in many religious traditions, such as Zoroastrianism and Buddhism, as well as in the more popular philosophical schools of late antiquity such as Stoicism and

Neoplatonism. Another version of dualism, which spread rapidly during the early Christian era, was Gnosticism, with a man called Marcion establishing a gnostic church in Rome by the middle of the second century. Baptised Marcionites were rigorous in the pursuit of self-denial, and were distinct from the mere believers who looked forward to being baptised later in life.

The Manichaen interpretation of dualism was named after Manes, who lived in third century Persia. According to Manes the point of any religious practice is to release particles of light that Satan stole from the World of Light and which now lie imprisoned in the human soul. So Jesus, Buddha and Manes himself had all been sent to assist in this task. To achieve this release requires extreme asceticism, including a commitment to vegetarianism. Within the Manichaen sect there was a hierarchy with an elite class of the "elect" ascetics being supported by the rank-and-file "hearers" – an obvious parallel with Marcion's movement and a pattern which would recur with the Cathars.

The Cathar beliefs were similar to Manes' at several points, though the exact nature of their link to Manichaeism remains a matter for debate. The Manichaen sect is known to have spread rapidly to Egypt and Rome, and then during the fourth century to the rest of North Africa, and for a time the man who became St.Augustine was an adherent. It is known that an offshoot survived in Chinese Turkestan into the 10th century. However, it is disputed to what extent it influenced the Bogomils of the Balkans, a group which later succumbed to persecution and was converted to Islam under the Ottomans. Nor is it clear how far the Bogomils influenced the subsequent Cathar beliefs which took root in Lombardy and, most famously, in Languedoc. Regarding the latter it is likely that crusaders brought some variant of Manichaenism home from the Levant to Albi, the town where it really flourished and which gave its name to the Albigensian heresy.

Whatever the origins, the main features of the Cathar faith are clear enough. Its dualism saw the visible world of matter as inherently evil, created by Satan. Only the invisible and spiritual are good, for this is the realm of the true God - the God of light. Humans were originally angelic beings and fell from that state, but nevertheless they retain a divine spark of light within them. Their fate is to suffer a cycle of reincarnations until they escape by achieving ascetic perfection. Damnation means being condemned to live again on this corrupt earth: hell is here and now as opposed to being in some afterlife.

I was intrigued by certain aspects of the belief system, not least the apparent contradiction that it is ascetic, anti-materialist and vegetarian (ie in theory it denies the possibility of any goodness in creation) yet in practice it seemed to allow very libertarian sexual morals. At first sight this is a contradiction, as is the concept (real or imagined) of substantial material treasure belonging to the Cathar community. To some extent these tensions are resolved by the idea that every individual has to decide for themselves whether to renounce the material world for a life of self-denial. Hence the simple hierarchy within Catharism, with the serious ascetics forming a class of *parfait* ("perfect") whilst the other believers (*"credentes"*) supported them. Access to the *parfait* status was through receiving the "*consolamentum*", a special blessing which could only be conferred by another *parfait*. The rank-and-file *credentes* waited and hoped to be cleansed at the end of their lives when they received the *consolamentum* themselves, just prior to death. The *consolamentum* was thus the rite of initiation and more besides: in effect it was baptism, confirmation, ordination, sanctification and possibly extreme unction all rolled into one. Its administration, from one *parfait* to another, was almost a of parody of the Roman Church's concept of an apostolic succession. Strictly speaking it was only those who had received the *consolamentum* who were Cathars, and they did not use the name to refer to themselves. It used to be assumed that the name "Cathar" was derived from the Greek *catharsis*, meaning cleansing or purity. However, it is now thought that it comes from a crude Germanic play on words from the 12th century, insinuating that the heretics worshipped and abused cats. Even the name *parfait* was itself a Catholic insult – delivered in the sneering sense of "the oh-so-perfect ones." The Cathars saw themselves as "good men", "good Christians" or "true Christians."

These titles were not likely to cut much ice with the established Church, of course. The Cathars might have seen themselves as "true Christians" but their faith contradicted the orthodoxy of Roman Catholicism at every turn. The classic Christianity of the Roman Church was monotheistic, of course, even allowing for the mysterious subtleties of a Trinitarian Godhead. In the Church's sight creation is essentially a good thing, even if it has been compromised into a fallen state. And the compromise was resolved through the incarnation of God in Christ, the second person of the Trinity, born of the Blessed Virgin, who revealed the heavenly Father and died to redeem creation before rising from death. Moreover Christ had instituted the sacraments, supremely the Mass, and had delegated spiritual authority to his apostles and their direct successors. So in the eyes of Rome the Cathars were heretics, pure and simple. It was not just a question of differences in theological opinion either: the Cathars were a real threat to the power, privilege, wealth and influence of the Church. They could not be tolerated for very long.

In purely theological terms the Cathars denied virtually every important tenet of orthodox belief, and they reckoned that the Roman Church, in worshipping the creator of matter, was actually worshipping the Devil. The Pope was more or less an agent of evil, and the priesthood and sacraments were null and void. From the Cathar perspective the Church reeked of fraud, corruption and hypocrisy. The wealth, trappings and sumptuous buildings of the Church were simply further evidence for its satanic nature. The Cathar concept of antimaterialism, which saw asceticism as the only road to salvation, rendered the whole apparatus of the Catholic Church redundant at a stroke. Moreover the austerity and poverty of the *parfaits*, who avoided meat and milk as well as marriage and procreation, were a standing rebuke to the degenerate behaviour of many Catholic priests. Likewise the Cathar conviction that women could be fit to be spiritual leaders was obviously corrosive of the prevailing ideology in the Church.

The challenge which the Cathars posed to the Church was not just theological and theoretical: it had no end of practical implications. It goes without saying that the Cathars considered themselves exempt from paying tithes or taxes to the Church. To make matters worse they were pacifist, at least initially, and therefore condemned the crusades to the Holy Land - crusades which had proved to be such a useful mechanism for asserting papal authority and increasing the Church's wealth. Nor was the Church the only institution with vested interests coming under threat. The Cathars also condemned aristocratic fortunes. However, far more subversive was their belief that they were exempt from taking vows, because in a feudal society virtually every contract or obligation was underwritten with a vow. This meant that the Cathar beliefs had the potential to undermine the entire social and economic system. This potential was reinforced by the concept of reincarnation, as there was less imperative to show respect to an overbearing noble if the latter was likely to return in the next life as a peasant, or maybe as a sheep or a pig.

So it was not just the Roman Church but the whole of medieval society which would be compromised if Catharism were to spread too far too fast. In the Middle Ages religion was the all-pervasive foundation for society: heresy was seen as a cancer which had to be cut out because an individual's false belief threatened those around him, and might bring divine wrath down upon a previously prosperous place. In many instances in western Europe persecution was initiated spontaneously by secular princes and lynch mobs before the Church itself stepped in and took over the orchestration of the pogrom.

One of the issues which intrigued me was why did Catharism spread? Or more specifically, why did it spread so spectacularly here, in Languedoc and Roussillon, where by the year 1200 the Catholic Church had been retreating for fifty years? I was troubled by the paradox that whilst Catharism had the potential to subvert the whole fabric of feudal society, it was nevertheless embraced by most of the nobility in this region. The best answers I had come across were to do with the anticlericalism of the nobility and the fact that, by the standards of the age, the nobility here were relatively small fry, at least compared to the landowners in other parts of what eventually became France. They did not perceive Catharism to be a great threat to themselves. It was far more of a threat to institutions which were large, distant and keen on centralization, and of these the Catholic Church and the French Crown were two obvious examples.

The Languedoc of the 12th century seems to have been a rather peculiar place, with a tolerant feudalism, small nobility and independent towns. It was prosperous but anarchic. Trade in the Mediterranean and a cash economy went hand-in-glove with a degree of urbanisation and a taste for luxury and refinement. In 1200 Toulouse was the third largest city in Latin Christendom, surpassed only by Rome and Venice. The wealth within the area attracted predators, but at the same time there was little in the way of central authoritarian control and no overall feudal army. Private warfare became an endemic problem, and mercenaries were sucked into the fighting as the petty nobility sought to bolster their forces. The fragile social cohesion was further weakened by the inheritance practice with its constant subdivision of land. Lacking the northern system of primogeniture the south saw its estates constantly being broken up into a mosaic of smaller and less viable entities. Of course the whole business was complicated by the medieval ties of kinship and feudal vassalship, but the net effect was that even the greatest landowners were left presiding over extensive territories but with limited powers. One exception, and therefore a source of jealousy, was provided by the monasteries: their communities did not die and so their estates remained intact. This fuelled anti-clericalism amongst the nobles at the same time that their own anarchic behaviour made it harder for the Church to impose its authority and stifle the spread of heresy. All things considered it is possible to argue, as Jonathan Sumption did in his 1978 book "*The Albigensian Crusade,*" that Languedoc's society was already past its peak and in decline before the crusade arrived.

Every commentator mentions the culture of the troubadours, these being itinerant poets and minstrels who saw the local Occitan language as the natural medium for poetry and love. The language, which was literally the "*langue d'oc,*" was of course a powerful symbol of defiance against an expanding French kingdom which was centred on Paris and the Ile de France. The troubadours' favourite themes of romance and war did not square exactly with the asceticism and pacifism of the Cathars, but that was hardly the point. The significant thing was that the troubadour culture epitomised a Languedoc which provided fertile soil for the Cathar movement. The Languedoc of the 12th century was not a democracy in any modern sense, but it did provide a relatively loose and tolerant version of feudalism, and members of all social classes seem to have been receptive to Catharism. It drew support from nobles and peasants, from merchants and shepherds alike.

No doubt different people were attracted for different reasons. The nobility saw the opportunity to improve their position *vis a vis* the Church. For the peasants and shepherds it was the austerity and sincerity of the *parfaits*, operating in close proximity to the rural poor, which impressed. Nobody relished paying tithes or taxes to the Church, and even those nobles who remained loyal to the Church through conviction might be equally reluctant to do the Church's bidding and persecute their subjects. The heretics might well be their kinsmen, people who had grown up alongside them and were living exemplary lives: to that extent the forces of social conservatism helped the Cathars more than the Church. (Likewise on the other side of the Pyrenees a ruler such as Pedro of Aragon might have been a good Catholic, but he was still reluctant to create problems for himself by persecuting his subjects). The degree of toleration north of the mountains was remarkable for its time, even extending to the Jews in some measure. However, the very atmosphere of tolerance which enabled Catharism to spread also proved, in the long run, to be its undoing, and also led to disaster for Languedoc. Weakened by toleration the region could not unite effectively enough for long enough to withstand the onslaught when the Church, the Crown and the barons of northern France eventually took concerted action and invaded the south with the fire of certainty in their bellies and no tolerant intentions whatsoever. It could be argued that the Cathars fell victim to 13th century moves towards greater lawmaking and codification: steps along the road towards the more centralised nation-states of the Early Modern period. Be that as it may, the Cathar convulsion had one indisputable long-term effect in that Languedoc was subsumed into the kingdom of France.

It was a curious thought, as I crossed the Col de Port and descended towards Tarascon-sur-Ariege in suffocating heat, that without the Cathars I might not be in France at all. It is conceivable that without the Albigensian heresy and its consequences I might now be walking through Spain, or possibly through an independent Catalunya or some sort of Greater Provence. It can be misleading to read history with hindsight: you know more or less what happened and if you are unwary "what happened" takes on the aura of inevitability, with the story becoming teleological. Likewise a casual glance at an atlas makes it look inevitable that France and Spain should meet along the natural barrier of the Pyrenean watershed, but it did not have to be that way. It was Richelieu in the 17th century who articulated the concept of a France with natural frontiers at the Rhine, Alps and Pyrenees. In the 12th century the geopolitical realities looked very different, for the Massif Central was a huge barrier to the expansion of the centralising northern kingdom which had its focus on Paris. Meanwhile the English Crown held much of western "France" and the Holy Roman Empire encroached to the Rhone. Languedoc was culturally closer to Aragon than to France, and with good communications southwards into Spain it was orientated towards trade in the Mediterranean. Roussillon regards itself as part of Catalunya to this day.

With so many imponderables in my head I turned to another intriguing issue: the role of women. Frankly I found them confusing. I mean that I was unclear over their significance in the spread of Catharism, and the information I had gleaned seemed to be contradictory. O'Shea suggests that one factor in the Cathar's (initial) success was that the movement offered women far more than the Catholic Church could. It gave them opportunities to be leaders rather than mere breeders. Indeed the whole Cathar saga is remarkable for the number of high-powered women who played significant roles in the events, though it must be said that not all of them were on the Cathar side. The argument would be that the Church and its hierarchy were trying to elbow females out of the picture. The standard theology of creation presented women as one of God's afterthoughts, and implied that they were not one of His brighter ideas. The cynic might argue that the increasing veneration of the Blessed Virgin Mary was something of a sop to women, designed to compensate for their loss of rights and privileges in both the Church and in society. By way of contrast the Cathar theology was more affirming of women, at least in theory, and it was reinforced by the fact that Languedoc had traditions which saw Mary Magdalene as a significant character, both as an apostle more or less on a par with Peter and as a supposed visitor to the region. However, there seemed to be more than one opinion on the role of women in all this. Le Roy Ladurie's study of Montaillou emphasised that whatever the theories of the Cathar faith, in practice many Cathar men were dismissive of women and remained pretty much unreconstructed misogynists. Even if that was their attitude, it still seems to be the case that Catharism enabled some women to come to prominence as spiritual leaders. In this they were aided by the fact that the imperative of secrecy made Catharism very much a thing of hearth and home: Catholicism was obviously practised more openly in public buildings.

Whatever the truth of the matter, I was unlikely to discover it in my current position. I was sitting on the ground with my back against the closed door of somebody's private garage, a short distance down the road from the eccentrically-named hamlet of Prat Communal. Shovelling peanuts into my mouth I tried to delay the moment when I would have to get up again, put on my rucksack, and step out of the shade into the blistering heat of the afternoon. As the day progressed, and as I

246

descended towards the village of Saurat, the temperature rose inexorably. Meanwhile I had plenty of questions revolving around each other, and I was hoping that in some way my journey into the Cathar heartland might provide clues or pointers to possible answers. I was not over-optimistic, because I knew that whatever the bedrock truth might be, Catharism in this area had subsequently been buried under umpteen layers of mud. Much of the muddy deposit of fantasy and legend had been laid down by commentators who had particular axes to grind and who were unscrupulous regarding historical truth. In other words they had their own anachronistic agendas which they were keen to impose on the Cathar story. I also knew that I was unlikely to unearth genuine fossils, so to speak, amongst the souvenir industry which has grown up on the back of the Cathar legend. And it is in the nature of historical research - indeed any research – that every time you find an answer it just leads to two or three further questions. Nevertheless, drawing closer to Montsegur, even with all these provisos in mind, I sensed a growing anticipation. Indeed it was this anticipation that was sustaining me through an increasingly unpleasant afternoon as I approached Tarascon. Eventually I reached a roundabout at the end of the motorway from Toulouse. From there it was a hot, dusty and noisy stretch of road into the town, inhaling fumes as the lorries thundered past. There were a multitude of roadsigns pointing the way to Andorra, and it pained me that this landlocked mountain kingdom was yet another Pyrenean oddity which I would have to bypass for lack of time.

Tarascon has one or two distinctions. A couple of miles away lies the cave at Lombrives, which is the largest one open to the public anywhere in France. The town also produces a delicious aperitif called *Hypocras*, which is one of those concoctions with exotic ingredients and the inevitable secret medieval recipe which has been handed down within a select clique

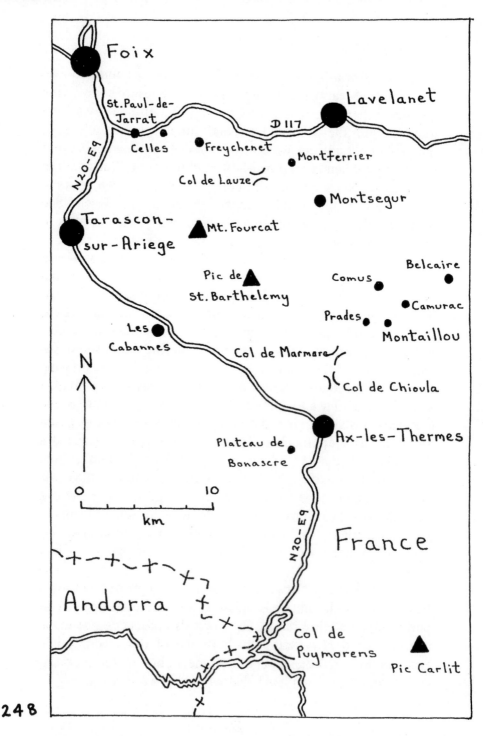

Tarascon-sur-Ariege to Ax-les-Thermes.

through the centuries. The waitress back in Massat had introduced me to this beverage, which is served cold and is mightily refreshing. However, the march to Tarascon had been grim, and so was the cheap hotel which I found. The woman running the place made some comment which implied that I was a bit naïve turning up in the town and expecting to get a bed when the Tour was so close, but nevertheless she found me a room. Tomorrow the great cycling event would be passing through Ax-les-Thermes, just fifteen miles down the road, before ascending the last hill of the day to the finish at Plateau de Bonascre. One of my ambitions for my journey had been to see the Tour in the flesh, but its route into Ax was from the east, over the Col de Pailheres, so there had been no chance for me to intercept it on foot. It had occurred to me that I could always stay two nights in Tarascon, and take a daytrip to Ax on the bus. It would not compromise my attempt to cross the country on foot, as the bus would be bringing me back to the same point in the evening. Nevertheless, I instinctively shied away from the idea of using any such machine during my journey. However illogical it might seem, I felt the bus-ride would be a compromise which would somehow affect the purity of the walk, and I remembered that on Nicholas Crane's epic journey he had followed the same discipline. The fact was that I was stranded a day's walk away from Ax. If I had travelled faster earlier in the expedition, or for that matter if I had set out a day earlier, I might have seen the Tour. But it was not to be. I was not too disappointed, because for one thing I was not relishing the thought of a second night in this particular hotel.

So my decision was made. Tomorrow virtually the entire population of Tarascon would be going off to see the Tour, and I would be walking alone in the opposite direction, heading north on the road towards Foix. My target for the day would be Montsegur itself, and it lay due east about twelve miles away as the crow flies. In theory I could navigate across the mountains to reach it, but I was reluctant to attempt this alone when I was not familiar with the terrain. The factor that really put me off was the weather forecast. The following day was going to be another boiler, and there would not be a scrap of shade on Mont Fourcat or the Pic-de-St.Barthelemy. By staying lower down and following country lanes I would be increasing the distance but getting the benefit of the shade for some of the time, and the navigation would be easier.

I tried to rehydrate with a couple of drinks in the hotel bar. The television was running the inevitable reports on the day's action in the Tour. It had been an individual time trial, and surprisingly Armstrong had been pushed into second place by Ullrich. Having absorbed this information I moved out into the square and settled at a table in the shade of a large marquee-type awning. I was pleased when I realised that the menu included pasta in the form of a *carbonara* dish. I could see that the following day would be a long one, and I was hoping to add to the value of the carbohydrate with a good night's sleep. In this I was thwarted. It was a Friday evening and the town centre throbbed with noise and music, much of it emanating from the bar beneath my room. The other problem was the pain in my feet and lower legs. I simply could not find a comfortable position for them, and I tossed and turned on the bed for at least three hours before I dozed off. The anticipation of Montsegur and further thoughts about the Cathars didn't help either.

I might have had plenty of questions about the Cathars, but some things were clear enough. For a start it was painfully obvious that by the close of the 12th century the Roman Church could not afford to tolerate the heresy for much longer. It was also clear that when the Church acted, through the Albigensian Crusade and then the Inquisition, it set a baleful precedent for the future treatment of dissent in Europe. The Church's initial

250

response had actually been more civilised, and took the form of Domingo de Guzman, the future St.Dominic, who travelled from Castile on his own mission of persuasion to the heretics and engaged them in dialogue on more or less reasonable terms. But he did not get far. In spite of Dominic's personal poverty and goodness, and in spite of his generosity in building a convent for Cathar women who renounced the heresy, he only converted a few dozen people. Eventually Pope Innocent III decided it was time to stop pussy-footing around. The papacy had not enjoyed good prestige during much of the 12th century and Innocent saw himself as the God-given instrument who would do something about it.

The ensuing action was concentrated into a relatively short period of time. The Albigensian Crusade really began with the sacking of Beziers in 1209 and ended with the Treaty of Meaux twenty years later. There was a further military sequel with the siege of Montsegur, the last great Cathar stronghold, in 1244. After that it was just a question of mopping up, and by 1258 Queribus and Puylaurens, the last Cathar fortifications in Roussillon, were under royal control. (For the record, the remainder of Roussillon was taken from Spain by Louis XI in 1463, but his successor Charles VIII handed it back thirty years later. It eventually reverted to France, once and for all, at the Treaty of the Pyrenees in 1659). However, the Crusade's military campaign only went part of the way towards stamping out the Cathars. The late 13th century saw a further resurgence of the movement, focussed on the upland village of Montaillou, and it was the activities of the Inquisition which ultimately proved more effective in eradicating the heretics.

The common perception of the medieval world is that it constituted a long nightmare of barbarity between the Classical age and the Renaissance: a nightmare characterised by darkness, superstition, poverty, misery, cruelty, dirt and disease. The Albigensian Crusade and especially the

251

Inquisition are archetypes for all this, along with the crusades to the Holy Land, the burning of witches and the Black Death. Of course such a view is something of a simplification. The Classical and Renaissance worlds could be savage too, to say nothing of the Modern era. And the medieval age had its redeeming features in its dynamism and energy, its monasteries and literature, and its concepts of romantic and courtly love.

No doubt there can be an equal and opposite danger of romanticising the medieval past too: a wilful desire to see the Middle Ages in terms of chivalry, castles and knights in shining armour. It can be tempting to sanitise the warfare of the period by comparing it with the subsequent development of more efficient weaponry, thus portraying medieval conflict as relatively harmless. In fact the reality was one of brutal tactics and horrific weapons. Armed conflict was often resolved via siege and massacre. Boiling oil was poured from fortifications whilst the bodies of horses and men were catapulted over walls to spread disease – a primitive version of biological warfare. Any wound was liable to turn septic and lead to gangrene. Yet even by the standards of the age the atrocities of the Albigensian Crusade, with its mass burnings and systematic blindings, stand out as particularly ghastly.

There is little danger of romanticising the Inquisition, which in its Roman and Spanish manifestations was to terrorise large swathes of Europe and Latin America for centuries. Our awareness of subsequent history makes the Inquisition seem even more insidious. The apparatus of the twentieth century totalitarian state - the atmosphere of fear and control, of secret police, of people denounced by neighbours and colleagues, of relatives disappearing in the night, of kangaroo courts in which the accused is effectively guilty unless proven innocent – all this was road-tested centuries earlier and starting in Languedoc. Yet for all the unimaginable terror inculcated by the Inquisition, the thought which disturbed me most was that it had worked. From the Church's perspective the Inquisition was a success; the Albigensian heresy was wiped out and by the middle of the 14th century the Cathars of Languedoc had vanished. It was an unpalatable thing to contemplate.

So what actually happened during the crusade? Innocent III was elected in 1198 and it was not long before his patience had run out. It was time for action and he persuaded the reluctant King of France, Philippe Auguste, to provide the muscle for it. The critical incident which triggered the onslaught took place in January of 1208. The Count of Toulouse, Raymond VI, was a man whose deepest religious convictions were unclear, but it is known that he had a stormy confrontation with the papal legate, Peter of Castlenau, at St.Gilles near the Rhone. The following morning, as Peter was preparing to cross the river, a lone horseman bore down upon him and drove a lance into his back. Peter was thrown from his mule and died almost immediately. The assassin fled, but was identified as one of Raymond's servants. Whether Raymond had ordered the slaying was far from clear, but at any rate he was the prime suspect. The subsequent invasion was launched in the summer of 1209 led by the Archbishop of Narbonne and a new papal legate called Arnaud Amaury, who was the sort of character that, in another era, would have loved the smell of napalm in the morning. In 1209 the invasion forces included barons from the north of France, no doubt enticed by the prospects of booty and land, and English mercenaries. Their opponents would be organised by the seigneurs of Languedoc, of whom the leading light, besides Raymond, was his nephew Raymond-Roger Trenceval, Viscount of Beziers and Carcassonne. Unfortunately for the southern cause these two men were bitter rivals already, and as the crusading hoard advanced down the Rhone Valley Raymond sought to save his own position by making his peace with the invaders and redirecting their wrath against his nephew's territory.

Beziers was in fact the first target. The city was besieged and taken, with the entire population of up to 20,000 being massacred. It was the Hiroshima of its day. One chronicler recorded that Amaury was asked how the attacking troops were going to distinguish Cathar from Catholic inside the city. His notorious response – "Kill them all; God will recognise his own" – may well have been apocryphal, but as a soundbite it summarised the tenor of the campaign all too well. As for the chanting, the favourite anthem was *Veni Sancte Spiritus*, a hymn ascribed to Innocent III which had been adopted by the Cistercians and was popular in northern France.

The next siege, at Carcassonne, saw the emergence of Simon de Montfort as the leading Catholic enforcer. He was a professional crusader from Normandy, the second son of an Anglo-Norman couple who had bequeathed Leicestershire to him. This inheritance was of little use to him, as the Plantagenets on the English throne would not countenance the claims of a noble who lived so close to their enemies in Paris. So Simon had to make do with his relatively modest estate near Rambouillet until the crusade gave him the opportunity to expand his lands through conquest. The Leicester inheritance was eventually taken up by Simon's fourth son and namesake, the very man who championed the baronial cause in England leading to the signing of the Magna Carta.

Carcassonne soon fell to the elder de Montfort. He was a brilliant and ruthless military leader, and within a few years his campaign of atrocities had terrorised Languedoc and left him in control of virtually all of it. Raymond VI was driven out for a while, along with his son who was yet another Raymond. However, Simon did not have it all his own way by any means. His forces were small, like most medieval armies, and as he campaigned back and forth across Languedoc he was hampered by the forty-day rule which meant that crusaders had to serve this period of time to earn their indulgences from the Church.

Once they had survived their forty days in the wilderness many were keen to go home immediately. Another problem was the distraction provided by the simultaneous crusades to the Holy Land, which drained away potential recruits and resources and diverted them to a cause which held a greater emotional appeal.

Simon stuck resolutely to his task in a series of campaigns characterised by ambush and skirmish, siege and massacre: indeed the only clash really resembling a pitched battle was his victory at Muret in 1213, which saw the death of Pedro II of Aragon. It was at Toulouse, in the summer of 1218, that Simon himself met his end. In the heat of battle he went to the aid of his brother Guy, who had just stopped a crossbow bolt with his groin. At that moment a rock propelled from a mangonel on the parapet struck Simon and took most of his head off.

Following Simon's death the younger Raymond succeeded his father as Count of Toulouse and managed to regain some territory. But his success was only temporary. The year 1226 saw a fresh invasion organised by the new and fanatical Parisian king Louis VIII. By now the invaders were no longer the polyglot crusading host of 1209: they were to all intents and purposes the army of the French Crown. By 1229 Raymond had been forced into a costly public humiliation, travelling to Meaux near Paris to accept the terms of the Church, and most of Languedoc was *de facto* annexed to France. (The remainder of Languedoc would become French in 1271 when Raymond's daughter died childless).

The military campaign alone was never quite enough to stamp out Catharism, especially in the remote foothills of the Pyrenees. The second phase of the offensive was the Inquisition, authorised by Pope Gregory IX in 1233 and set up under the Dominicans. The Order had only been founded in 1206, and whilst Dominic had been a reasonably gentle soul his followers became far more aggressive once they got going, to the extent that the Pope suspended their over-enthusiastic activities in 1237. Three years later they were back in business, and it led to drastic consequences. In May 1242 the Cathar Peter-Roger of Mirepoix gathered a band of knights from Montsegur, rode to Avignonet, and butchered the eleven chief inquisitors in their sleep. The inevitable retaliation took the form of the siege of Montsegur.

I first caught sight of this notorious place from the Col de la Lauze, which is four miles away. Even from that distance the castle was unmistakable, perched on a rocky peak which has steep sides and a summit over 1200 metres in altitude. I was approaching from the north-west, and from that angle and distance the castle had a fairy-tale quality which was at odds with its grisly history. The original fortifications had been put up by Guillaume the Short Nose, sometime Duke of Acquitaine. The castle was then rebuilt as a Cathar bastion by Raymond of Pereille, a local lord with several *parfaits* in his family. The request to rebuild it had been made in 1204, before the Albigensian Crusade was declared, so its construction was either down to remarkable foresight or possibly the desire to provide a secluded retreat for the Cathar "good women" or *parfaites*. Either way it served well as a safe haven during the ensuing upheavals. The castle was remote and it must have looked invincible.

As the activities of the Inquisition had begun to bite the population of the castle had increased, along with that of the community around it, for many Cathars were living in caves and huts on the summit of the mountain. Early in the 1230's Guilhabert of Castres asked Raymond of Pereille whether his fortified village could become the centre of the faith. By 1240 over 200 *parfaits* were living in and around the castle. Life there must have been quite colourful, for these Cathars, who included both men and women, devoted themselves not just to prayer and fasting but to work. Many were not only ascetics but artisans, producing goods such as blankets and candles to

256

support the community. Some were herbalists and doctors. The place also functioned as a retreat centre for *credentes* from the surrounding region. In some respects it was operating much like a Catholic monastic community. Of course the Cathars' opponents regarded the place in a less charitable light: to them it was a notorious nest of heretics and they christened it "that synagogue of Satan."

In addition to the *parfaits* there was a garrison of anything up to 200 knights and soldiers at the castle. Some of these had relatives amongst the *parfaits* whilst others were mercenaries, and a number had their families with them. The military leader was Peter-Roger of Mirepoix. On the spiritual side Guilhabert of Castres died of old age in the late 1230's - quite an achievement for a Cathar leader in those days - and was succeeded by Bertrand Marty.

Staring up at the castle today one can only wonder at the labour involved in its construction. Presumably the stones were quarried from the summit, so at least they did not have to be lifted up the mountain. The building was never particularly large, and would have been crowded during the siege with nearly five hundred people living in and around it. It was certainly not designed with comfort in mind. The other Cathar strongholds of Puylaurens, Peyrepertuse and Queribus all lie east of Montsegur, more or less on a direct line to Perpignan, and all were larger. To reach the castle is not easy even today: the path from the car park ascends 180 metres at an average gradient of 1 in 4. One guidebook warns, "the climb really is quite dangerous and the descent is worse." When I walked up it on a misty Sunday morning I found it straightforward enough and figured that whoever wrote the guidebook could not have experienced the *Chemin de la Mature* or the *Corniche des Alhas*. Having said that, I did not have to reckon with the way being barred by hostile Cathars. To attempt the ascent weighed down with armour and weapons, and with defenders hurling missiles from above, would have been a different matter altogether. The only realistic approach is this pathway from the south-west, and it would have been easily blocked. In my case the sole obstacle which might have delayed my progress was a little kiosk where you were supposed to pay a few euros for a ticket, but it was only manned from nine o'clock in the morning and I passed it at eight-thirty. (On my subsequent descent I found the kiosk occupied, but the official inside refused to take any payment).

When I reached the castle I was disappointed to discover that in spite of my early start I was not the only tourist up there. The mist and swirling cloud frustrated my attempts at photography, but added something to the atmosphere. The castle was bare and bleak, and consisted of little more than four walls without a roof. It reminded me of the Carreg Cennen castle in South Wales which I had visited several times as a child, except that as a piece of architecture Montsegur was less sophisticated. However, it was of course the Cathar history that added the interest, and I tried to imagine the desperation experienced by its defenders as their opponents closed in and their fate was sealed.

The siege began in May 1243 on the Feast of the Ascension – exactly one year on from the massacre of the inquisitors which Peter-Roger had organised at Avignonet. The besiegers were led by Hugh of Arcis, backed up by Peter Amiel who was Archbishop of Narbonne, and by the Bishop of Albi. The affair rapidly became a stalemate. The besiegers had 10,000 men but even these were not enough to completely seal off the two-mile perimeter of the mountain's base. Defenders could get in and out, with daring, using the steep scrubby ravines on the mountainside. Moreover the terrain clearly made it impossible to deploy siege engines such as trebuchets. On the other side the garrison also had its problems. It was difficult to bring supplies in on any scale and, with the *parfaits* being pacifists,

Peter-Roger had command of less than one hundred able-bodied defenders. Skilful use of the terrain enabled him to ward off the assaults, but sorties were out of the question and he could ill-afford any losses.

With the cold and dark of winter closing in the besiegers became just as demoralised as the besieged, and around Christmas of 1243 Hugh of Arcis resolved to break the stalemate with a bold and desperate project. His target was the bastion of Roc de la Tour, a spike of stone at the eastern end of the summit ridge, several hundred yards from the main castle and quite a bit lower in altitude, and the volunteers were a group of Gascon or Basque mountain men. Under cover of darkness, and in total silence, they scaled the cliff to the east. The guards at the bastion were surprised and killed, with some simply being tossed off the cliff. The next morning the Gascons saw the dizzying drop and swore that they would never have made the ascent in daylight.

Daybreak must have brought dismay to the Cathar defenders, for the writing was now on the wall. Having gained a bridgehead on the top of the mountain the attackers were rapidly reinforced and as the snow swirled they began to inch closer to the castle itself. Their next move was to winch up parts of a mangonel which was quickly reassembled, and soon stones were flying into the main defences.

Finally Peter-Roger accepted that there was no realistic prospect of relief, and on 2nd March 1244 he surrendered. The capitulation involved a fortnight's truce during which lay people could leave the castle with their past crimes forgiven. This measure of mercy seems to have been symptomatic of the recognition, on both sides, that check-mate had been achieved. The military dimension of the Albigensian Crusade had reached a decisive conclusion. The people leaving the castle were questioned by the Inquisition, and their evidence provides the historical knowledge of what happened at both Avignonet and Montsegur.

For the *parfaits* there would be no mercy. They had two weeks to decide whether to recant and subject themselves to the Church's just and gentle rule. In the meantime their enjoyment of the view was no doubt spoiled by the sight of the Archbishop's men, far below, toiling away in a snowy clearing as they stacked it with dry wood. Whatever one thinks of the Cathars' theology, it is touching that not one of them asked for the Church's mercy. Indeed, on 13th March a further twenty-one *credentes* (drawn from all ranks of feudal society) came forward and asked to receive the *consolamentum*: they were choosing to join the *parfaits* and die. And so on 16th March some 220 people were led from the castle in chains and herded onto the giant pyre. At a word from the Archbishop burning torches were thrown in amongst them, and within a few minutes the Cathars had been engulfed in flames.

After this barbecue the castle walls were levelled, and then at a later date rebuilt by the Catholic Guy de Levis, so the structure visible today is not the one that was standing there in 1244. The idea that the current building's walls and windows are aligned with the sun, and based upon some secret Cathar knowledge, is nonsense. Yet it seems that the bonfire at Montsegur had hardly died down before the mill of myth and legend began to roll, fuelled to some extent by the horrible finality of the mass immolation. Imbert of Salas, testifying to the Inquisition, claimed that two Cathars had smuggled some treasure out of the castle around Christmas of 1243, possibly taking it to caves at Sabarthes near Foix, to the north-west. The remainder of the Cathar treasure was supposed to have been spirited away on 15th March 1244 by four *parfaits* heading over the Col de la Peyre to the south.

Part of the problem in assessing the Cathars - or simply in trying to understand them - is that their memory has been hijacked by no end of subsequent movements. Maybe this was part of the price they paid in getting wiped out so comprehensively, as they have had no direct descendants to speak on their behalf. Instead they have been portrayed as forerunners of the Protestant Reformation, of Occitan nationalism, of pacifism, of feminism, of vegetarianism and of the New Age, to name but a few. They have been admired by civil libertarians, by Nazis and by cults such as the Order of the Solar Temple. They have inspired awe and occult respect, and have acted as a magnet which attracts weirdoes of virtually every stripe. Of course there is a big problem of anachronism here. Just as the castle standing at Montsegur today was constructed after the Cathars had been extinguished, so a multitude of later interest-groups have sought to co-opt the Cathars to their causes, thus projecting their own agendas backwards through the centuries.

The legends surrounding the Cathars have developed over time, growing at an almost exponential rate. Today "Cathar Country" is well established as a tourist attraction which draws money into the local economy. Indeed the whole saga, at least since the 19th century, adds up to a miserable tale in which a colourful period of history has been exploited and manipulated, often with scant regard for what actually happened. For that matter it also provides us with numerous salutary examples of human gullibility.

Until the mid-19th century the Cathar debate was fairly low-key. The Protestants portrayed the Cathars as forerunners of the Reformation. The Catholics argued that the Cathars had not been Christians at all. Liberal historians emphasised Languedoc's troubadour culture and the horrors of the crusade. However, the Cathars' profile was raised during the 1870's with the publication of Napoleon Peyrat's "*History of the Albigensians*." It was Peyrat more than anyone who created the myth of the Cathars, of Montsegur, and of lost Pyrenean treasure.

Peyrat had been born locally in the Ariege in 1809 and under the Third Republic he devoted himself to writing polemics against what he regarded as an undemocratic and reactionary Catholic establishment. Unfortunately Peyrat's talent as a writer was not matched by an equal diligence in seeking out the truth. When he came across the Cathars he was delighted, because they furnished him with a pile of fresh ammunition for his propaganda. Peyrat proceeded to portray 12th century Languedoc as highly civilised and inhabited by freedom-loving democrats who were then crushed by the barbaric Catholic invaders. Moreover, as 19th century French nationalism had already served up Joan of Arc as an icon, Peyrat proceeded to invent an Occitan heroine in the shape of "Esclarmonde" who was a conflation of several historical figures. In this way the cult of Montsegur was well and truly launched, and linked to the concepts of secret caves, tunnels and hidden treasure.

If Peyrat had received the Cathar story with joy, his own work was in turn very attractive to anybody seeking to promote the Occitan language and Languedoc nationalism. Earlier in the 19th century French and German scholars had been rediscovering the old Provencal languages and their troubadour poetry. These included the Languedoc dialect, later called Occitan. For the region's nationalists a work which portrayed 12th century Languedoc as an enlightened place was obviously very helpful.

By the end of the 19th century the Cathar legend was getting mixed up in some of the more murky undercurrents in European philosophy. Orientalism and the occult gained in popularity and the Cathars were portrayed as the guardians of some preclassical eastern wisdom: after all, reincarnation is a major plank in eastern religions. By now the Montsegur treasure was mutating into a deposit of ancient knowledge and spiritual revelation. This sort of idea was advanced by Josephin Peladan, an occultist who equated Montsegur with Montsalvat, the holy mountain of Wagner's *Parsifal* and *Lohengrin*. The concept of a Pyrenean Holy Grail was now on the horizon.

The horrific loss of life during the First World War boosted interest in spiritism and the paranormal. The Montsegur of the interwar years attracted spiritualists, occultists and Occitan nationalists in equal measure. The local leader, Deodat Roche, was largely responsible for creating the concept of "Cathar Country" which we see today. One of Roche's followers, Maurice Magre, was a writer of speculative history and Cathar novels who worked to make Montsegur famous. Indeed, on my ascent to the castle I had come across a plaque in his memory, located a few metres off to the left of the steep path. It recorded that Magre had died in 1941. Before his death Magre had endowed the place with a further dubious legacy in that he had introduced Otto Rahn to Montsegur.

Rahn's 1933 book *"Crusade against the Grail"* assembled all the existing Pyrenean Holy Grail stories and compared them with *Parsifal*. There were several stories in circulation, including the old tradition that Mary Magdalene had brought the grail to Languedoc. For Rahn, not only was Montsegur obviously Wagner's Montsalvat, but he equated *Parsifal* or Percival with Trenceval – referring back to the Cathar Viscount of Beziers and Carcassonne who had been the first Languedoc noble to face the onslaught in 1209. Rahn also had a guardian for his grail, none other than Peyrat's heroine Esclarmonde.

By 1937 Rahn had returned to Germany and joined the SS. His second book, *"The Court of Lucifer,"* was another Grail and Cathar effort. This time, inevitably, his Cathar heroes were Nazis – true Aryans of pure Nordic blood. Rahn seemed to see the grail as something which conferred mystical power and possibly as a way to portray Christ as an Aryan hero done to death by the Jews. Strangely the end of the Second World War, and its result, did little to put the lid on all of this nonsense. If anything the stories were embellished yet further with Nazi sympathisers claiming that Hitler had been part of a neo-Cathar sect and that German engineers had excavated Montsegur during the war to retrieve the grail.

There seems to be no end to the ability of the Cathar legend to adapt and evolve, transforming itself into whatever is required to fit in with the spirit of the age. Indeed, the variety of contradictory movements which are drawn to the place can itself be used as evidence, by any and all of them, that "there must be something in it." By the 1960s hippies were coming to Montsegur, and it was vegetarianism, feminism and free love which were being emphasised. However, the occult dimension never seems to go away for long, and a British psychiatrist called Arthur Guirdham claimed that several of his patients in England were exhibiting signs of being reincarnated Cathars. Guirdham himself claimed to be Guilhabert of Castres.

Meanwhile the Montsegur treasure received a new lease of life with the publication of Baigent, Leigh and Lincoln's popular occult detective story *"The Holy Blood and the Holy Grail."* This picks up on the peculiar goings-on at Rennes-le-Chateau, near Carcassonne, at the end of the 19th century where the local priest, a man called Sauniere, suddenly began living and spending extravagantly. (The relatively mundane truth of the matter seems to be that Sauniere had conned various local notables into leaving him money in their wills). In the book Sauniere had, of course, discovered Montsegur's treasure and was selling it off, besides blackmailing the Vatican for good measure. The book hints that not all of the treasure has been recovered, so today Rennes-le-Chateau, like Montsegur, is vulnerable to fortune-seekers with shovels.

The spiral of weirdness and gullibility does not end even there. A couple of religious cults have emphasised their links with the Cathars and Montsegur before committing mass suicide. In one instance this apocalyptic ending was timed to coincide with the receipt of messages from the Hale-Bopp comet.

Standing in the ruins of Montsegur and meditating upon all this I felt dizzy. My head was spinning with the effort of trying to bend my brain around it. "Where's the surface?" I wondered. It was fascinating but depressing to trace this tortuous tale of the bizarre. For one thing Montsegur and most of the other "Cathar" castles in Languedoc and Roussillon are anachronisms – they were constructed after the heretics were wiped out. Yet New Age visitors still stare at them, convinced they are looking at solar temples which fell victim to the nastiness of the established Church. The whole thing smacks of "castles in the air."

However it was curious how certain ingredients recurred throughout the saga. I was not thinking about Cathar treasure or the Holy Grail: it would be relatively easy to spread a rumour about such things which would then be repeated and would grow and embellish itself, developing a self-generating tradition all of its own. I was more disturbed by the elements in the background, of reincarnation and mysticism, of spiritism and the occult. I felt uncomfortable here at Montsegur. I knew that it would be impossible to disentangle all the threads which had been woven together in the truth and legend surrounding this place, but I wondered about the simple fact that so many people had come here who were already dabbling in the spiritual realm in all sorts of dubious ways, arguably bringing a range of unwholesome influences and concentrating them at this one spot. One feature which remained consistent throughout the whole Montsegur saga was the profoundly unchristian nature of virtually everything assosciated with the place.

I had my own slightly odd experience as I wandered outside the walls. Moving west on the northern side of the summit I passed a few feet above another visitor. She was dressed in a white tee-shirt and purple shorts and was reclining against a rock. With her eyes closed and a beatific smile on her upturned face I presumed she was in a state of meditation or prayer and was careful not to disturb her. Five minutes later I came back in the opposite direction, and glanced down to see the same tee-shirt and shorts, the same closed eyes and expression. But this time it was a man. I stared at him for a minute, taken aback. I could only imagine that a couple who liked to dress the same were visiting the place together and each had taken their turn to rest at the same spot whilst the other one wandered around the ruins.

I was glad to be descending the hill and moving on. I was leaving the castle with few of my serious questions about the Cathars answered. I had been disturbed by the story of the crusade and by the thought of the Inquisition's activities, and particularly by the unpalatable fact that these appear to have worked effectively. Yet as I descended the path towards the car park I was not so sure which side had won. Certainly on 16th March 1244 it looked like game, set and match to the Catholic Church. But today, early in the 21st century, the Roman Church appears to be struggling in France in many respects, certainly in terms of numbers attending worship, vocations to the priesthood, and the enthusiasm which the majority of the population express for its dogma. On the other hand the New Age and the various disparate spiritualities of the postmodern era seem to be gaining ground. It would be stretching it to say that the Cathars really won after all, but it seems clear that they are not going to just fade away and be forgotten. At the bottom of the steps I came upon a memorial to the Cathars. It was a small monument in stone and wood with a few flowers, standing on the probable site of the clearing where the holocaust had taken place, and the flowers were fresh.

Chapter 10.

Sex, lice and clergymen.

The walk from Tarascon to Montsegur had been a tough one, and it eventually took over ten hours on a grillingly-hot Saturday. In the relative cool of the morning I had made rapid progress north through Bompas and Mercus, following the main road alongside the Ariege in the direction of Foix. Meanwhile dozens of cyclists streamed past in the opposite direction, mostly in small groups. All were decked out in the colourful lycra of the top professional teams, and all were heading down to Ax-les-Thermes and Plateau de Bonascre to see the big event.

At St.Antoine I stopped for a coffee before executing a ninety-degree right-hand turn and continuing east towards St.Paul-de-Jarrat. I was congratulating myself on my clever tactics. By going north and then east I had kept the bulk of the mountains between myself and the ascending sun for much of the morning. But it was too good to last, and I found I was now exposed on a stretch of straight treeless road. Turning right again at Celles I proceeded up a narrow lane, but the temperature was climbing faster than I was and I felt tired long before I reached the tiny settlement of Freychenet.

From there it was a simple case of following the lane as it twisted across the countryside, snaking in and out of the woods. Barely a single car went past during the next couple of hours, and as the afternoon grew hotter I got progressively weaker. The lane seemed interminable, and I became obsessed with the idea of cold drinks. Eventually I reached the so-called

Col de Lauze. This was little more than a T-junction between a couple of farmyards, but it did at least afford me my first glimpse of Montsegur, four miles away but unmistakable. On the downhill section of road beyond the col I passed a reservoir which looked pretty much dried up. Another twisting and wooded section of road brought me at last to Montferrier and the merciful sight of a bar. As I devoured half a litre of beer I questioned the barman and established that there was no guest-house or hotel nearby. So the die was cast: I would have to continue to the village of Montsegur itself.

The main road from Montferrier to Montsegur was about three miles, and it was uphill all the way. I had not appreciated this with my casual reading of the map, and it came as an unpleasant revelation. After the first mile the refreshing effects of the beer had worn off and I was not feeling at all strong. I struggled on, for there was no alternative, but at one point on a steep hill I lay down to rest at the side of the road. It was a relief to remove the burden from my legs for a few minutes, and I lay there grinning stupidly at the few cars which went past, hoping fervently that the drivers would not stop and cause me further embarrassment. When I stood up again I immediately staggered backwards two or three strides as the weight of my rucksack dragged me back down the gradient. Gritting my teeth I drove forwards up the hill. The road was leading to the Col de Montsegur. From this angle the castle on the mountain-top looked magnificent, and I knew that with a blue sky and the sun behind me I ought to be taking photographs. Some excellent shots were in the offing, but I was far too exhausted for photography to be an option. No energy could be spared for fiddling with a camera. "Lord have mercy" I gasped in dismay as I passed a notice indicating that it was still a full kilometre to the col. "Why does everywhere in the Pyrenees have to have a col?" Somehow I covered the last few hundred metres and sank down again, this time in a field of yellow straw and stubble next to the road. I was now directly beneath the plug of rock which was crowned with the infamous and archetypal Cathar stronghold. "So that's what I've come to see," I thought. "A pile of stones on a hill."

After about ten minutes of collapse I struggled to my feet and continued through a car park and along the road, which was at last going downhill. I knew I was virtually out on my feet, and I hoped sincerely that I would not vomit as I entered the village seeking a bed for the night. An advertising-hoarding on the edge of the settlement indicated the presence of a hotel at the centre, but when I reached it there were no signs of life. A notice on the door announced that it was closed for the day. No doubt the owner and staff had gone off to see the Tour. However, around the corner I came upon a small group of people drinking unde a parasol outside what appeared to be a private house. I sank onto a plastic chair alongside them and requested a lemonade from a woman of late middle-age who seemed to be running a simple bar from her kitchen. I gulped it down and ordered an orange juice, simultaneously establishing that the woman's home functioned as a guest-house, of a sort, and that there was a room which I could take for the night. Once I had despatched the orange juice she showed me the way upstairs. It was an old-fashioned and rambling building, and its management-style appeared eccentric, but it was a sanctuary nevertheless.

Having made use of the shower I descended once more to street level and settled under the parasol to imbibe more liquid. The group which had been there previously had disappeared indoors to eat, but I had no appetite and ate nothing all evening. However I drank steadily, some of the time talking to a rather sad-looking grey cat which was lying on the ground in the shade and appeared to have had part of its nostril torn off. By the time I eventually crawled into bed I would have consumed three-quarters of a litre of lemonade, half a litre of orange juice and a large volume of water.

In the meantime two giant Englishmen had rolled up in a large car, seeking accommodation for the night. After some protracted negotiations they managed to secure a couple of rooms. It transpired that they were journalists who were following the Tour, hoping to write a book about it. Their press passes enabled them to drive to the finishing area each day and watch the action from there, either following the television coverage with the other journalists or seeing it relayed onto the giant screens which entertained the crowd. They were seeking to include esoteric material on the areas which the Tour was passing through, so Montsegur was a good candidate for inclusion on that basis. One of them had a background in music and on a previous stage of the Tour they'd gone to pay homage at Jim Morrison's grave. They arrived hot and tired, but they had had a good day. The crowds around Ax had been enormous, and even with a police escort it had taken them an eternity to get clear of the traffic jam once the day's cycling was over. But the hordes of spectators had been good-humoured and lacked the aggressive edge which the journalists had noticed amongst the Germans and Dutch in the Alps the previous week. As for the action, they reckoned it had been the best day of the Tour so far. Three Spanish riders had broken clear and one of them, Carlos Sastre, had taken the stage win and claimed his fifteen minutes of fame. But the real battle was unfolding behind him. Ullrich, surprise winner of the previous day's time trial, had put in an attack on the final climb of the day, with about four kilometres to go. For a while Armstrong had been unable to respond, and the crowds had gone wild. Eventually the Texan staged a recovery of sorts and limited his losses to a few seconds, but Ullrich was turning the spectacle into a genuine contest for the first time in years.

As one of the journalists said, few people in Britain have any idea of just how massive the Tour really is. For three weeks every summer this combination of a circus and a migration rotates around France, and every year it grows bigger. There's nothing remotely like it in Britain, or for that matter anywhere else on earth. Talking to the journalists I knew I had missed out on something by failing to see the Tour at first hand, and I felt an uneasy sense of loss. Having said that, I was getting enough drama of my own. I might not have heard the crowd roar as Ullrich attacked, but at the same moment Armstrong was struggling to respond on the climb to Bonascre I too was fighting hard as I forced myself up the road to the col at Montsegur. There was no crowd to watch me, but in the morning my own private tour and torment would continue nonetheless.

In fact the morning began easily. I had slept well and woke refreshed, again pleasantly surprised at my powers of recovery. Twelve hours previously I had been at the limit, but now I found my appetite for exploration restored. After breakfast I slipped out of the guest-house. My green rucksack remained in my room, and without its weight I sailed back up to the carpark and col with ease. It was an overcast and misty morning, and the humidity made me sweat as I ascended to the castle itself, but that was a minor irritation. Descending to the village once more I collected my gear, settled my bill with the lady who owned the "hotel", and then spent some time studying in the village's museum. It was stocked with a good range of artefacts and numerous books about the Cathars. I bought a few postcards and left Montsegur somewhat bemused and possibly a little disappointed. I had anticipated that the place would be thriving with hotels, cafes and souvenir shops, and that it would be a throbbing mass of hippies, eco-hikers and general weirdoes. In the event the only visitors I saw around the village were middle-aged and elderly tourists who looked pretty harmless. As for the village itself, if you subtracted the castle and the museum you were left with a sleepy backwater: there was little else to hint at its violent and gruesome history.

I left the museum at coffee-time: outside it was still a grey Sunday morning. After a brief struggle to find the correct trail I headed east on a path variously described as GR107, number 7B, the "*Sentier Cathare*" or the "Path of the Good Men." It led through thickly wooded country for a couple of miles before emerging at Pelail. A sharp right-hand turn had me going south along a narrow lane and past a large party of people who were engaged in a family picnic. After another mile or two the road ran out and I continued up the Gorges-de-la-Frau. The way was increasingly steep, narrow and rocky, and the air humid and oppressive. Eventually the gradient levelled off, the gorge opened out and I came to the village of Comus. Some kind of Sunday afternoon jamboree was in progress with people playing games such as *boules* on a flat area of grass. In the village square I purchased a couple of drinks in a temporary marquee opposite a stage supporting sound equipment. Litter was lying around and I guessed that there had been a concert or party the previous night. Between Comus and Camurac I came upon yet another strange weekend event. Young men were racing up and down rough hummocky terrain on funny little machines which appeared to be a cross between a tractor and a motorbike. Each of these quadbikes had four large tyres and an engine that generated speed and noise in equal measure. A considerable crowd was enjoying this entertainment, which appeared to be well organised.

In Camurac I located a *gite d'etape*. It was deserted but unlocked, and following some instructions on the door I let myself in and took a shower before attempting to wash my increasingly revolting clothes. A while later the proprietor of this establishment appeared and proceeded to set up tables for a private dinner party. He was clearly expecting a couple of dozen guests and I agreed to make his job marginally easier by going out to eat at a slightly odd bar-cum-restaurant at the end of the village. I had returned and retired to bed before the dinner party even began, and it continued uproariously into the early hours.

I was the only person sleeping in the *gite* that night – or rather failing to sleep. After a solitary breakfast I checked out and walked the mile or so to Montaillou. Inevitably it was very different from how I had pictured it in my imagination. As you read about a place you cannot help building up mental images of it, and if you subsequently manage to visit the site you always find it is at odds with what you were anticipating. It can be difficult to believe you are actually in the correct place at all. That had been the case at Montsegur and it felt similar here at Montaillou.

Pottering around the place I soon realised that there was not a vast amount to see. The modern settlement is a reasonable size, having had something of a revival in its population over recent years, but on this Monday morning there were few signs of life. Colourful posters proclaimed that the village would be hosting a medieval festival for three days in August, but as I was there on 21st July it would be no use to me. I wandered up towards the most prominent feature, which is the ruin of the castle or chateau at the top of the hill. In fact nothing remains today except for three sides of the old keep. The medieval village would have been a cluster of buildings near to it, and indeed there was evidence of some recent archaeological work on the summit of the hill, with several shallow pits having been dug. Presumably these excavations were an attempt to trace the foundations of the medieval houses. At least the archaeologists would have had relatively easy access to them, as it was just a case of removing grass and topsoil. They would not have been impeded by the presence of contemporary and occupied housing, as the modern settlement is lower down the slope.

There were no other visitors at the keep, save one elderly couple who were strolling around. As I stood in the grass on that sunny Monday morning I tried to imagine how the place would have looked in the early 14th century. The huts crowded around the chateau would have added up to no more than a few dozen homes. The population in the year 1300 was roughly 250, with these being almost entirely farmers, peasants and shepherds. The evidence suggests that Montaillou was a largely isolated and introverted community, a farming village shared by humans and animals alike. The farming was mixed, with wheat, oats and hemp grown on the terraces on the hillside. There was no mill in the village in medieval times, and grain had to be transported the six miles south to Ax-les-Thermes to be ground. Much of the farming was pastoral, involving sheep, whilst the woods around the village provided building material, fuel and supplementary food in the form of snails, mushrooms and hazelnuts. The diet was basic but reasonably nutritious, consisting of bread, pork and soups made from cabbages, turnips, beans and pears. (Cathar *parfaits* were supposed to be vegetarian, because the consumption of meat could interfere with metempsychosis, ie the circulation of souls through reincarnation, but this prohibition did not extend to *credentes*). Hygiene was non-existent, and of course there was no running water or electricity. It was a difficult mental leap to visualise a community in which nobody ever had a bath and hardly anybody was literate.

It seems that a dominant feature in everyday village life was the *domus*. This word denoted house and home, hearth and family, with all these concepts used almost interchangeably. The domus could be a nuclear family or an extended family, or possibly both at different times, and it was the entity which gave people their sense of belonging. By 1300 there were about forty such houses in the village, and the majority were Cathar or had at least been strongly influenced by the heresy at some stage. Conversion, either to Catharism or back to Catholicism, often took place on a household basis rather than as an individual decision. The network of Cathar families supported each other and provided havens for visiting *parfaits*.

Back out in the sunshine I settled down on a low wall to soak up the atmosphere of the village and to reflect on my experiences. On the road from Montsegur three things had been playing on my mind. They were sex, violence and clergymen. It seemed that these three phenomena had reared their heads repeatedly during the entire pilgrimage from the Atlantic. They formed a peculiar triangle in which the three corners were constantly orbiting around each other. At Montsegur it was the clergy-and-violence side of the triangle which had been prominent. Here in Montaillou it was the clergy-and-sex axis which would demand attention.

Regarding violence it was Arnaud Amaury who had been the most colourful example. Presiding over the genocide at Beziers was only the first of his atrocities during the Albigensian campaign. By 1212 he had moved on to Spain and was leading 40,000 men to the battlefield of Las Navas de Tolosa for one of the truly seismic confrontations in Spanish history. One is left with the impression that being a priest and a papal legate cramped his style. In attitude and spirit Amaury is a more suitable candidate than the saintly Dominic to be seen as the father of the Inquisition. But he was by no means the only cleric who found warfare more inspiring than worship. At the siege of Termes Simon de Montfort was accompanied by the most skilful military engineer in France – a man called Guillaume whose specialities included undermining fortifications, building siege towers and developing catapults. In his spare time Guillaume was the archdeacon of Paris. At the siege of Penne d'Agenais he devised the largest trebuchet yet seen. Guillaume enjoyed his work so much that in 1212 he refused the bishopric of Beziers so that he could stay with the crusade.

Another monk with an appetite for military adventure was Durand, the Bishop of Albi. He played a decisive role at the siege of Montsegur itself, for the dismantled mangonel which was hauled to the summit of the mountain and then reassembled with such devastating effects was Durand's own design. For that matter one of the contemporary chroniclers of the crusade was Guillaume de Tudela, another man who seemed unfocussed in his priestly calling but who admired the manner in which trebuchets could deliver death over considerable distances.

To the modern mind the concept of bishops dressed in armour and leading men into battle, or simply inciting others to greater violence, seems bizarre and repulsive. Certainly such behaviour sits uneasily with the eirenic thrust of much of Christ's teaching. However, up to a point it is unfair to judge their behaviour by our standards. Times have changed, and as we look back at the medieval warrior-clergy we view them through a lens which has been shaped by the Enlightenment. As the late Lesslie Newbigin argued, one of the most profound effects of the Enlightenment was to create a deep division in western culture. On one side of the divide is the public sphere which recognises supposedly objective scientific facts. On the other side is the private sphere of values and opinions, and it is to this realm that religious belief is relegated. Thus in modern culture faith is marginalized and it is portrayed as a purely subjective phenomenon, of little relevance to "real" life. The fault-line between the public world of facts and the private world of values runs through modern society at every level: one simple example would be the assertion that "the Church should keep out of politics."

This post-enlightenment perception of reality can be criticised from various angles. Indeed Newbigin's thesis is not immune from criticism itself, and one could argue that even in the few years since Newbigin's death our society has actually moved on from modernism into a post-modern mentality, where faith and spirituality are still viewed as relative but are nevertheless seen as having a valid contribution in public life. But these are arguments for another day. In the Albigensian context the relevant point is that the pre-enlightenment world had a more integrated view of the cosmos. The medieval mind was not prone to inventing artificial divisions between religion and politics, or between faith and action. God was real and he was involved in every aspect of life, and so were his agents, even when it meant bringing divine vengeance to bear on the enemies of the deity.

To digress in a different direction one could consider the current phenomenon of Muslim fundamentalism and jihad-inspired violence which has broken out in various parts of the world and, most spectacularly, in New York on September 11th of 2001. No doubt the violence has numerous causes and involves various grievances against the West, some of which are more valid than others, and all of which are coloured by a perception of the western world which dates back to the crusades of the Middle Ages. But it has also been argued that Muslim terrorism is not triggered entirely by resentment or fear of western hegemony: it can also be seen as symptomatic of a deep cultural struggle within Islam as the faith confronts the reality of the modern world. One response is to seek to adapt to modern life: another is to retreat into fundamentalism: maybe there is a spectrum of other options too. The point is that the Islamic world-view has traditionally been a more integrated one in which the faith pervades every aspect of life, and it should be respected for that. It has avoided the tendency of the post-enlightenment West to divide reality up and store it away in a series of separate boxes.

Regarding the medieval Christian clerics, one can observe that unless a clergyman adopts a thoroughly pacifist position he must allow for a just war to be a theoretical possibility. And if it is a theoretical possibility there may be occasions when it becomes a practical necessity. Whether the Albigensian campaign fulfilled the criteria for a just war is dubious in the extreme, and a question worthy of debate in its own right. (One could draw a neat historical parallel and say that the crusade did not fulfil all of the classic criteria for *jus ad bellum,* but that in Rome's perception the Cathars constituted a serious long-term threat just as much as Saddam Hussein's Iraq was assessed to be a threat to the interests of contemporary Washington). Whatever the truth in either case, if a priest is convinced that a particular campaign is justifiable then participating himself is no more reprehensible than sitting on the sidelines watching others do the killing on his behalf. Having said that, it is the enthusiasm for violence displayed by some of these characters which is alarming: it went well beyond the just conduct of warfare (in an age which had quite sophisticated codes for acceptable military activity) and entered the realms of atrocity. The behaviour of men such as Amaury was not that of a soldier but that of a war criminal. One of the most potent factors was the certainty with which the medieval clerics believed they were on God's side, which in turn meant that God was on their side. That conviction can easily propel people into the most appalling behaviour, in which almost anything is justifiable as a means to an end. The largest mass burning of the Albigensian campaign, indeed of the entire Middle Ages, took place when Amaury and de Montfort rounded up 400 Cathar *parfaits* in Lavaur. As the victims died horribly in the flames Bishop Fulk of Toulouse led his followers in the singing of the *Te Deum Laudamus.* No doubt the screams of the dying were extra music in his ears.

However, it was the activities of another ecclesiastical hard-nut, a man called Jacques Fournier, which eventually wrapped up the Cathar drama and inadvertently provided historians with a priceless insight into medieval daily life as it was lived in this very village of Montaillou. Fournier came from humble origins in Saverdun, just eight miles north of Pamiers. His uncle was abbot of the Cistercian monastery of Fontfroide near Narbonne, so Fournier too resolved to become a monk, and in time he succeeded his uncle as the abbot. By 1317 he was Bishop of Pamiers, and after nine years there he was promoted to the Diocese of Mirepoix. He then became a cardinal and in 1334 he was elected Pope at Avignon. As Benedict XII he initiated the building of the Palace of the Popes in Avignon, and commissioned Simone Martini to paint the frescoes.

It was Fournier's work at Pamiers which had repercussions for the Cathars of Montaillou, not his subsequent meteoric rise to the papacy. The Diocese of Pamiers was coterminous with the lands of the Comte de Foix, an estate which itself corresponds to the modern *department* of the Ariege. When Fournier became the bishop his diocese was a relatively recent creation. Indeed it had been set up by Pope Boniface VIII in 1295 precisely because of fresh outbreaks of Catharism in the area. Boniface reckoned that a new, compact diocese would be more effective in stamping out the heresy, and so the Inquisition set to work there. The early campaigns were led by Geoffrey d'Ablis, a capable and methodical Dominican who was Inquisitor for Carcassonne.

The Cathar revival, centred on Montaillou, had been largely the work of the Autier brothers, Pierre and Guillaume. These two *parfaits* lived only a few miles away in Ax-les-Thermes and had made regular but discreet visits to Montaillou, trusting that its Cathar majority made it something of a safe haven. A pastoral visit might be for teaching and encouraging their flock, or sometimes to administer the *consolamentum* to a dying soul:

279

either way they would try to arrive and depart in secret. (Dying could be a tricky business in a place where the *parfaits* wanted to administer the *consolamentum* whilst the Catholic clergy were seeking to provide the last rites: believers from both faiths might have to fight off the unwanted attention of the other side). As is so often the case with underground movements it was betrayal which brought the Autiers to grief. A man called William Peter Cavaille had kept quiet about his Cathar faith whilst languishing in jail in Carcassonne, but upon his release he found that fellow *credentes* were refusing to lend him money, and he took his revenge by putting the Inquisition onto their scent. By 1309 d'Ablis had carried out an unprecedented raid on Montaillou, sealing the village off with soldiers and arresting every inhabitant over twelve years of age. A number of people were imprisoned and their testimony recorded. By 1310 a dozen *parfaits* had been picked off and sent to the stake. Pierre Autier himself was caught in 1309, and interrogated for ten months. In April of 1310 the Inquisition burned him in front of the cathedral in Toulouse.

Geoffrey d'Ablis had proved an effective Inquisitor. But it took Fournier, with his incisive mind, his attention to detail and his excellent interrogation skills, to work out the full extent of the heresy within Montaillou. When he became bishop in 1317 he brought fresh energy to the case, starting with the depositions obtained by d'Ablis and proceeding by means of his own interviews. His work was systematic and shrewd, and as a native of the Ariege he had the massive advantage of being fluent in the local Occitan dialect and thus being able to detect the subtle nuances in the evidence he was obtaining. Fournier's records were unique, and his subsequent elevation to the Papacy led to their preservation in the Vatican, to the delight of historians. They enable us to hear medieval peasants speaking for themselves, albeit under conditions of stress and duress, when the bulk of their contemporaries were illiterate and could leave no written record of their lives. It was the mass of precise detail in Fournier's records which enabled Emanuel le Roy Ladurie to reconstruct almost every aspect of Montaillou's daily life in his classic work of the 1970's. Fournier himself was so thorough and detailed in his own investigation that he too seemed to be taking a sort of academic interest in the sociology of the Cathars in the place.

Some bald statistics may serve to clarify the extent of the Inquisition's work under Fournier. His court in Pamiers sat on 370 days between 1318 and 1325. It carried out 578 interrogations, of which 418 were examining the accused and the other 160 were taking evidence from witnesses. These sessions concerned 98 alleged cases of heresy, which between them implicated 114 individuals. Of these people all but twenty appeared in person before the court. Roughly sixty percent of the accused were men and forty percent were women.

Montaillou supplied 25 of the accused, plus several witnesses. In other words a quarter of the people who appeared before Fournier's Inquisition were from this one village. Three further accused came from the neighbouring and larger village of Prades. Fournier's method was to summon a suspect to the court by sending a message of denunciation to the village. When the suspect arrived in Pamiers statements would be taken, and any unsatisfactory explanations would be followed up by sharper questioning under oath. Fournier had various threats which could be brought into play, such as imprisonment, the confiscation of property, sending the victim on a penitential pilgrimage or requiring them to wear a yellow cross sewn onto their clothing. One can imagine that he was a subtle and sinister interrogator, adept at playing the "hard man" and "soft man" roles alternately as he pieced together the fragments of the jigsaw and a picture began to emerge. Having said that, he seems to have had a measure of sensitivity. He only had one man tortured, which was pretty restrained by the standards of some inquisitors. Many *credentes* appealed to him for clemency and received it. However, unrepentant *credentes* and especially *parfaits* could expect no mercy. His court eventually sent five people to the stake. One was Guillaume Fort from Montaillou. The other four were Waldensians from Pamiers itself.

This fact intrigued me. When I had entered Cathar Country one of my basic questions had been about the spreading of the heresy: why had it been so popular here in Languedoc and Roussillon as opposed to elsewhere in France? Now that I had reached Montaillou the question had been focussed in onto this one place: why had the heresy revived itself here as opposed to elsewhere in the region? An obvious factor would be that Catharism had more chance of flourishing in the geographically remote uplands, well away from the towns where the Inquisition would be vigilant and could maintain a more efficient surveillance. Yet the separate heresy of Waldensianism seemed to do better in the towns, even in Pamiers under the very nose of the bishop. Maybe there was a clue in the origins of the Waldensian movement. It had been started in the 12th century by Peter Valdes, and its alternative name had been "the poor men of Lyons". Could that name hint at it being a more urban phenomenon, drawing its natural supporters from artisans and apprentices? It was a theory, at any rate. It is debatable whether Catharism or Waldensianism constituted the greater threat to the Catholic Church. In as much as the Waldensians rejected the idea of priests as mediators between Man and God they were more akin to the later Protestants than the Cathars were – the latter retained the concept of mediation using the *parfaits*. If Languedoc has any link from the heresy of the 13th century to the Calvinism of the 16th it is more likely to stem from the Waldensians than from the Cathars.

In the case of the Cathars their revival in Montaillou seemed to owe more to the lack of strong feudal oversight. The local lord and *chatelain* (military officer) was a man called Berenger de Roquefort, but when he died in 1299 his widow, Beatrice de Planisolles, moved out of the castle and lived in the village. There seems to have been little in the way of class division between noble and peasant within Montaillou: there were too few people and they were living too close together. The nobility of the uplands were relatively poor, and some of the peasants there were relatively rich. Nor were there any militant Catholics in the village, at least not after one dangerous potential informer, Arnaud Lizier, had been murdered. It was a claustrophobic place, and to some extent it mirrored the totalitarian coercion of Church and Inquisition down in the towns but in reverse. To be suspected of being a Catholic informer could be dangerous in Montaillou.

If the village had been totally Cathar and totally united then the heretical faith might have survived there indefinitely, or at least for a good deal longer. But in fact the village was not monochrome and it was far from united. The divisions may not have been those of a Marxist-type class struggle, but nevertheless the community was riven with conflict. In fact the village was a veritable soap-opera which would make most of our current television dramas look tame by comparison. When le Roy Ladurie's work was published in 1975 the village became famous. Its fame was not based on the Cathar heresy or tales of buried treasure, and not based on lurid fascination with the Inquisition and its torture techniques. Montaillou became famous because of sex. It seemed that everybody who lived there had been involved in it. Or maybe the interest was triggered more by the fascinating juxtaposition of sex and lice. People in Montaillou, especially the women, would delouse each other whilst sitting on the doorsteps of their homes. There was no bathing in medieval Montaillou, and all the carnal lust was being played out between characters who were carrying around their own personal ecosystems of fleas, flies and mosquitoes.

The village seems to have been rife with every variety of heterosexual activity. The impression one gets is that the peasants had a somewhat innocent attitude to the whole business: if sex was pleasurable to both parties then it could not be disagreeable to God. The pleasure conferred innocence. There were no prostitutes as such in the village: access to these would be only be possible whilst visiting the occasional fairs in the nearby towns. Again there does not seem to have been any strong moral objection to money changing hands: the payment could be justified as partly financial and partly in pleasure. Nor was concubinage seen as necessarily objectionable. On the whole the morals seem to have been lax compared to later centuries. But if it was a permissive society it was not on the whole a promiscuous one. Marriage seems to have been largely respected. The only mention of homosexuality in Fournier's records concerns an instance in Pamiers, not Montaillou, and in a milieu which was urban, clerical and slightly elitist. The village also had a taboo against incest, and sex between first cousins was banned. This could be a bit tricky, because if a ban on incest is going to be upheld then people need to know who is related to whom, and in a society with high illegitimacy rates and no computers it was quite difficult to keep track of exactly whose genes were mixed up together.

A case in point was an incident in which a woman called Raymonde Testaniere escaped a rape attempt by an Arnaud Vital by protesting that she had born children by Vital's cousin, and therefore the intercourse would be incestuous. Rape was certainly a danger for young women, and on one occasion a Bernard Belot tried to rape Raymonde, the wife of Guillaume Autier. This led to a row between the two men, and Belot incurred a hefty fine from the officials of the Comte de Foix.

And Beatrice de Planisolles, the wife of Berenger de Roquefort and thereby *chatelaine* of the village, was herself raped by Pathau Clergue, a brutal and illegitimate cousin of the village priest. However, one might wonder whether the incident was entirely without her consent, because when she was widowed the following year she became Pathau's mistress for a while before dumping him in favour of the priest himself.

It is recorded that Beatrice once said "you priests desire women more than other men do." She was well qualified to judge. Having transferred her affections from Pathau to his cousin Pierre she slept with the priest in the church on Christmas night and then regularly for another two years. Eventually she broke with Pierre Clergue and married Othon de Lagleize. After further affairs she was widowed for a second time, and again took a priest as a lover, this one being called Bartelemy Amilhac. Her career more or less reflected the romanticism of troubadour poetry, which did not portray marriage as a happy or loving business and asserted that passion would only be found outside it.

Eventually Beatrice fell foul of the Inquisition, and ended up as Fournier's star witness. During July and August of 1320 she had nine sessions of interrogation, until exhaustion compelled her to confess her guilt. She admitted her affair with Pierre Clergue, which had happened nearly twenty years earlier by that stage. But the sensational part of her testimony was not that Clergue had failed to keep his vow of celibacy. It was that his lust for her body had been accompanied by attempts to capture her soul by denigrating the Roman Church. Pierre Clergue, the village's Catholic priest, was himself a Cathar.

Of all the lice in Montaillou, Pierre Clergue was undoubtedly the largest. He is the central character in the entire drama. The Inquisition record lists at least a dozen women who were his mistresses at one time or another. One was his sister-in-law. Four others consisted of two pairs of sisters. His insatiable appetite extended to taking women in the sulphur baths at Ax-les-Thermes. Back in the village he deflowered a virgin called Grazide Rives and maintained a relationship with her for several months. He then married her off to a man called Pierre Lizier, but continued to know her carnally until Lizier died four years later. Apparently Lizier said that he accepted his wife's continuing liason with the priest, but he would not accept her doing it with other men. Perhaps, following the murder of his relative Arnaud Lizier, he was resigned to the fact that it was not wise to cross Pierre Clergue, who was operating almost like a lord of the manor exercising his right to the village virgins on their wedding nights. On my way into the village I had stopped to study the graveyard at the little Romanesque chapel of Notre Dame de Carnesses. The burials here were relatively recent ones, dating from the last couple of centuries. As I read the gravestones I found that every other surname was Clergue, or some double-barrelled variant of it. Whatever one may think of the promiscuous priest there is no denying that his behaviour was effective as a strategy for spreading his genes amongst succeeding generations.

It is possible that Clergue had some attractive qualities, and he did not force himself on women through physical violence. A more cynical view is that he did not need to. His position as the village priest gave him enormous power, for if a woman rejected his advances he could threaten to denounce her to the Inquisition. As a seduction technique, "sleep with me or get burned at the stake" is somewhat lacking in charm. By any standards his behaviour was greedy and selfish. Nor was it just a case of satisfying lust. Power gave him sex, but in turn sex gave him power as he tightened his grip over a network of women who could be useful as informers and as denouncers of his enemies.

At this point the plot thickens yet further, for Pierre Clergue's brother Bernard was the *bayle* or bailiff in the village. In other words he was the legal representative of the Comte de Foix, and acted as an enforcer who collected the various taxes, tithes, rents and dues which were owing to the Comte or the Church. So between them the two brothers controlled the spiritual and temporal affairs of the village and could exercise a virtual monopoly of power at a level below the feudal or manorial. The lack of feudal oversight enabled them to tighten their stranglehold and ensure that their clan remained dominant. They were operating like a pair of gangsters, with Pierre as the dominant partner or Godfather. His tentacles extended into every aspect of village life: in Montaillou all roads eventually led back to him at some point.

Pierre Clergue's links with the heretics, and his access to the Inquisition, meant that he could play both ends against the middle and increase his own power, wealth and influence in the process. Tithes were a key issue. For a while the Clergues were collecting them and simultaneously "protecting" the population from their full effect. They did this by collecting only a percentage of the sums due. This was then split, with some of it going to the Church, some being siphoned off for their *parfait* friends, and some simply being retained for themselves. So everybody was happy, at least until 1317 when Fournier became bishop and declared that henceforth tithes would be collected in full. This gave the Clergues less room for manoeuvre and undermined their racketeering even before Fournier moved to attack them directly. The Clergue gang's position was too good to last, and eventually the Inquisition closed in and Pierre had to choose between betraying the Cathars or going down with them. Inevitably he opted for the former, using the opportunity to take further revenge on his enemies in the village. Fournier put him behind bars, and he died in prison a year later. Bernard was also incarcerated for a time and released, dying in 1324. Beatrice de Planisolles, the priest's former lover, spent fifteen months in prison before

Fournier released her. As the Clergue gang were eclipsed the Azema clique rose to prominence in Montaillou, helped by the fact that they were good Catholics and distant cousins of Fournier.

I was intrigued to know how Pierre Clergue had justified his despicable activities. Obviously he did not take his clerical vow of celibacy very seriously. In fact he once said "I am a priest, I do not want a wife," implying that he wanted all women. It seems that celibacy was predominant in the lowlands, but in the mountains clergy concubinage was largely tolerated. However, Catholic theology and attitudes were not so relevant in any case, granted that Clergue was a Cathar sympathiser. He was probably not the most thorough Cathar theologian either: his attitude seemed to be that he could do whatever he liked during his life because when he approached death the *consolamentum* would absolve him.

It comes back to the paradox I had noted earlier, that in theory the Cathar theology encouraged celibacy and asceticism, but in practice it often led to the exact opposite, with extremes of amoral or immoral behaviour. Clergue's attitudes had brought me closer to understanding the logic of the problem. In the stricter versions of Catharism any sexual act was wrong – even for a married couple. Indeed marriage itself was wrong. Everything was wrong. But there's the rub. If everything is sinful and condemned, then no activity is really any worse than any other. And granted that a human being has to be doing something, they might as well be doing whatever gives them pleasure. In any case the *consolamentum* would provide salvation at the end of one's earthly life. The logic is summed up in the old maxim that "since everything is forbidden, everything is allowed." A similar sort of pragmatism prevailed when it came to having children. A theology which forbade marriage and procreation should have reduced the birth-rate dramatically, but in fact it failed to suppress the peasants' spontaneous desire to reproduce. In a context where the work was labour intensive and illness kept the death-rates high, children were an economic necessity.

One of my other questions had been about the role of women in spreading the heresy. Le Roy Ladurie had emphasised that women had a tough life in a medieval village, especially when they were young. Male chauvinism was strong, especially in the mountains and regardless of whether the males were Catholic or Cathar. Wives were more or less possessions, (ideally possessions which would bring a good dowry with them into their new *domus*), and they were liable to suffer beatings. They were discriminated against in so much as their assigned tasks were seen as inferior, whether it was cooking, collecting water, gardening or bearing children. They were the principal delousers, and they were expected to lay out the dead. Educationally they were the equals of their menfolk, in that neither group had any schooling anyway. As is the case in many cultures down through history, it seems that generally the men had the power whilst the women did much of the work that enabled everyday life to happen.

There may have been a measure of female solidarity and anti-masculine feeling in the village. Occasionally a woman would succeed as a head of household and thus establish a matriarchal *domus,* and the menopause helped them to gain respect as they were then regarded less as mere sexual objects. The spread of Catharism required both men and women. It was largely down to the ministry of itinerant *parfaits,* of whom virtually all were male, but once the heresy was established within the village the females had a role to play. Daily life was very much centred on the hearth and home which were the women's workplace, and it was here that the network of Cathar households was sustained. In any case the population of the village would have been largely female at any given time, especially with the high mortality rates which meant that a male of fifty would have

289

been an old man. In a society where marriages were typically between men in their twenties and girls in their teens there would also have been a preponderence of widows.

The other key players in the spreading of the heresy were the shepherds. The term "shepherd" was ambiguous, because almost everybody in the village was involved with keeping sheep as part of their mixed farming. However, there was also a nomadic underclass of specialist shepherds, who were a rough bunch and very much at the bottom of the social scale. They were engaged in transhumance with flocks of hundreds of sheep, and were employed by individual farmers. The economics of the business could get quite complicated. Money was used, but so was barter, and the bartering could involve sheep or wool. Moreover the shepherd might own a few of the sheep in the flock himself, or he might be hiring some of them on a sort of sharecropping basis. So in theory an individual shepherd could be functioning in several roles simultaneously. He could be an employee, an owner and a hirer of sheep all at the same time. Whatever his exact role, he was unlikely to be well disposed towards the Catholic establishment. A major source of peasant resentment against the Church was the infamous sheep tithe, or *carnelage*. This tax was enforced vigorously by Fournier and hated by the shepherds.

Groups of shepherds would club together to form a *cabane* – a hut which functioned as a temporary home and as a base for simple co-operative activities, such as making cheese from the ewes' milk. Like *"domus"* the word *"cabane"* denoted both a place and an institution which conferred a sense of belonging. Unlike the *domus* the *cabane* was temporary and a purely male set-up. A typical *cabane* might have several shepherds and two to three hundred sheep at any one time. Even whilst he belonged to a *cabane* a shepherd might treasure the links he'd got, through birth or marriage, to a more permanent *domus* in the village.

The shepherds lived an unstable life. They were paid in money or kind, and might change their master regularly. As nomads they could not accumulate wealth in the form of heavy possessions: it had to be cash or sheep. They were in any case poor, and some of them regarded poverty and equality as ideals. Many were too impoverished to marry. But the life had its compensations - with freedom to wander in the fresh air they were to some extent beyond the range of feudal oppression, and they could enjoy nourishing food and good friendships. The rhythm of their lives was set by the transhumance, and by seasonal activities such as lambing and shearing. And of course their lifestyle was ideal for spreading heresy and for smuggling disguised *parfaits*, as they roamed over considerable distances and could cross the Pyrenees into Spain. Indeed, the last phase of the Cathar drama depended upon a network of escape routes and safe houses which stretched down into Aragon and Catalunya. Refugees from Montaillou and Ax-les-Thermes formed a Cathar colony at San Mateo, in Tarragona, nearly two hundred miles south of the Ariege.

The last of the Cathar *parfaits* was himself a shepherd. Guillaume Belibaste was a rough character who had killed another shepherd in a fight. He then became a *parfait*, but was still something of a rascal. When his mistress Raymonde became pregnant Belibaste tricked his loyal but simplistic friend Pierre Maury into marrying her for a few days in order to cover his own misdemeanour. As a *parfait* his sexual relationship with her was, of course, inappropriate. But Belibaste's days were numbered. Even the haven at San Mateo was not far enough away from the Inquisition. A visitor from the Ariege called Arnaud Sicre overheard some women talking, and recognised their Montaillou accents. He infiltrated the group to win Belibaste's confidence before luring him, along with Maury, back across the mountains. Belibaste was captured and burned in 1321.

Belibaste's death marks the final extinction of Catharism and pulls the curtain down on the Montaillou soap-opera. It had been a place of conflict and betrayal, of conspiracy and murder, of passion and lust. It had the classic ingredients of drama in any age. I felt I had come closer to the Cathars here than I had ever managed at Montsegur. Standing in the grass in the hot sun I stared into the archaeologists' excavation pits and wondered whether I could slip back through a time warp and see the Cathars gathering around a hearth to discuss issues of faith, or maybe hear Beatrice de Planisolles cooing "you priests desire women more than other men do." In a sense I had met her and met Pierre Clergue, thanks principally to le Roy Ladurie's research and to the more recent efforts of Rene Weis, whose research and fieldwork have extended the story through the pages of his book "*The Yellow Cross.*" I felt that these Montaillou characters were alive and real, even across a distance of seven hundred years, and they seemed more plausible and less alien than the rather remote people involved in the Crusade and at the siege of Montsegur.

As I left the village my final thought was a slightly uneasy one. Montaillou has provided a fascinating insight into medieval life, but I was wondering whether it was truly typical of its age. Like it or not, its social environment was recorded in detail precisely because it was atypical – it had a Cathar majority and was thereby the exception rather than the rule. The Catharism in Montaillou was also atypical, in the sense that it did not belong to the main wave of heresy which swept Languedoc in the late twelfth century but to a small revival a full century later. And that revival was itself facilitated by unusual conditions, principally the weakness or absence of effective feudal oversight. These qualifications made me wary about reading too much into this one location, but nevertheless this single upland settlement has opened a window for historians into a lost world.

I left Montaillou and followed the sheep trails south towards Ax-les-Thermes, traversing the very hillsides which would have been familiar to the shepherds Pierre Maury and Guillaume Belibaste, to the Autier brothers, and to the other *parfaits* who had travelled in disguise across the uplands of the Ariege on their clandestine missions seven centuries ago.

Chapter 11.

The road to the monastery.

My route south over the Col du Chioula brought me down into Ax-les-Thermes. The first hotel I tried was full, and the second was empty and had every appearance of having gone out of business for good. Eventually I found the Roy Rene Hotel and booked in for two nights. The woman who was running the place accompanied me upstairs to show me my room. This was an act of considerable courage as it meant sharing the confined space of a tiny lift with my steaming carcase and disgusting clothing, to say nothing of the giant green rucksack. It was a decent hotel run by pleasant people and their food was excellent.

The following day was a Tuesday and it was designated for rest. In fact it was the 22nd of July, one calendar month since I had left St.Jean-de-Luz, and I was three-quarters of the way across France. In the centre of Ax I had a haircut and pottered around a large bookshop, browsing through countless publications on the Cathars. Also I took the opportunity to catch up with the British newspapers. These were dominated by the death of Dr David Kelly. The story which had just broken seemed to have all the ingredients for the plot of a thriller. A body had been discovered in rural Oxfordshire, apparently the victim of a suicide. It turned out to be the country's chief expert on biological weapons and a veteran of three dozen visits to Iraq. A complicated character who supposedly shied away from publicity and loved his work: a

294

person who, according to his friends, was a man of integrity and warmth.

The story I pieced together from the mass of reports and analysis was that Kelly had been involved in producing the British government's dossier on Iraq's supposed Weapons of Mass Destruction. The main allegation was that the government had wanted the evidence to be spiced up for propaganda purposes. In other words they were seeking to gild the lily to persuade a reluctant public to support the war. It was being suggested that Kelly had said or implied as much to a BBC journalist called Andrew Gilligan, and possibly to other people. Gilligan had broadcast the allegations on the radio, thus triggering a conflict between the government and the BBC.

Most people are cynical about politicians and their motives at the best of times. It is difficult not to be. In a grubby world everybody fights to promote and protect their own perceived interests, which by extension means the interests of the group, class or party to which they feel they belong. Every politician will talk in terms of "acting in the national interest", but of course it is self-evident to each of them that "the national interest" coincides with their own election or re-election. The power and influence which accrue, and for that matter the financial rewards, are just incidental consequences of bearing these great burdens of responsibility on behalf of lesser mortals. The ends will always justify the means. All power corrupts.

Not everybody behaves totally cynically all of the time. Maybe there are a few decent people left. Maybe Dr Kelly was one of them, though if the government was adept at spinning stories for the media one could equally well ask what Kelly was doing talking to a journalist in the first place. Whatever the exact rights and wrongs of this particular case, it was obvious to me that Britain has changed within living memory, in the sense that general standards of decency, politeness and consideration for others have declined markedly. The reasons for this are no doubt many and complex, and the increasing secularisation of national life has been both a cause and a result. Of course there has never been a time when Christian standards of behaviour were adhered to by everyone, or even by the majority, but earlier in the twentieth century there was a greater consensus on what constituted decent behaviour. Towards the end of that century these standards were largely overtaken by greed, selfishness and general nastiness. Discretion has been devalued: today if three people hold a confidential meeting it is likely that two of them will leak its contents to the media. Pernicious motives are acted on with a callous disregard for those who are hung out to dry or left to twist in the wind.

Nevertheless, even after I had devoured several newspapers full of depressing commentary, I found that pride in my country still ran deep. At dinner that night I saw that the hotel's menu had been augmented with a little slip of paper which was, I assumed, a slight on British beef. The paper had a computer-generated picture of a cow, and three lines of information, arranged vertically:

"Nee en France.
Elleve en France.
Abbatu en France."

In other words "the beef in this restaurant was born, reared and slaughtered in safe conditions here in France." My biro was upstairs in my room, otherwise I might have been tempted to take it out and add a fourth line:

"Vomite en France."

That evening I dined on fish, gently humming Elgar to myself. Patriotism may be the last refuge, but it can be a mightily seductive one.

The morning after my rest day I felt a bit low, conscious that the bulk of my time on the expedition had slipped away. But

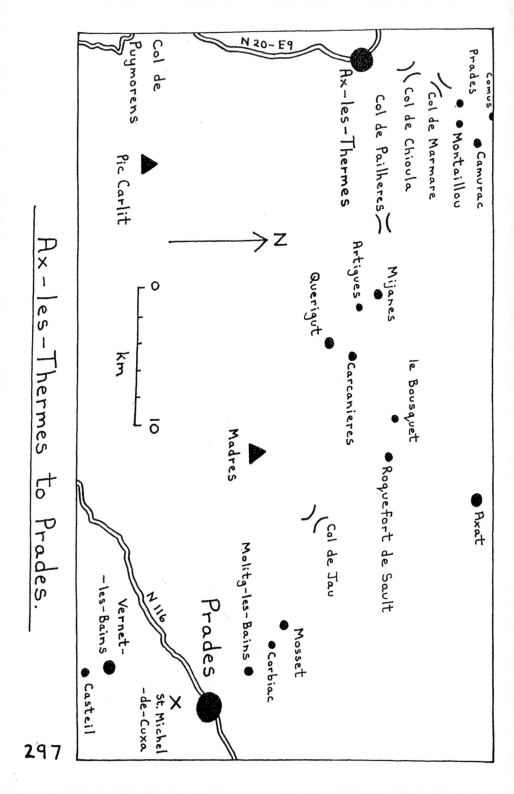

Ax-les-Thermes to Prades.

297

once I had left the hotel and got moving it was easier to be positive. There were still nearly two weeks remaining, and that in itself was a longer "holiday" than I had enjoyed for many years. I bought more water, filling my containers to their full three-litre capacity, and I set off up the road and out of Ax-les-Thermes. A signpost indicated that it was 37 kilometres to Querigut, which was my chosen target for the day. It was a daunting prospect in warm conditions and with a major col en route. Indeed, the Col de Pailheres was high, at an altitude of 2001 metres. By the time I reached it I had ascended four-and-a-half thousand feet in four-and-a-half hours. I had not passed a café or shop all morning, and there was nothing at the col except open hillside. It had been a tedious walk up the road, following the route of the previous Saturday's Tour stage in reverse. The final part of my ascent struck me as increasingly Spanish as the terrain opened out into grassland with the odd clump of rocks on the skyline. There were few trees and no shade. The col was almost deserted. Strange to think that just four days ago it would have been swarming with spectators as the Tour cyclists heaved themselves over it and shot off down the long descent to Ax, which was now eleven or twelve miles away behind me. Beyond the col I followed the narrow road down a long succession of twists and hairpins, sickened by the amount of graffiti which the cycling fans had painted on the tarmac. Names of favourite riders and teams, slogans and cartoons: some of it was clever but most of it was just a brainless mess.

I was aiming for Querigut because I believed, from the map, that I would find a hotel there. Nothing was marked on the map for Mijanes, but I wandered around this village and was on the point of leaving when I discovered the delightful Relais de la Pailheres. I bought a beer and enquired about a room for the night. In the bar area the television was relaying the inevitable Tour coverage. I had arrived just as the extraordinary Tyler

298

Hamilton was entering the outskirts of Bayonne, riding alone to a stage win with his broken collarbone. Hamilton's courage was becoming legendary. He had previously completed the *Giro d'Italia* with a broken collarbone, enduring dreadful agony by grinding his teeth together so hard that he had to get eleven of them crowned. Tyler's teeth had become famous, and had probably done more to restore American credibility in the world, or at least in the eyes of the French, than any amount of effort by the State Department.

The hotel at Mijanes was friendly and clean; a maze of a building on several levels with corridors and rooms at crazy angles. It had character and excellent cuisine. I was hanging around in the bar waiting for dinner when suddenly it grew dark outside. Heavy clouds were gathering around the hills and at 7pm precisely the storm broke. From the window I could enjoy the lightning, thunder and the lashings of rain: I have always found it's a beautiful feeling to watch a violent storm if you are under cover with all the hatches battened down. After that my dinner tasted even better, though when I ordered half a bottle of *rose* the waiter produced one of 50 centilitres rather than the normal 37-and-a-half. Not a massive problem, but it contributed to a slightly sore head the next morning.

I left Mijanes by crossing a substantial bridge over a stream which had been swollen by the previous evening's rain. Increasingly I was feeling that a shadow hung over the expedition. It had been there more or less since Bagneres-de-Luchon, when I had reached the half-way point. The simple fact is that once you have passed half-way, measured either in time or distance, you know that you are closer to the end than the beginning. And you find that time is accelerating too. If the expedition had been six years long instead of six weeks I would probably have experienced the same sensation after three years.

The logic is inescapable. If the walk is a metaphor for life then the end of the walk can only be a death. There is no way you can get around that. So I sensed a mixture of emotions crowding in together - satisfaction at the distance already covered; relief that the end was coming closer; anxiety that no injury or sickness should rob me of my triumph; and above all sadness. You may well experience some good days towards the end of an expedition, but what you can never recapture is the sheer raw excitement of being at the beginning, when the whole trip lies ahead of you. And you appreciate that beauty all the more when you are past the half-way point. Youth is indeed wasted on the young.

I also felt a sadness when I thought that I had achieved a certain level of fitness, and yet I was bound to lose it again. In all probability I would never be this fit again, because I would never get this length of time off work to devote to a strenuous physical activity. And besides, I would only grow older. I loved the physical exercise even whilst I hated it. The pain and exhaustion can become addictive, in a strange way. When you have suffered you want to feel that your suffering was significant; that the fatigue was an investment in some sort of account on which you can draw in the future. Herb Elliott, the famous Australian athlete of the 1950s who held the world record for the mile, once wrote about his concept of the "pain reservoir." He saw this as something akin to a lake which he could fill up during training and then draw on in competition. You do not want to feel that the training you have undergone in the past was a meaningless suffering. So you go on and train more, seeking to push your fitness further and make the pain of the past count towards something.

Of course a human being also needs a target to train towards, whether it is an Olympic medal or just walking the length of the Pyrenees. It is impossible to get seriously fit and to stay fit for no reason. The human desire for training can be a deep one,

300

closely allied to the drive for self-improvement and a better life. But the training has to be directed towards a tangible goal if you are going to maintain the motivation. Maybe it is also linked to the instinctive desire to clutch at immortality – the futile illusion that if a man fights hard enough against his waistline he can delay the aging process and lengthen his days indefinitely. And there's also the feeling that maybe, one day, you will have to face some unforeseen and extreme ordeal and will have to fight to survive, in which case you want to be that bit better equipped to do so. Yet whatever the motivation to pummel one's body, the "mental anaesthetic" or simple amnesia plays a crucial role. If the human brain could accurately recall the true awfulness of yesterday's pain then there would be no *Tour de France* today, as no rider would be prepared to get back on his bicycle.

Around 11 o'clock I paused for a break, sitting on a bench beside the road and looking back across the countryside in the direction of Mijanes. My mind was churning over the possibilities for the book I was intending to write. Indeed, I was already wondering whether I could produce a second one. This would be a more theological treatise, and would have the title *"Meditations on a Molotov Cocktail."* My idea was to trace the construction of a petrol bomb starting from the lowest level, that of the atoms and molecules in the fluid which had been formed through geological processes countless million years ago. Of course these inanimate particles of matter have no awareness of either their own existence nor the purpose to which they are being put. Ascending through the various levels of complexity one could trace the glasswork and design which has gone into the moulding of the bottle, and so on until one reaches the more interesting questions which concern the person throwing the item, and what factors are influencing his activity and purpose. I was aware of Pascal's comment that a tree or a rock does not know itself to be miserable whereas a

301

human being does: our awareness of the very misery of our lives is proof of Mankind's greatness. At the most interesting level is the motivation of the person throwing the bomb: here we have one collection of atoms and molecules which are themselves aware of their own existence and are also intent on incinerating another similar example of self-conscious life. If I got around to writing my paper the intention would be to counter any naïve scientific reductionism and to examine where God fits into all this, and into the different layers of complexity and levels of truth within the universe we observe and strive to understand.

In the meantime I had a more immediate task on which to concentrate. For a couple of hours I worked my way across country on meandering lanes, through the little villages of le Pla, le Puch and Carcanieres. From there I descended into the heavily wooded gorge of the Aude. It was an oppressive place, for the valley was narrow and dark. The overcast weather had helped my progress through the morning, but now I found that the low-lying cloud and general greyness were a grim addition to the atmosphere in the canyon. The humidity and darkness added to a vague and disturbing intimation of evil in this place. I hurried south along the D118 for about a kilometre, contemplating the fact that the river flowing in the opposite direction would eventually reach Carcassonne and its fairy-tale mock medieval walls. The original walls had been the work of the Visigoths, but in the 19th century they were rebuilt by Viollet le Duc, with his efforts supported by Napoleon III. I smiled to myself as I recalled how Miles Morland had mentioned the project and described the result as the creation of "the first Disneyland."

The road had little traffic but nevertheless it was a relief when I could turn off it and begin to ascend the opposite side of the gorge. I did not have to go far to gain some height and I sensed my feeling of oppression was being left behind. I stopped for lunch – a few biscuits and grain bars – and studied the map. My destiny for the afternoon would be to follow a country lane which appeared as a great yellow loop on the map, running north then east and finally south as it joined a string of villages such as Le Bousquet and Roquefort-de-Sault. A few measurements revealed that it would be a daunting 26 kilometres from my current position to the Col de Jau, and the final eleven of these were one continuous climb. In the event this last ascent was a bitter and tedious slog, most of it conducted on a narrow road surrounded by thick forest. Finally at 5pm I sensed that there was more light above me and to the sides. The trees were thinning out as I came to the top of the rise, and after another few minutes I was on the col and studying a sign which welcomed me to the *"Pyrenees Orientales."* At this point I was passing from Languedoc into Roussillon. I paused in a chilly wind to consume the last of my food for the day's hike, and then I continued south for a couple of kilometres down a forest track, aiming for a *refuge*.

When I located the *refuge* I quickly realised that it was going to be basic in the extreme, for it consisted of little more than a dark hovel of a farmhouse. Inside I encountered a Dutch family, who reinforced the impression of primitive surroundings by telling me that the owners of the place were out in the woods collecting mushrooms. I made use of the freezing shower and resigned myself to a rough night, for it was a grim contrast with the accommodation I had found at Mijanes twenty-four hours earlier. In the shower the lyrics of a Billy Joel song came back to me – "we had the Midas touch, until we met the Dutch."

Drying myself off I felt happier, for I was imbued with that warm glow which only a cold shower can produce. And the accommodation I had found was at least shelter against the rain which had begun to blow through the forest just as I had arrived. Eventually the woman who owned the place returned from her foraging expedition, accompanied by a teenage daughter and several other guests, and she set about preparing a meal. It was obvious that mushrooms would be a major ingredient. The mother and daughter seemed immensely good natured and soon had an open fire going, which added to an atmosphere of earthy acceptance and toleration.

At dinner I shared a table with the Dutch family, who were ambling across the countryside with a donkey carrying their luggage, somewhat akin to Robert Louis Stevenson in the Cevennes. The parents were pleasant company, and as their two boys were quite young they were only covering about ten miles per day. One of the children was asking who had first thought the earth was round. The ensuing discussion was in Dutch, so I could not really follow it, except that Columbus'name came up several times. My contribution was to say (in English) that I thought the ancient Greeks had tried to calculate the radius of the planet by using the lengths of shadows cast by poles at different latitudes, but I wasn't too sure whether my recollections were accurate or just imagination.

That night I shared a dormitory with the Dutch contingent, and I rested well as I huddled in my sleeping bag on a mattress. At dawn I was up and away before any of them had stirred, and I never got to meet their donkey. I was facing another thirty long kilometres to Prades, though it was at least downhill all the way. The highlight of the morning was a good second breakfast which I consumed in a bar in Mosset. I was now virtually on the "Green Line" - that peculiar French invention which exists purely so as not to be the Greenwich meridian. Therefore I must have been due south of Paris. I also admired the architecture of Mosset and took a few decent photos from below the village, for from that angle it was reminiscent of the classic Mediterranean hilltop settlements which one can see in Italy. It was an odd impression and it was reinforced later in the day as I paused to admire the red tiled roofs of Campome further down the valley. I love the combination of terracotta tiles with stone walls and dark wooden window-shutters. Repeatedly on my journey I had noticed how even a few strategically placed flowers could enhance a building's appearance. It might not be the purple bougainvillea of the Riviera, but nevertheless a couple of window-boxes or hanging-baskets could add a splash of colour and break up the angular shape of a boringly square building. And the illusion of suddenly being in Sicily was strengthened when I passed through Molitg-les-Bains in the early afternoon. This incongruous place had several expensive hotels crammed into a narrow gorge and surrounded by Italian-style gardens. I had laughed openly as I enterred Molitg, for I had come upon a bizarre roadsign which demanded *"Silence and Prudence."*

The other highlight of the day was passing through Corbiac, about a mile down the valley from Mosset. This was the location of a medieval monastery, bought and renovated by a British writer called Rosemary Bailey and described in detail in her book *"Life in a Postcard."* As I approached Corbiac I could see that the building was set back fifty metres or so from the road, and had a couple of cars parked outside. There was also a van of some sort at the western end where a couple of figures were visible at work. The air was still and I fancied I could hear snatches of English accents, but I was not sure.

Bailey's book tells how she was travelling in Roussillon in 1988 and came upon Corbiac, which was ironic because she would have been falling in love with the place at exactly the same time that I was traversing the eastern Pyrenees. Over the following years, accompanied by her husband and infant son, she had restored the monastery to the point where they could inhabit it on a permanent basis. Part of the attraction had been the 13th century Romanesque chapel with its frescoes, though this section of the building had suffered the indignity of being used as a barn and cowshed after the Revolution. During its history the monastery had seen a couple of rebuilding initiatives, with the most significant taking place under the Augustinians at the end of the 16th century. Indeed, the opening chapter of Bailey's account contains a useful description of the daily routine of a monk at that time, as the cycle of worship was interspersed with meals, manual labour and prayer. It was certainly a tough regime, with seven or eight daily offices in addition to the Mass, bitterly cold conditions in winter, and fasting for much of the year.

In her descriptions of Corbiac Bailey returns repeatedly to several constant companions; not just to the ghosts of bygone monks but to the awesome presence of the Canigou mountain and to the biting chill of the *Tramontane* wind as it howls down the valley from the Pyrenees. The location seems to exude a quality which is not merely of antiquity but of timelessness. The pattern of the monastic worship is tied to the cycle of night and day as the earth rotates, and through the occasional festivals it is linked to the greater progression of the seasons, year on year. The spiritual life of the community is plugged into the rhythms of the natural order, as though withdrawal from worldly ways has enabled a deeper engagement with the world. Far from being an escape to privacy and seclusion, the cloister is revealed as a place of raw pain and vulnerability, as one stands exposed before God. Of course it all reflects one of the central paradoxes of the Christian way – the mystery that death leads to life; that the crucifixion leads to the resurrection; that dying to self leads to life in a more fulfilling sense. All four gospels contain sayings of Christ to the effect that "whoever would save his life will lose it, but whoever loses his life for my sake will find it."

As I examined the monastery from the road I was thankful that it was summer, and I did not have to contend with the icy *Tramontane* stripping the leaves from the trees. I was sorely tempted to go and knock on the front door, but a sign warned that it was private property and access was forbidden. Besides, I figured that the occupants were probably sick of people turning up unannounced and saying "I read your book and I've come to see your house." All I could say would have been "I read your book, and now I'm walking across France and hoping to write about my journey, and like your late brother I too am an Anglican clergyman." Hardly enough to justify interrupting the restoration work. So I contented myself with a few photos of the distinctive bell-tower construction and the curved outside of the apse at the east end of the chapel.

Wistfully I plodded on towards Prades. It was now Friday afternoon and when I reached the town it was being baked under a searing sun. Funnily enough this was the birthplace of Thomas Merton, the American monk whose experiences as a Trappist formed the basis for his classic 1948 book *"The Seven Storey Mountain."* (Merton was destined to meet an end that would be ridiculous almost to the point of being comical. At the age of fifty-three he was electrocuted when the Trappists sent him to an interfaïth conference in Thailand. It seems he had just climbed out of a shower in Bangkok when he tried to switch on a faulty electric fan. It is rather sad to think of a spiritual genius disappearing in a flash of blue light and a puff of acrid smoke). Prades was also the place where the famous cellist Pablo Casals had settled when he fled from Franco, and when I arrived I found that the town was gearing itself up for its annual Casals Festival of Chamber Music. Prades seemed to be considerably smaller in real life than it looked on the map, and I was anxious to find a hotel and secure a room because it would have to be home for three nights. I had arranged to stay at the monastery of St.Martin-du-Canigou from the following Monday, so for better or worse I had a whole weekend to kill in Prades. I was relieved when I discovered "Les Glycines" which was set back slightly off the main street, the Rue General de

Gaulle. I asked what the name meant, and was told that the *glycine* was a purple plant. I had been wondering whether it was something to do with cats, because the hotel was overrun with pictures, ornaments and sculptures depicting furry felines. Clearly the owner of the place was cat-crazy, and it reminded me of my own Smokey, half a continent away. At dinner I asked the waitress about the number of cat-items in the entire hotel. She reckoned the total was about seventeen hundred.

Upstairs in my room I lay on the bed watching television. George Clooney reappeared, still dubbed into French, but this time he was the captain of a fishing boat in a film called *"The Perfect Storm."* I had seen the film before so I switched channels and caught two short episodes of a series called *"Crime"* featuring detectives in Paris. As luck would have it I saw several instalments of this particular offering, on successive Friday evenings in different hotel rooms, and quickly I realised that the plot was always going to be more or less the same. I was also bemused by the fact that these policemen had a habit of wandering around the streets in a team of six as they discussed their latest case.

On the Saturday morning I lazed around the pavement cafes reading the English newspapers. I also walked around the town centre in search of a new tee-shirt, thinking I would make myself a little more presentable when I reached the Canigou monastery on the Monday afternoon. However I failed in my quest, as even the large supermarket on the eastern edge of the town had nothing suitable at a decent price. Instead I returned to my hotel room with three new pairs of socks. On the television the Tour was about to reach its *denoument* with the final individual time trial. The French phrase *"contre la montre"* has a nice ring to it. The course was going to be 49 kilometres from Porniac on the Atlantic coast inland to the centre of Nantes, and Armstrong was starting with an advantage of 65 seconds over Ullrich. The experts all seemed to agree that Ullrich would win the stage, but not by enough to overhaul Armstrong's lead in the overall classification.

As a further element of interest the showdown was going to be complicated by the weather. The commentators on the TV were wrapped in cagoules and Porniac looked as though it could have been anywhere in the west of Ireland on a wet autumn day. For the first time in the entire three weeks the cyclists would encounter rain, and moreover it was heavy and it was coming in on a blustery wind. The event unfolded through the course of the afternoon, with the riders setting off at intervals until finally Ullrich and Armstrong took to the road, three minutes apart. Their times at the various checkpoints revealed that they were very evenly matched. At no point did Ullrich look like he would claw back a significant chunk of his rival's lead, and in the end he lost about ten seconds when he failed to negotiate a roundabout, fell, and slid across the glistening road into some restraining bales. So Armstrong triumphed by a few seconds, virtually ensuring his fifth consecutive Tour victory. In fact the pair only finished third and fourth on the day's stage. Victory was claimed by Britain's David Millar, which was some compensation for a fiasco during the opening Prologue three weeks earlier. On that occasion Millar had been poised to win, and thus to take the yellow jersey, but he had been thwarted by a mechanical failure which was quickly attributed to the failings of the management of his Cofidis team. During the three weeks since that disappointment Millar had persisted with the Tour in spite of suffering a bout of bronchitis, so maybe there was a measure of justice in his success at Nantes. Second place had been claimed by the remarkable Tyler Hamilton who thus elevated himself, along with his crowned teeth and broken collarbone, to fourth place in the overall rankings.

The Tour looms over everything. It is always there in the background and whenever you glance at a newspaper or

309

glimpse a television screen it is right there in your face. Nobody is allowed to forget it for long. At breakfast that morning in the hotel dining room I could hear it being analysed on the radio in the kitchen. It occurred to me that when I had set out on my walk, the Tour had not even begun. Yet the event is so pervasive that this very realisation surprised me. In fact I had reached Lescun before the Tour even got going, and I was struggling up the *Chemin de la Mature* on the day that Millar almost won the Prologue. My personal Tour had begun a full fortnight before the cycling, and it would continue for a further week after the surviving riders had reached Paris.

That Saturday evening I ate dinner in the hotel and was retiring for an early night when I idly flicked the television on again. In this way I caught the last twenty minutes or so of a French documentary about the ascent of Annapurna in 1950. Archive footage recorded harrowing scenes as Maurice Herzog and his companions, Terray, Lachenal and Rebuffat, retreated from the mountain minus various fingers and toes. The commentary seemed to be saying that at the time, just after the Second World War, France desperately needed some heroes and these hapless alpinists supplied the need. It was a sad business, and I fell asleep reminded of the afternoon I had spent in the railway station in Bordeaux, sick and sunburned, sixteen years earlier.

On the Sunday I was due to meet up with some old friends who were in France on holiday. It was good to be with them again, even though it felt slightly surreal because previously I had only ever seen them in Surrey. They were part of a houseparty which had taken over a villa for a few days and transformed it into an outpost of the Home Counties. After a swim, a drink and a pleasant lunch we played billiards, inventing our own rules for a curious little table with no pockets. I ended up playing against somebody who was reputed to be on the Oxford Diocesan Board of Finance. I was keen to ask him about the financial implications of the Jeffrey John affair, and whether it was true that if John had taken up his post as Bishop of Reading the diocesan income would have dropped by forty percent as disgruntled evangelical parishes withheld their "quota" payments. But I thought better of it. My opponent was on holiday too, and indeed he had probably come to France hoping to escape from this theological controversy and its attendant financial headache.

After some thunder and rain had passed over I ambled back to "Les Glycines", thinking I might spend the evening listening to Mozart's Requiem in the church in the town centre. It was due to be the highlight of the opening day of the Pablo Casals festival. However, I did not yet have a ticket, and my plan was scuppered when the hotel took too long to serve my evening meal. I was not too disappointed, being thankful at the prospect of another early night. The television news informed me that Armstrong had duly ridden into Paris to claim victory on the Champs Elysees. In some respects his triumph had been more impressive than those of the previous couple of years, because he had been forced to fight for it whilst lacking the aura of invincibility. And he had now joined the most exclusive club in cycling, that of the five-time Tour winners. There seemed to be something significant in the fact that none of his heroic predecessors – Anquetil, Merckx, Hinault or Indurain – had managed to go on to a sixth victory, and I could not imagine Armstrong achieving it either. Maybe there is some invisible barrier there which limits even these supreme athletes. But you never know. The pundits were embarking on an exhaustive analysis of the three weeks just gone. They reckoned that the decisive turning-point had come six days earlier on the climb to Luz-Ardiden. Armstrong, whose overall campaign was looking vulnerable in the face of Ullrich's renewed strength, had collided with a spectator and gone down. The Texan's instinctive response was to remount and, in a burst of crazed

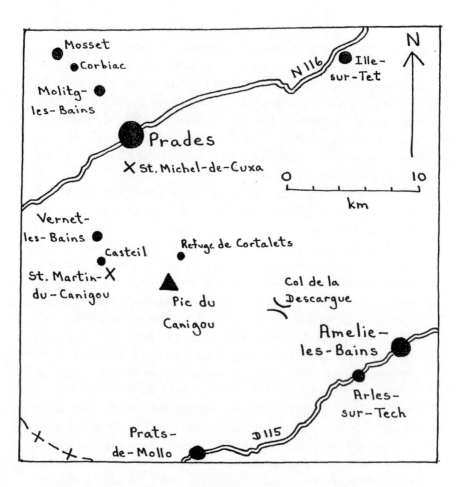

Prades to Amelie-les-Bains.

adrenaline, to storm ahead and win the stage, thus re-establishing his overall lead and making a powerful psychological statement at the same time.

I have always found the end of the Tour sad, and tended to see those last laps on the Champs Elysees as a depressing spectacle rather than an exciting finale. They signal that it is all over for another year; a link with France and the summer and the Alps and Pyrenees is being broken again. It is a tiny bereavement every year – not a major one but a bereavement nevertheless – just as the beginning of the Tour is a resurrection of hope and adventure at the beginning of July. Every year the opening prologue is followed by a relatively flat first week as the Tour beds down, but you know that the mountains lie ahead. And when all is said and done it is the mountains that really make the Tour. Take away the Alps and Pyrenees and what is left would not be half the spectacle, half the drama or half the heroism. The history, tradition and heritage would be immeasurably diluted. Great things are done when men and mountains meet.

The following morning I checked out of Les Glycines, bade farewell to the countless cats, and walked west along the Rue General de Gaulle. At a simple junction I turned south and began to ascend, working my way out of the town through the suburb of Codalet and on past the imposing abbey of St.Michel-de-Cuxa. I should have paused for a couple of hours and taken a tour around the place, but I was anxious to make progress and reckoned that as I was making for another monastery in any case I could probably afford to bypass this one. Nevertheless the sight of the high walls and square tower at St.Michel-de-Cuxa raised monastic issues for me, and prompted me to reflect on my expectations of St.Martin-du-Canigou. As I trudged on along the lane I gradually managed to distil my thoughts into three questions. The first was the one I had identified weeks earlier whilst I had been approaching

Roncesvalles: whether there was a communal dimension to monastic life which could serve as a counterbalance to the (potentially selfish) individualism of the pilgrimage? The second area which intrigued me was whether monasticism itself was an outdated anachronism, or whether it might still be relevant today. Indeed, might it be more relevant than ever in the 21st century in our so-called postmodern culture? The third question, which obviously was linked to the other two, was the more personal one of whether I could see the monastery as a way forward for myself, either as a resource for future retreats or even as some sort of a vocation.

Passing St.Michel-de-Cuxa also reminded me of Patrick Leigh-Fermor, the man who had walked to Constantinople and then spent the Second World War stirring up trouble for the Germans in Crete. By the 1950s he had resurfaced in northern France and was spending several months as a guest in the Benedictine Abbey of St.Wandrille de Fontanelle. He wrote about his experiences there in a slim book called "*A time to keep silence.*" I had read a 1982 reprint of the book and noted the warnings implicit in Leigh-Fermor's updated introductory chapter. In effect he said that even after two or three months in the monastery he was still poorly qualified to write about it, having acquired only a superficial acquaintance with monasticism. Indeed at least one monk had criticised him for writing at all, regarding it as an intrusive and indiscreet abuse of his time in the community.

This criticism was probably unfair, to the extent that Leigh-Fermor was really writing about his own experiences and impressions rather than seeking to offer a definitive account of monasticism. So I resolved to follow Leigh-Fermor's example: it seemed to me that if I recorded my own impressions of my time at Canigou they would be valid in their own right, though of course it would be regrettable if they gave a misleading account of the monastic life. Indeed I was painfully aware that

314

Leigh-Fermor's sojourn at St.Wandrille had been two to three months: my time at St.Martin would be a mere two or three days and so my experience was bound to be a relatively superficial one. Of course I shared one thing with my illustrious predecessor in as much as neither of us had taken any monastic vows: like Leigh-Fermor I would be only a guest within the monastic walls and this too would mean that my observations were inevitably going to be somewhat skewed.

Some of Leigh-Fermor's observations made for interesting reading. When he arrived at the monastery he was apprehensive and when he got inside he found the first few days painful and depressing as he adjusted to the rhythm of life in the place. The simplicity of the food and the lack of wine combined with the regular worship to present a bleak prospect. However, his walk across Europe and his activities during the War had shown that he was an adaptable character, and adapt he did. Rapidly he came to appreciate and to enjoy the regime. Having spent much of the first week sleeping and working off a weight of residual tiredness he found that five or six hours sleep per night were perfectly adequate and quite refreshing. He was in an environment where there were no demands on his nervous energy, and he was insulated from the countless urgent and (usually) trivial intrusions which assail us in everyday life and which do so much to erode its quality. So he rapidly sensed a greater freedom and work became easier. It was interesting to note that Leigh-Fermor was writing in the 1950s: one can only assume that "the tyranny of the urgent" has become even more oppressive since then as the pace of life has accelerated.

The same dynamics applied to the monks of course. Leigh-Fermor observed that they seemed to have a deep contentment about them and that on the whole they appeared very healthy in spite of the frugal conditions. They were serious about meeting God at a deep level, not just superficially, and they seemed to have a genuine decency and goodness. My own thought here

315

was that this was all fine as far as it went: I knew from my own very limited spiritual experience that it is easier to be holy when you are not responsible for anything. The problem and challenge which many committed Christians are facing today is how you achieve some sort of holiness in the midst of all the urgency. And the next obvious question would be about what one means by "holiness" in any case? I could accept that for some people the pursuit of holiness would entail a withdrawal from everyday life into an enclosed space such as a monastery. But that could not be the whole answer, nor is it an appropriate strategy for everyone. I tended to suspect that "holiness" itself is less to do with withdrawal from life and more to do with engagement in life - but an engagement in which the believer lives close to God and thereby sees things increasingly from God's perspective.

That was not to say that the monks had chosen some sort of easy option. As Leigh-Fermor himself argued, to accuse members of religious houses of cowardice, on the grounds that they have run away from the world, is absurd. On the contrary they are people of courage. Of course there is a sense in which a monastery functions as a haven, and a visitor casually spending a few days or weeks there might regard it as a blissful escape from other pressures. But it is a different matter for the monk or nun who has taken serious vows and committed themselves to the regime. They are entering a place where there is no hiding from God or from oneself, and from which there is no going back. Not every Christian is called to it. Having said that, is not the life of the monk just one extreme way of living out the call to a holy lifestyle which confronts all those who wish to call themselves Christians?

Obviously the pursuit of holiness is one of the fundamental features at the root of monasticism. The whole movement developed from hermits such as Saint Antony in the Egyptian desert, and during the 4th century in particular their influence

316

spread to the West. Then came the Rule of Benedict which was the first detailed monastic legislation adapted to European needs. It superceded all other previous rules, and meant that from the 8th to the 12th centuries the Benedictines were dominant in western Europe. Benedict himself had lived from approximately 480AD to 550 in central Italy. As a young man he had been appalled at the licentiousness of life in Rome, and he had withdrawn to a cave at Subiaco to live as a hermit. A community gathered around him and in time he established a dozen monasteries, each with an abbot and twelve monks. By the year 525 local pressure had forced him to move, and he settled at Monte Cassino. It was here that he wrote the famous Rule, thus regulating the spiritual and administrative aspects of his monasteries.

Of course Monte Cassino was destined to achieve even greater fame during the Second World War, as the town was a strongpoint on the German Gustav Line, blocking the entrance to the Liri Valley and thus obstructing the Allied advance on Rome. The Benedictine monastery dominated the town and was bombed into rubble only to be rebuilt after the war. Benedict's Rule, with its 73 short chapters, had long been famous in its own right, and many of its provisions were pretty strict. It prescribed seven times of prayer per day, plus times of manual labour and reading. The monks would keep only the barest of possessions, and could not wander far outside the monastery. There was to be silence at mealtimes. Everything was geared to free the monks from the world and to enable them to devote their time to worship and prayer. Benedict himself did not think that the Rule was particularly tough, or at any rate he believed (following Christ's teaching) that the pathway to life must necessarily be narrow, steep and rugged but that as one progresses along it God's grace makes it easier to persevere.

The Benedictine lifestyle makes no sense without a regard for the value of worship and a belief in the efficacy of prayer. The same can no doubt be said about the other contemplative Orders such as the Cistercians and Carthusians which emerged later on. (The Franciscans, Dominicans and Jesuits had a different emphasis, and were more interested in action of one sort or another outside in the world). However, the most extreme development of the Benedictine tradition came with the Trappists, who seemed to revel in subjecting themselves to suffering. This could include not just the extreme silence for which the Order became proverbial, but committing themselves to grindingly tough manual labour and seeking to survive extremes of heat and cold. Hair shirts and self-flagellation were other refinements. All of this left little or no time for reading or study. Leigh-Fermor actually spent some time in a Trappist foundation and felt that the old joke that Trappists took four vows – poverty, chastity, obedience and ignorance – was rather unfair. Nevertheless, it was clear from his writings that he did not find the Trappist regime as attractive as the Benedictine. I suspected that my instincts would be similar to Leigh-Fermor's: that the Benedictine set-up was more humane whereas the Trappists would have an intellectual poverty that was withering rather than emancipating. The psychology behind the Trappist behaviour would no doubt furnish a thesis in its own right. Studying the Cathars I had noted various links and parallels between clerics and soldiers, and indeed there are areas of overlap between the spiritual and the military life. Now I wondered whether the Trappists saw themselves in a similar way to the modern special forces: ie as a sort of elite for the real hard men of the monastic world?

Another interesting dimension in Leigh-Fermor's observations concerned the awareness of death and its proximity. He wrote that with the monks' lifestyle death would be an easy change to adjust to, though he wrote *that* early in his account, when he was still feeling overwhelmed by depression and loneliness in the place, so maybe it was a somewhat jaundiced comment. The more positive angle on it was to say that the monks lived every day as though it was their last, and indeed how could one feel more "alive" than that - a poignant observation from a man who had spent half of the Second World War behind enemy lines. From the monks' perspective life in this world was, in any case, only a fleeting moment before eternity. So it made sense to use it in worship and prayer, in saving one's own soul and praying for the souls of others. The lifestyle meant renouncing the pleasures of this life, which are considered meaningless anyway, and confronting death head-on. So part of the psychology was to keep death ever before their eyes and to pray for a holy death. Each day was regarded as life and death in microcosm, with death represented by sleep and followed by the little miracle of resurrection when one awoke the following morning.

Patrick Leigh-Fermor's description of St.Wandrille had a sting in its tail. He had found adjusting to the place difficult, but he wrote that when the time came to leave it he found readjusting to "normal" life outside the monastery far more painful and depressing. He described the world outside the monastery as "an inferno of noise and vulgarity." Staring out of his train window as he travelled back into Paris he saw billboards advertising drinks, and regarded them as personal insults far more than as symbols of freedom.

I stopped on a straight section of road just beyond St.Michel-de-Cuxa, pausing for a few minutes to take a couple of pictures of its prominent square tower before I trudged on. As was usually the case after a "day off" I was feeling sluggish and was struggling to find any comfortable rhythm for the first hours of my walk. Rightly or wrongly I had come to attribute this phenomenon to having taken on board a weight of extra food during the rest day and stored it as fat in my body. On this occasion I had made matters worse by having two days of rest in a row and having eaten correspondingly more without taking any real exercise. After a cup of coffee in Taurinya I felt slightly brighter and plodded on along the twisting lanes towards Fillois and Vernet-les-Bains. All morning the view ahead was dominated by the Canigou massif. From Prades it had looked quite close, but I knew this was a trick of the bright light, for the summit was a good ten miles away. Even from that distance the Canigou seemed to exude a mighty presence. Walking towards it was an odd experience, as I had the strange sensation that I was not getting any closer to the mountain but that nevertheless it was growing larger. I was bemused and disorientated, and put it down to the twisting nature of my route combined with the alterations in perspective as I worked my way round the north-western edge of the massif.

I entered Vernet-les-Bains with caution, remembering Nicholas Crane's warning that this was where he had stayed in the worst hotel of his life. Crane's book did not reveal which hotel that was, but I was taking no chances and had arranged my schedule so that I need only risk lunch here. And so it was that I consumed a leisurely *plat du jour* outside one of the bars. I had no idea what sort of food I would encounter at the monastery, so I reckoned it might be wise to get a good meal inside me before I arrived.

After I had eaten my fill I pottered around the centre of the place which the English had once called "The Paradise of the Pyrenees." They had colonised it during the years before the First World War, drawn by the sulphur springs and led by Lord Roberts, who had won his Victoria Cross during the Indian Mutiny. In fact he was more famous for his exploits in Afghanistan, for in 1880 he had led the expedition from Kabul to relieve Kandahar, marching his men three hundred miles in three weeks through blazing heat and fighting a battle at the end of it. More recently he had rounded off his military career by winning the Boer War. By the time he reached Vernet he was Earl of Kandahar, Pretoria and Waterford. Of more immediate interest to me was the fact that in 1911 "Lord Bobs", with Rudyard Kipling as an accomplice, had led a party of thirty people up to St.Martin-du-Canigou to see the restoration work at the monastery. But life in Vernet had been too good to last. The outbreak of war in 1914 had killed off this Edwardian idyll overnight as the English deserted it for Blighty and signed up in droves for service on the Western Front. In fact the war killed off Lord Roberts too, for he succumbed to a cold whilst on a morale-boosting visit to the troops.

From Vernet-les-Bains it was uphill to the little hamlet of Casteil. Again I felt laboured in my walking, no doubt an effect of the heat combined with the food and wine I had absorbed at lunchtime. In Casteil I found a souvenir shop where I bought and drank a tin of iced tea. I also bought mineral water and filled my containers to capacity, before purchasing a quantity of biscuits and chocolate. The latter were a further precaution against any Spartan living conditions at the monastery, and if it turned out that I did not need them to supplement the monastic diet then they would always be useful as supplies when the walk resumed beyond St.Martin. So I was heavily laden as I ascended the final mile, up a smooth concrete track that climbed one thousand feet in a spectacular series of bends going up the side of a gorge. The bottom third of the ascent was hideously hot as the sun reflected off the rocks. Incredibly this track was used regularly by four-wheel-drive vehicles going to and from the monastery. It was barely wide enough for a car, and had no railings or barriers whatsoever. At numerous points there was nothing beside the grace of God to prevent vehicles toppling over the edge. Higher up the hillside this dizzying pathway went into forests of chestnut and oak and was marginally safer. I was certainly thankful for the shade which these trees afforded, for I had been dripping with sweat all the way from Casteil. During the ascent I encountered numerous groups of tourists walking in the opposite direction as they came down from St.Martin. Most of them said *"bonjour"*; a few giggled; and one or two could not refrain from open laughter. No doubt this was triggered by the outlandish sight of my sunglasses, my hat and the giant green rucksack.

Two-thirds of the way up I paused at a neat little Romanesque church beside the path. This building had been restored in the late 1970's and a quantity of bones had been dug up, so the best guess was that it had been a burial chapel, pressed into use when the monks up at the monastery had run out of suitable land for burying their deceased comrades. The view was superb and Vernet-les-Bains looked very small and distant. From there it was only a few hundred metres to the Abbey itself. I had felt apprehensive about my arrival for several days, for I had very little idea what I would find there and I was unsure what sort of reception I might get. I tried to tell myself that my trepidation was really little more than fear of the unknown. At least the people at St.Martin knew I was coming, for I had followed their instructions and phoned them from Tarascon ten days previously to confirm my time of arrival.

I decided that I had to be ready for anything. I half-wondered whether I would be searched at the monastery door and my secret supplies of food confiscated. I also cast my mind back to Patrick Leigh-Fermor's arrival at the Abbey of St.Wandrille and I identified with some of his fears. Like Leigh-Fermor I did not relish the prospect of a theological grilling. After all, St.Martin was a Roman Catholic foundation and I wondered whether I was still harbouring a few primitive Protestant prejudices which would come to the surface during my stay. I found myself imagining what it would be like to be stuck in a cell and tied to a chair whilst a couple of fifteen-stone nuns shone a lamp into my face and asked me what I really thought of Jeffrey John:

"I don't know," I stammered. "I've never met the man!"

"But you must know something! You'll have to do better than this, you snivelling English heretic!"

"Well I can't. You've got to believe me!" I knew I was gibbering in a pathetic attempt to gain time. Then I had a brainwave and clutched at fresh hope. "But wait a minute – yesterday I was playing billiards with somebody from the Oxford Diocesan Board of Finance and he said"...........

"*What?* You expect us to believe *that?*" My interrogator drew closer, eclipsing the light from the lamp. "This is your final warning!" she hissed. "Sister Gertrude is an expert with the electrodes!"

The second nun emerged from the shadows and spoke for the first time. "The pain will be exquisite," she said softly. "I can assure you of that."

"Be reasonable!" I croaked.

The first nun smiled through a mouthful of broken and yellowing teeth. "The time for reason is over, Englishman, and so is the Week of Prayer for Christian Unity. Now you talk!" Her laughter, when it came, was a horrible mirthless cackle.

"You can't do this to me!"

Actually I thought the interrogation scenario was unlikely. The Roman Church has the allegiance of more than one billion people around the globe, so it hardly needs to worry too much about the strange theological contortions of its pint-sized Anglican cousin.

In the event my welcome was a friendly one. After presenting myself to the people on duty in the Abbey shop I rapidly gained access through the locked front door and into the monastery itself. My hosts were pleasant but made a minimum of fuss, which I liked. I was escorted into a building perched on the edge of the gorge. A steep staircase and a long corridor led to my room. It was furnished with a bed, a desk and a couple of chairs in addition to a cupboard and a washbasin in the corner. If anything it was more comfortable than I had been anticipating, and like all the other rooms it had a nameplate on the outside of the door. I was now Saint Matthew. I was quite pleased by this - particularly when I noticed that if I had been put in the next room I would have been Saint Bridget.

It took only a few minutes to settle in, emptying the rucksack and arranging its contents around the room. I felt relieved to have got into the monastery, and satisfied to be where I was. This abbey had been a major target ever since I had left the Atlantic coast, and now I had reached it. In spite of some ordeals along the way I had actually got there, and more or less on schedule too. I decided to celebrate with a shave, and as I scraped the foam from my face I saw in the mirror that something had changed during the course of the expedition. An old identity had been slipping away and a new persona had been replacing it. Now, here at the monastery, I could see it clearly. The Yesterday Man had gone, left behind somewhere in the central Pyrenees. In his place the Mad Monk had arrived.

Chapter 12.

Mad Monk at Canigou.

My attempt to shave had shown me that the plumbing in my room was antiquated, if not actually medieval. There was no warm water and no plug for the basin, so I simply used cold water running from the tap. The problem was that the cold water kept cutting out too. My room was at the end of the corridor on the upper of two floors, so it was probably at the end of whatever circuit of pipes had been installed in the building. When anybody in another room turned on their tap it meant I lost the pressure in mine. I decided to accept this stoically. After all, my room was more comfortable than I had any right to expect, and the electric lighting meant that I had got at least one innovation which a medieval monk would not recognise.

I took a more detailed look around the room. On the desk lay a page of information for guests. Amongst other things it described the monastery bell, and I would indeed soon discover that there was no avoiding the bell when it was rung. The information sheet (loosely translated from the French) said "when you hear the sound of the bell, you can consider it to be like the call of God. It will be time for an office (ie worship in the chapel) or time for a meal." I wondered about the last bit. If the meals were "like the call of God" it raised the question of what sort of food would be served.

I sat on the bed, weighing up whether I was likely to survive the meals and the worship, and wondering whether I could cope with two-and-a-half days here. Again I felt a measure of insecurity: insecurity that in this environment, peopled with characters professionally dedicated to the pursuit of devotion, the shallowness of my own spiritual life would be exposed.

For I had no illusions. I knew that when it came to serious prayer and worship I was only an amateur. Of course I might dabble a bit, here and there, taking a dilettante interest in different types of prayer, but compared to people who took serious vows and devoted life and soul to contemplation of the divine I knew I was only dipping the odd toe into the water. At home my prayers and Bible reading were mostly incorporated into the daily office of Morning Prayer, to which I would normally devote about thirty minutes. Of course that was better than nothing, and on odd occasions it could be supplemented by other devotional events during the course of the day, but really it was thin fare.

It seemed to me that my walk actually provided an analogy, albeit an imperfect one. At home my normal physical training would be, on average, a jog of about an hour every other afternoon. For the last few months before the expedition this had been replaced by a walk with boots and rucksack, averaging perhaps two hours. None of my training walks had exceeded four-and-a-half hours. And I thought I was getting reasonably fit on that regime. Indeed, compared to most people my age I was pretty fit. But in the Pyrenees even the shortest walking day had been getting on for five hours. Most had been seven to nine hours, and on one or two horrendous occasions they had been eleven hours. As a result I had moved through various pain barriers to new levels of fitness, or at least to new perspectives from which discomfort that was previously intolerable had come to be accepted. From my new vantage point I could see that an extra couple of hours effort, late in the day and with no food and little water, might not be an attractive prospect, but it could be accepted with a grimace and a shrug. And all this was in mountainous terrain, whereas my training at home had been largely over flat courses. Here in the Pyrenees I had risen closer to the level of a professional athlete, not in terms of performance but in the sense that my body was always either training or recovering from training. And that is surely one of the things that seperates the professional athlete from the amateur. The amateur can train, and maybe train hard, but when he stops training he has to go back to work. His body has less chance to recover between sessions. For the true professional everything is orientated towards recovering fully so that the next training session is of maximum benefit. And as you rise through the various levels of fitness and pain you can appreciate with greater sensitivity just how your body is feeling. You can sense whether it is having a good day or a bad day; whether there is energy in reserve or not. It is like fine-tuning an engine or a musical instrument.

The analogy with prayer is not perfect, of course. For one thing prayer is about a relationship with God, and for another it involves God's grace. Prayer is a different business from walking, but the analogy holds to some extent. And the point of the analogy is that you cannot hope to become a spiritual giant overnight, even if you aspire to such a thing at all. You cannot move from a ten-minute "quiet time" one day to hours of contemplation the next, any more than the occasional jogger can decide to go out tomorrow and run an Olympic marathon. It just does not work like that. One has to build up slowly and steadily, and no doubt there are any number of pain barriers along the way. I thought again about Thomas Merton and his "*Seven Storey Mountain.*" I had never read the book, but I liked the title as it seemed to imply more or less what I suspected, and what my intimation told me must be the case. As I thought about the prayerful life I knew I was working more from intuition than personal experience. I knew that as a "pray-er" I was the equivalent of the amateur jogger, and it would be foolish to aspire to behaving like a full-time "religious" or "contemplative" overnight. More than that, any such attempt would be more likely to leave me discouraged and depressed. Better to be realistic and work up to it gradually. In one way I was pleased that my stay in the monastery was only scheduled for a couple of days, as it removed any silly notion of trying to become a spiritual heavyweight.

This logic gave me fresh courage, and I decided that I should no longer hide in my room but go out and explore my new surroundings. As I wandered around the complex of buildings my first impression was how small they were in real life. Prior to my visit I had seen several photographs of the place, but invariably they made it look much larger. In the cloisters a party of thirty or forty tourists was embarking on a guided tour with one of the monks, so I merged into the back of the group hoping to learn about the history of the abbey.

The monastery of St.Martin-du-Canigou is named after Saint Martin of Tours, a fourth-century Roman soldier who had met a naked beggar. Martin had used his sword to divide his own cloak in two, giving one half to the beggar and retaining the other half for himself. When his military service was over Martin was baptised and ordained by Hillary of Poitiers before taking up the life of a hermit and living in a solitary cell near Liguge. His holiness drew others to him, and a community formed. Somewhat reluctantly he was prevailed upon to become Bishop of Tours in 372AD, and for a while lived as a hermit in a cell next to a church. Distracted by curious visitors he was compelled to withdraw to Marmoutier, where he established a monastery as a centre for evangelising rural France, much of which was still pagan. The rigour of life in his monastery made it a training ground for bishops, and Martin himself would travel back into the city on Sundays to pray with the mentally ill, the dispossessed and other outcasts. Most of what is known about Martin comes from a popular biography of him written by Sulpicius Severus, and this book spread

Martin's fame throughout western Europe. Martin (who of course pre-dated Benedict) stimulated monasticism throughout the West and created a template for the holy men of the Dark Ages. He died in 397AD, and achieved the curious distinction of being the first non-martyr to be venerated as a saint. Equally remarkable was the fact that he managed to become the patron saint of both soldiers and pacifists.

The monastic history of the Canigou site dates from about 1000AD. Guifred Cabreta, Count of the Cerdagne, began the construction of an abbey designed to receive a community of Benedictine monks. There were two consecrations, in 1009 and 1014, owing to the peculiar design of the place. In effect Guifred built two churches, one on top of the other. Today the lower one is a crypt whilst the upper one functions as a chapel. They were both consecrated in 1009, but then both were extended to the west, which prompted the second ceremony five years later. Guifred's design, with one church on top of the other, caused headaches for the engineers. Originally the lower church had granite columns, but these were unable to bear the weight of the upper church and had to be reinforced with stonework. When the buildings were extended the engineers avoided a repeat of the problem by simply using stonework rather than columns. The whole project was finished in 1030 with the completion of the tower. This large square structure was destined to survive for only four centuries, for in 1428 it was badly damaged by an earthquake. It was rebuilt but is now thought to be slightly shorter than the original. Two tombs near the base of the tower are those of Guifred and his second wife Elizabeth. They had retired to the monastery in 1035 and Guifred, who had himself become a Benedictine monk, was reckoned to have dug out the tombs himself in anticipation of their deaths.

The Abbey's history was by no means always peaceful – indeed it was often turbulent as it was vulnerable to any number of brigands and bandits in addition to whatever feudal armies were marauding around the Catalan hills. The occupation by the Benedictines ended in 1782, just a few years before the Revolution, when the last five monks asked permission to leave. After their departure the Abbey quickly fell into ruin. Local people looted the site and amongst other items they carted away the capitals (carved stone column heads) in order to decorate other churches and even private homes.

The restoration of the place during the 20th century was really due to the initiative of two remarkable men, each of whom devoted thirty years to the project. In 1902 the Bishop of Perpignan, Monseigneur de Carsalade, bought the ruins and began a programme of work which would run until 1932. He managed to recover most of the missing capitals and set them on columns on the south side of the cloisters. (In Nicholas Crane's book it mentions how, during the visit organised by Lord Roberts and Rudyard Kipling, an Irish lady had to be restrained from taking one of the capitals home as a souvenir and using it as a sundial). The capitals depict a curious mixture of scenes. Some show animals, mostly lions. One has a dog and a monkey extending their paws in friendship whilst a snake, the symbol of jealousy, appears between them as a cause of discord. Another purportedly shows a mitred abbot being thrown into hell. The cloisters are also odd in that they are open to the outside. Normally cloisters are closed, to mark separation from the world, and this had been the case with Guifred's original building. However, Monseigneur de Carsalade decided to have the cloisters open to let the sunlight show the capitals to full advantage, and this had the additional benefit of allowing a view across the gorge to the south.

The second phase of the restoration ran from 1952 to 1982 and was the work of a Benedictine monk, Father Bernard de Chabannes. By the time he had finished the abbey was more or less in the condition visible today. Then in 1988 the Diocese of Perpignan invited the Order of the Beatitudes to take over the buildings and to establish a community there. The Beatitudes were a relatively recent creation: they only dated from the 1960s as they had been established in the wake of the Second Vatican Council and were a product of the charismatic renewal movement within the Roman Church. Their name had changed even during this brief history, for originally they were "The Order of the Lion of Judah and the Immolated Lamb." Apparently the "Lion of Judah" was based on a verse in the Book of Revelation. Quite where the "Immolated Lamb" came from I was not so sure: maybe it was a belated recognition that the Church in these parts had sometimes displayed a propensity for setting people on fire. Anyway, the name changed in the 1980s when it was realised that "the Lion of Judah" might compromise the work of the Order in Africa and Asia as it could antagonise Muslims. There was also a cult in Britain which had adopted the same name. In any case the less ferocious "Beatitudes" (the name comes from the opening verses of the Sermon on the Mount) was deemed to be a better expression of the Order's desire to work amongst the poor, and it certainly sounded less intimidating than the previous title.

Swiftly I found out that the Order of the Beatitudes has thirty religious houses in France and a further thirty or forty around the world. The community living at Canigou consisted of about twenty people, but many of the houses are considerably smaller. It is an unusual Order in that it is mixed: it includes both monks and nuns. For that matter it also mixes "religious" with lay members who have not taken the full vows of poverty, chastity and obedience but who have nevertheless made a commitment to the community. The lay members are also both sexes and, surprisingly, included married couples and even families with small children. Nor are members necessarily attached to a single place, for it is usual to move from one house to another every few years. Whilst I was at Canigou the community there consisted of about twenty people, equally split between males and females and more or less equally divided between religious and laity. The latter included two married couples, and a priest was resident on the site. Apparently "the Beatitudes" had only received their final and full recognition from the Pope two months before my visit. This recognition as an official Order had come at the end of a long campaign, and it did not surprise me that the Pontiff had needed time to get his head around the legal and practical difficulties involved in such unusual domestic arrangements.

Besides incorporating men, women, children, clergy, religious and laity, the Order also made for a cosmopolitan international mixture. At dinner on my first evening I spoke to two nuns, one of whom was Italian and the other Austrian. I met a Polish man, and then a Welshman who had been a neighbour of Rowan Williams in Brecon and who had been studying at seminaries in France and Spain. The conversation at dinner was mostly in French, with snatches of Spanish, English and German. The atmosphere was easy-going and tolerant, with a minimum of fuss. I spoke to a young couple from Barcelona who had been lay members of the community for about eight years. They asked about the Church of England and its policy of ordaining women, but there was no antagonism that I could detect. There were various other visitors and guests present besides myself, principally two women from Bergerac near Bordeaux who were roughly my age and were tall and slim.

Dinner was actually taking place in the open air, in a triangular garden outside the kitchen door. It was enclosed on two sides by the monastery buildings, whilst the third side had a low stone wall and a drop of several hundred feet into the gorge. It was on this vertiginous terrace that I first met "King." He was one of the largest dogs I had ever seen. In fact I thought I recognised him from one of the carved capitals in the cloisters – the one which depicted a "devouring lion." At first I took him to be a large Saint Bernard, but in fact he was a cross between a Pyrenean sheepdog and a German shepherd dog, probably with a few other genes mixed in for good measure. He looked as though he had been fed regularly on steroids, and it emerged that he had got his name from King Kong. I first saw him when I was standing with my back to the low wall above the dizzying drop, and one of the monks was warning me that the dog could be a bit awkward with strangers. As I was receiving this advice King was getting a simultaneous talking-to from a diminutive nun who was about half his size. I could not hear all of it but it was clear that the enormous hound was being told he had to behave. During dinner I noticed that the great dog looked a little agitated, but it was normal policy for him to wait for the humans to finish their meal before he got his food and walk. There was also a grey cat living in the monastery. It appeared from time to time but I was never quite sure how it got on with the dog. I also wondered what King made of the pervasive and deafening monastery bell when it was rung. Presumably he was used to it.

As we finished dinner the sun was slipping away and the warm evening was turning into a chilly twilight. There was a sense of peace about the place; a peace which had descended emphatically when the day's final party of tourists had left the abbey earlier in the evening. I was already learning that the tourists were a big factor in life here. I commented on what I had noticed about the evening peace, and then immediately I regretted it and feared that I might have caused offence: after all offering a welcome to visitors is a large element in the monastic tradition. But one of the nuns confirmed that my observation was pretty accurate. In many ways this was a difficult location in which to pursue the religious life. Whatever else it might be, the abbey was home for the members of the community, and it was difficult if one of them unlocked the front door to go out for a stroll and found several tourists fighting to get in. If you went to pray in the chapel you might have a party of forty tourists taking photographs of you. In fact, the nun said, she never went into the chapel on Sunday afternoons, as it was more peaceful to pray in her room. When members of the Beatitudes moved to Canigou they were warned about the tourist factor. The community was coping with the problem by letting in parties of thirty or forty people at a time for quiet guided tours, and there would be five or six such tours per day.

At least, that was the case through the summer. Winter was much quieter, but if tourists were no longer an issue there were other problems, most obviously the low temperature. By all accounts the abbey could get desperately cold. The heating for most of the complex was electric, and it was expensive without being terribly efficient. The insulation was also poor in most of the buildings. I shuddered in the evening chill, and commented on the fact that we were now sitting in shadow in a gorge on the north-western side of the Canigou massif. "That's right," said the nun. "March is a lovely month because that's when the sunshine returns above the mountain's ridges." She reckoned November could be quite pleasant too, but for three months in the middle of winter it would be dark as well as cold.

I was pleased that I had survived my first day, or half-day, in the abbey. I had also had my first meal and found it basic but nourishing. The community were warm, welcoming and accepting of me as a guest. I had committed one small *faux pas* when I entered the chapel for worship earlier in the evening. I knew that Vespers was to be at 5.15pm, followed immediately by the Mass, so I got there early and chose a discreet place to sit, next to the side wall. Only when the community filed in and launched into their worship did I realise that they were segregated. Men were on the right of the chapel and women on the left, and of course I had chosen a seat on the left. But it was not a problem, and I was soon enjoying listening to the singing. There was little in the way of instruments to accompany the songs, but it hardly mattered as all of the people there seemed to be accomplished singers. The Order had its own corpus of musical material which had been written over the years, along with various settings for the psalms, and the small number of worshippers seemed to have no problem in producing beautiful harmonies. I was to find that open intercessory prayer and singing in tongues were ingredients in many of the services – features one might assosciate more with evangelical and Pentecostal worship – and these were blended easily with the more obviously Catholic elements such as the Rosary, prayer to the Blessed Virgin and the Adoration of the Sacrament.

I retreated to bed tired after a long day of exertion – physical, mental and spiritual. I felt contented and strangely at home. My first impressions of this place were warm and positive, and I knew I would not just survive the next two days but enjoy them.

I slept well and was awake before the monastery bell sounded at 7.15am. Having a wash proved almost impossible: everybody else in the building was getting up and using their washbasins at the same time so the water kept cutting out in mine. At least the toilet at the opposite end of the corridor was well stocked with paper and disinfectant, and it had a comprehensive calendar of saints on the wall. There seemed to be a saint for virtually every day of the year. Today, July 29th, was Saint Martha. I was pleased as I had always liked the story of Martha and her sister Mary and felt that there was a lot of psychological mileage in it. I remembered that I had once led a parish Retreat Day based on the characters of the two sisters from Bethany.

At breakfast I indulged in my usual large bowl of *café au lait*, with various bits of bread and jam, plus orange juice and yoghurt. I was sitting next to one of the French women from Bergerac. Her breakfast seemed to consist of a bowl of boiled water with something like a sprig of pine needles floating on the surface. "No wonder she's so slim," I thought. I was about to make a joke out of it, but decided not to. It can be difficult and dangerous translating humour across linguistic boundaries.

Whilst I was staying in the monastery my thoughts tended to go round in circles and they kept revisiting the same topics. This had been the case throughout the walk, but here at St.Martin the focus narrowed down to a few issues, such as prayer, vocation and the monastic vows. As with Patrick Leigh-Fermor's experience at St.Wandrille I found that being in a monastery raised questions about my priorities in life. In Prades a couple of days previously one of my friends from Surrey had asked what I intended to do when my current post expired:

"I don't know for sure," I said.

"Well, what do you want to do?" was Mannfried's follow-up question. I found it a tricky one to answer. My calling as a priest and even as a Christian was not about what I wanted as much as about seeking God's guidance and following what He wanted. Only such a course could lead to fulfilment. But as my friend reasonably said, God is unlikely to call you to something where you will be permanently miserable. There is a sense in which it is perfectly legitimate to ask "what do I want?" and "what would make me happy?"

My friends persisted with their interrogation. "Have you got a long-term ambition?" asked Christine.

"Yes, of course."

"Well, what is it?"

"To meet death cheerfully."

"Very commendable," grunted Mannfried. "But it may not help you much in your search for a job."

I wondered about that, and remembered how Leigh-Fermor had said that the Benedictine monks were encouraged to keep death ever before their eyes, and to pray for a holy death. The paradox was that this aspect of their lifestyle enabled them to be more alive than ever in the meantime. Rosemary Bailey seemed to have reached a similar conclusion in her thoughts about the monks of Corbiac, and about her late brother. The last line in her book had said that "perhaps it is only when you are ready to relinquish everything, as the monks were, that you can fully enter into the moment." It seemed to me that there was a certain kind of inexorable logic to it. After all, what is life in this world if it's not an extended exercise in preparing for death? I knew from my own experience as a priest and pastor that I was better at coping with funerals than weddings. Maybe it is more accurate to say that I always found it difficult to preach at weddings: you have to stand there and talk about God whilst everybody else sits there and thinks about sex.

For a while I had nurtured the suspicion that ultimately a monastery might be the happiest place for me. It was somewhere to renounce the pursuit of worldly pleasure and to concentrate on the worship of God, as part of a community dedicated to the same purpose. Of course the monastic vows look frightening. "Obedience" goes against our contemporary culture and, on the face of it, goes against our desire for self-fulfilment, though at one level it is quite pleasant having somebody to tell you what to do, provided they are also taking the responsibility for it. Children are clearly happier when they are receiving firm but loving discipline which sets boundaries for them. Indeed, one suspects that some youths who have known little love or discipline probably feel happiest in prison, where they find security for the first time.

Likewise "poverty" goes against the grain at a superficial level, though I suspected that there are different types of poverty. Making a conscious lifestyle-decision to renounce

337

wealth is very different from being born into crushing degradation and never having any choice about it. In my case I liked money, but I did not feel I was consumed by the desire to accumulate large amounts of it.

"Chastity" would not be a massive problem either, for I was generally content with my own company. On the current expedition I had only really experienced loneliness once, and that was in the departure lounge at Stansted when I sat there for an hour or so wondering what on earth I was doing. I was about to fly to a distant corner of Europe where I knew nobody and where all I had got for definite was the prospect of a taxi ride to a hotel which I had booked using the internet. But after I had boarded the 'plane I had not felt lonely at all. Solitude did not bother me, and I knew that being on one's own is not the same thing as loneliness. I was more prone to experience the latter when I was with other people, and indeed the loneliest place of all is to be part of a crowd. Occasionally towards the end of my rest days I had begun to feel a little dissatisfied, when I had cleaned myself up and washed my kit, eaten and slept, and when I was facing a second evening in the same restaurant at a table by myself. But that just meant I was keen to get going again the following day with the next stage of the march, and if the rest day had restored my appetite for the battle then it had served its purpose. If you can keep going, with hope in your heart, you don't walk alone. And sometimes, when the going was tough, I had found myself thinking about people I had known at different stages of my life – parents and relatives, friends and enemies, colleagues at work, people dead and people still alive, even teachers I had had in school thirty years before. Their presence was an encouragement and a challenge. With so many of them watching me I could never give up. "Since we are surrounded by so great a cloud of witnesses," says the writer to the Hebrews in the New Testament, "let us run with perseverance the race that is set before us." I could never return from the expedition and tell all those people I had failed. Defeat was not an option.

Of course another aspect of the walk was the presence of God: was He with me or not? I did not always feel like He was there, of course. When things are painful and you are weak He can seem all too absent. But you cannot just go on your feelings either, as they are not always reliable.

The existence or otherwise of God is probably the oldest philosophical question and the most fundamental one, and it is probably the most insoluble too. After all, different people live their lives in this world surrounded by more or less the same evidence and yet they come to diametrically opposite conclusions on the subject. Of course there is no conclusive proof either way. How could there be? How could this universe, with its constraints of space and time, generate proof for the existence of something which is by definition larger than the universe and exists outside that space and time? The universe may supply evidence, but not proof. People come to different conclusions, based no doubt on a multiplicity of reasons, but ultimately based (one suspects) on a deep and irrational gut-feeling. My gut-feeling was that it is absurd to suppose that the entire world around us is purely the chance product of a mass of accidents, with no purpose or intelligence behind it. Indeed, to believe such a thing would (in one sense) take a far greater measure of faith than to believe that the universe is the work of some sort of Higher Being.

Certainly there are some genuine atheists, who have thought things through in a thorough and serious way and decided there is no such Being, and one has to respect their opinion. But I suspect that there are not many people who are serious and consistent in applying their atheism. I remembered arguing with an atheist once, and feeling I had landed a significant blow when the conversation turned to the nature of love. The man admitted that he loved his wife. "But isn't that rather inconsistent?" I asked. "If your atheistic beliefs are actually true, how can you say you love your wife? With all due respect to her, if there is no God and life is merely the random result of accidents, what is your wife? She's just a rather complicated piece of mud with some electricity in it to make it move around." At this point I sensed that our discussion was degenerating in the direction of physical violence, as my opponent seemed upset that I had described his partner in these terms. He felt my comments lacked respect for her. But that was my point, of course. If his atheistic philosophy was accurate then there was no reason to show respect to his wife or anybody else: the logic of atheism leads coldly to the totalitarianism of a communist or fascist state. Of course dreadful atrocities can be committed in the cause of theism too – you only have to look to the Cathar saga to see that – but the point stands that the rational and consistent application of atheism undercuts any notion of human rights. Where there is no God there is no Man either.

I suspect that deep down the vast majority of people know that God exists, in some guise or other. There is too much in life and in our experience of life which tells us it is not purely the consequence of accidents. Obviously there is plenty to disturb and perplex us in this world, and the evidence God serves up for us can seem contradictory and confusing. It is difficult to resolve what He is doing, let alone why. But on balance it looks far more likely to me that He exists than that He does not, and if He exists then it has implications for everything.

"What do you want?" My friends had posed the question in the context of a discussion about jobs and career. But the question is legitimate as a broader one, applying to the whole of life. Of course one can duck the question by answering it superficially: "I'd like a good steak, a decent bottle of wine and a good night's sleep." But beyond that, what are the deeper desires in life? Possibly to find fulfilment by being in the right place at the right time, doing the right thing. But if God exists in a meaningful sense, then the deepest level of longing must (in theory at least) be to know Him and be known by Him, and to know that one is loved by Him.

In the first chapter of John's Gospel, Jesus poses the question to two people who are following him. They are in fact literally following him. We are told that they were disciples of John the Baptist who had seen Jesus and who got up to walk behind him. Jesus turns to them and says, in effect, "what do you want?" The interesting point is that they cannot answer the question, so they change the subject and ask him where he is staying. The two people do not know - or at least they cannot articulate - their deepest desires. Yet they are following Jesus, for something has drawn them to this person who is the Christ. Their answer to the question is, I suppose, half an answer. In asking "where are you staying?" they are really saying that they want to be with him.

At rock-bottom, the deepest desire is to know God and to be known by God, and to feel that one is loved and accepted by Him. As Saint Augustine famously expressed it, "You have made us for Yourself, and our hearts are restless until they find their rest in You." If that is really the case then nothing else in life will ever satisfy completely. The two disciples seem to have been feeling their way towards this sort of conclusion: they were drawn to Christ and wanted to be with Him, but they were unable to express that desire clearly as yet.

We too may be drawn to Christ for all sorts of reasons. Indeed we may never know the reasons, for how can we really ever be certain of our deepest motives for anything we do? Yet we are drawn. He calls us to "come and see where I am staying." It is a call to come and be with him. It is not a call, in the first instance, to do anything: just a call to be with him. In the third chapter of Mark's Gospel "he called twelve to be with

341

him." Later they would be sent out to do things; to preach and heal the sick and so on; but the primary calling was to be with him.

That evening I went to Mass in the chapel. The priest's homily was about Martha, for it was still her day. The talk was all in French but the priest spoke slowly and clearly, and it was not difficult to pick up his main point. Jesus was saying to Martha, "Here I am. Come and be with me. Sit here with me like Mary is doing. You are distracted by your good deeds. What you are doing has its place, but it's not all that important. Whilst I am here, it's important to be with me."

The monastery is about being. It's about being in the presence of God, and being in a relationship with God and with other people. The very existence of the monastery is something of a rebuke to the insane activism of the modern lifestyle. It is also a rebuke to the frenzied rushing of many clergymen. The 19th century Scottish pastor Murray McShane had a notice on his desk which said "my people's greatest need is my personal holiness." Surely that must be the case. What people really want and need from a pastor or priest is somebody who is used to being with God, and who can therefore bring something of the presence and peace of God into their lives. It is a sad spectacle if clergy run around like headless chickens in a state of manic activism, for when they arrive anywhere all they have really got left to offer people is their own busy-ness.

If the monastery is about "being" it is also about prayer and worship, and how these activities continue day after day and year after year, regardless of who comes and goes in the community. The worship and prayer have a life of their own and they continue, soaking into the fabric of the place. So the community has an ongoing essence and a continuity which is greater than any one person who is part of it. In one sense the individual is not important. The community of faith is the important thing, and it is greater than the sum of its parts.

This communal aspect intrigued me. Through community the members belonged to each other, and they belonged to an entity that was somehow larger than the mere total of its members. A simple analogy was provided by the stones in the monastery walls. Each stone was unique; each a different size and shape; each on its own useless in terms of providing shelter. Yet put together these stones combined for a purpose and they served as walls. The New Testament itself uses similar imagery, saying that Christ is himself the cornerstone.

I also sensed that some thought had gone into organising the community. It made good sense that the people I was meeting were not just members of the "community of St.Martin-du-Canigou." They were also part of the much larger Order of the Beatitudes, with its sixty or seventy houses, its liturgy, its own songs and ethos. And most of them would move between houses from time to time. So there was some healthy circulation of blood within the body, to use a different metaphor. It is possibly a better system than one where people just belong to one house and stay there permanently, for then there are dangers that the community might ossify or fossilize. Little empires get built up; tensions become entrenched; habits become so ingrained that they cannot be changed. No doubt any and all of these could still happen up to a point, but on the whole it is likely to be healthier if your particular house is only one of seventy and therefore less likely to succumb to introversion. Presumably the Order provides a measure of oversight from outside, so there is less danger of a single community going off at a tangent and developing into some bizarre cult of its own.

I wondered how the community really worked. During my walk I had made an interesting observation. Occasionally I had come upon groups of walkers and overtaken them, but I had never been overtaken by a group. Even if I was clearly carrying more weight I would still outstrip them over any distance. As I thought about this odd fact I realised that the reason was actually quite simple. If a group is going to remain together and continue to be a group then it has to walk at the speed of its slowest member. If I came upon a group of, say, ten walkers, then it was unlikely that all ten would be faster than I was. I was almost bound to be quicker than at least one of them, and therefore quicker than the group.

So how does a community make progress? It cannot always be constrained by the "speed of the slowest" principle. To do so would not, ultimately, be in the interests of the group or in the interests of any individual, not even the slowest one. It was another conundrum for me to ponder as I strolled around the cloisters and settled in the shade, relishing the silence before the next party of tourists was allowed in. Of course group dynamics will always raise tensions. In my case I had solved all such problems for my expedition at a stroke, by choosing to go alone. It was a decision I did not regret, though I realised that if I were ever to undertake such a walk again I might like to be part of a small team. Even with all the tensions and frustrations a journey is ultimately a richer experience when it is shared with other people. No man is an island, though there can be great advantages in being a peninsula.

In one of my earlier parishes I had been given a cactus plant as a present. It was a large one; roughly two feet high and quite heavy with its tub of gravel. Of course cacti come in all shapes and sizes, and mine had large flat lobes, almost as large as dinner plates. I placed it in a corner of the living room, next to the sofa in a position where it would benefit from any sunshine coming through the window. I knew that I was hopeless when it came to caring for plants. My uncle in South Wales had once got into the Guinness Book of Records for growing the heaviest onion ever recorded, but I had no interest in gardening and any plants unfortunate enough to end up in my house tended to perish quickly.

I knew that the cactus is a remarkable plant, capable of surviving for years in a hot climate with little rainfall. The long roots suck water from deep underground, and the thick leathery skin helps to prevent water loss, enabling it to survive prolonged drought. However, my particular cactus faced danger of a different sort. During a meeting in my home a heavily-built woman sat on the end of the sofa and almost fell off. The cactus took the impact and the top lobe was snapped in half. Mercifully the person involved avoided most of the prickles.

Following this accident I expected the plant to die off. But it survived, and even the part which had been damaged continued to grow. In time it went on to produce flowers. I felt that the plant was saying something about life: injuries may be painful but given time the majority of them heal up. I came to see my cactus plant as a sort of parable. Around the same time I was leading a small group for a number of young men, all of whom had particular problems and who had been damaged in some sense by life. The meetings were exhausting, and at least to begin with my main function was as a referee in the various disputes and arguments. But over time the people in the group became firm friends, and the cactus was a symbol for the group as much as for any of us as individuals. We were a collection of cacti: each had been damaged but we had found new life together and the life came in and through community.

So I was not entirely convinced that the individual always travels faster than the group. He may have a higher speed, but in the long run he may find he is merely going nowhere fast. After all, the Tour cycling demonstrated time and time again that an individual who has broken away is likely to be overhauled by the peloton. I had read somewhere that a similar effect is observable when birds such as geese fly together in a formation: as each bird flaps its wings it helps to create uplift for the bird following so that the potential range of the group is greater than that of a single bird.

Sensing that a fresh batch of tourists was about to invade, I abandoned the cloisters and decided to make use of the shower. It was now mid-afternoon. There was only one shower in my accommodation block but at this time of the day I should not have any competition for it. It was located downstairs, near the entrance to the building, and whilst it was basic it had worked well enough upon my arrival the previous afternoon. But this time it failed to perform to requirements. It waited until I had got my hair full of shampoo and then the water cut out. Once more I was left cursing the plumbing in this place. I tried everything but could only coax the tiniest trickle of water from the showerhead. For ten or fifteen minutes I struggled to use this miniscule supply to rinse the shampoo away. At dinner that evening I would learn that there had been a leak in a pipe somewhere else in the abbey, so the entire water supply had been closed off. Meanwhile I continued with my futile ablutions for a few more minutes before giving up. I wrapped my towel around my waist and emerged from the shower room into the corridor, immediately colliding with a nun. She was hurrying into the building on a mission of mercy to check the errant water supply. It reminded me of the incident in the bathroom back at the *refuge* at Lac d'Oredon, except that there was a curious reversal of roles. This time I was the one with the towel.

Somehow I got enough of the shampoo out of my head to present myself for Vespers and Mass. Earlier in the day I had attended a prayer session which had involved heavy use of the Rosary. The words were intoned repeatedly, in French, and after a while I found they had their own hypnotic rhythm. "Hail Mary, full of grace, the Lord is with thee; blessed art thou amongst women and blessed is Jesus the fruit of thy womb." The response, also repeated endlessly, was "Holy Mary, mother of God, pray for us poor sinners now and at the hour of our death." The *angelus* prayers, and the Adoration of the Sacrament which I had also attended, raised some obvious questions for anybody coming from a more Protestant background. In the chapel I turned over in my mind some of the issues, such as the appropriateness of praying to Mary, and the dogmas about her Immaculate Conception and Bodily Assumption. Obviously these were traditions which resonated with vast numbers of Catholics, but for which objective evidence was thin. It seemed to me that the issues were important at one level, and there was plenty of scope for debate over them, but at another level what did it matter what I thought in any case? Catholicism has a great strength in the way that it emphasises the Faith, (with a capital "F"). This is the Faith of the Church, as opposed to the faith (with a small "f") of the individual believer. It's no accident that the rise of Protestantism coincided with the development of the printing press and the translation of the Bible into the vernacular, and it quickly led to the situation where every believer had his own "paper Pope" and became his own arbiter of theological truth. Since its inception in the 16th century Protestantism has been bedevilled by division after division as churches have split and split again, sometimes over points of theological dispute but just as often over loyalty to leading personalities. In the Catholic worship I experienced a little of the joy of being part of something universal – plugging into the Faith which had supposedly been believed by all true Christians at all times and in all places.

During the Adoration of the Sacrament I contemplated the consecrated wafer in the monstrance, and enjoyed inhaling the incense which was wafting around. But even if I had not enjoyed the worship I would still have felt it was a valuable discipline to attend it. The point about a discipline, and the value of it, lies in the fact that you do it when you feel like it and you do it when you don't feel like it. Either way you do it. Again the feelings and opinions of the individual on a particular day are less significant than the fact that the activity continues and is ongoing. And if a discipline is pursued over time it may become a habit and become more natural, with the consequence that you actually feel more like doing it anyway.

Again I could see an analogy with physical exercise. Since I was a teenager I have been running regularly. I suppose it began at an age when I was full of energy and wanted to burn off the stress of homework and exam revision. Since then I have kept running, several times per week. Often I have not felt like going out to run, especially if it is cold, dark, wet or windy. But on the whole I have gone out regardless of the conditions. As a result I got fitter and was better able to run even when I was not in the mood for it. And often I found that whilst I had been reluctant to go out and train, I actually enjoyed it once I got going. The running, the effort and the pain became habits, and maybe even became addictive, and the fitness became a habit too.

Prayer is similar, in the sense that to make progress you have to persist with it whether you feel like it or not, because on many occasions you won't feel like it. That is when a Daily Office or something like St.Benedict's pattern of offices can be so valuable. Over time you get used to praying, and maybe reach a point where it feels odd if you are deprived of the opportunity to pray.

I suspect that nobody can really teach you to pray. You learn to pray by praying. Of course other people might provide advice, guidance and encouragement. But if you want to learn you have to do it. And it is probably easier if you are involved in a group or community which is also pursuing prayer: better than trying to go it alone. I was enjoying being involved in this community of prayer at Canigou, even if I was very much on the periphery of it. Of course I was not a proper member of the community: I had made no commitment to it and taken no vows. The service books were unfamiliar and everything was in French, except for some tuneful outbursts of *glossolalia*. In the chapel services I was hovering between being an observer and a participant, balancing in a position which was both privileged and uncomfortable. At the Mass I felt sad that I could not receive the sacrament because, of course, the Church of England is not in full communion with the Bishop of Rome. I did not know how the priest would have responded had I asked to receive the wafer, and I did not want to cause him any embarrassment. I suppose I could have asked for eucharistic hospitality on the grounds that I was an impossible distance from the nearest Anglican church and was missing the sacrament, not having received it for the duration of the expedition, but I did not think of that at the time. In any case, there was plenty in the worship which I was finding of value. I particularly liked the way each service started. The participants simply turned up at the appointed hour and began their time of praise with the minimum of fuss. It was logical really. The rest of their lives were dedicated to worship in one form or another, so what they did in the chapel was just a continuation of the prayer and contemplation in which they were already immersed. It was refreshing to have none of the ghastly "notices" which pollute Anglican services in England and turn so much worship into a mildly religious version of News at Ten.

Dinner that evening was going to be eaten in the open air again, on the triangular terrace above the gorge. As I was waiting for the meal to commence I was standing once more with my back to the low wall, with the gorge behind me, and I noticed that King was looking disgruntled. In fact he was looking at me. If he decided to charge then that great mass of meat and fur would rapidly assume the momentum of the irresistible force, and I knew that I was not the immovable object. My strategy for survival would have to involve standing perfectly still in the face of his thunderous approach. Then, at the last instant, it would have to be a quick side-step, and maybe I could twist around in time to see the great beast sailing across the wall and continuing in the general direction of Spain. And then gravity would have ministered to him. If there is such a place as a heaven for dogs King would have entered it in style, probably destroying several trees down in the gorge in the process. It would be a sad end, and I did not relish the thought that I might be held responsible for the demise of the monastery's great loafing mascot. Fortunately at that moment the animal was distracted, as one of the monks emerged from the kitchen carrying a bowl of food and a large bone for him.

After dinner I sat on a bench outside the chapel, on the level above the cloisters, and enjoyed the last warmth of the day's sunshine. Repeatedly I was drawn to the Romanesque architecture with its rounded arches and pillars, the square tower, the curve of the apse and the simplicity of the lines. The stonework was yellow and warm in the sun. In northern Europe the architecture came to be dominated by the pointed angles and arches of the later Gothic style. These shapes could bear greater loads, especially once they were reinforced by the flying buttress. But the design was not purely about the pragmatics of engineering. It was aesthetic too. In the north the pointed arches provided definition in the flat grey light. Here in the south the sunlight was brighter, and the arches could afford to be rounded and more "natural."

The Romanesque style (known as "Norman" in Britain) coincided with the rise of monasticism and the wave of church building in the 11th century. Surviving Roman ruins such as arenas, aquaducts and triumphal arches provided the models. The Roman basilica was the prototype for the standard church, with a central nave taller than the side aisles, thus allowing an extra set of windows above the rounded pillars and arches. Of course one of the finest examples of Norman architecture, with its stone barrel-vaulted roofing, is to be seen in Durham Cathedral. During my years in Surrey and Cumbria I made regular visits and found the cathedral to be a refuge: a sacramental place. Fleeing from the pressures and tensions of parish life I often found that the sanctuary knocker on the main door was appropriately symbolic. Entering the vast building I liked the sensation of being enveloped in the darkness with its subdued echoes. I would choose a pew in the nave, next to one of the columns with its simple but attractive decorative pattern, and I would sit for a while gazing at the stained glass of the Rose Window at the east end, high above the tomb of Saint Cuthbert. I was happy sitting there, and more so in the autumn or winter when it was raining or grey outside and the votive candles were flickering on their stands. For a few minutes I was back in the Middle Ages and fancied that I was somehow part of an invisible network of cathedrals; at the end of a spiritual line linking Durham to York and Canterbury and to the continent beyond. A line linking me to Rouen and Chartres and Paris, to Strasbourg and Cologne, and then over the Alps to Milan and Florence and ultimately to Rome itself at the other end of the chain. After a while I would return from this semi-hypnotic state and would wander around the cloisters and maybe around the peninsula above the River Wear. And if the weather was bright that was no problem either. The most uplifting days can be in autumn, when the atmosphere is clean and crisp with the first hints of frost. There is a freshness, for the autumnal rains have cleansed the air of the summer's dust, and in bright sunlight the leaves – brown and yellow and maroon – surpass description against the background of a blue sky. There is a paradox in the beauty, of course, for in soaking up the colours of those leaves I am staring at death, but at the same time the low angle of the sun casts long shadows and the orange quality of the light hints at glory. On such an afternoon it is obvious that God exists and it appears ridiculous to suppose otherwise - there is no need for superfluous arguments about the atheist's wife being a lump of mud.

My thoughts of orange light brought me back to Canigou, where the sun was now slipping away and the gorge was again being immersed in shadow. The same familiar issues and questions circled around in my head. What did I really want? Was the monastic community a way forward for myself, or a way forward for the Church as a whole, even in Britain in the 21st century? In a bout of vanity I allowed myself to daydream and tried to imagine building a Canigou-style monastery in England. After all, there's not much point being a mad monk if you are not allowed a few crazy dreams. Swiftly I came to the conclusion that the idea was impractical: it would cost a lot of money and the Romanesque architecture might look out of place in Milton Keynes, or wherever. Nevertheless, a place of seclusion and solitude, of stillness and peace; a place of worship focussed on the sacraments, in which prayer is natural and continuous; a community which offers simple hospitality; surely these ingredients are still as relevant today as they have ever been.

One of the abbey guidebooks described the work of the second great restorer of St.Martin-du-Canigou, the Benedictine monk Bernard de Chabannes. At the end of his restoration project the monk received a warm and generous letter of appreciation from Henry L'Heureux, Bishop of Perpignan, (and therefore a successor of the first great restorer, Monseigneur de Carsalade). In his letter Bishop L'Heureux wrote:

"The experience of all those who have seen the sun rise and the twilight descend upon this Abbey nestling among the crags of Canigou, is to have known indescribable beauty, nature inviolate, a silence so complete that the voice of another Being can be heard, the voice of the God of Sinai and Tabor. Who

352

will say that this dialogue is not modern Man's most fundamental need?"

I agreed wholeheartedly with these comments, except that I might quibble with the inclusion of the word "modern." Modern Man, whoever *he* is, does not need the dialogue with God any more or any less than his ancestors - or any more or any less than those generations as yet unborn.

By now it was getting chilly on the terrace above the cloisters, so I retreated indoors and went to bed.

Chapter 13.

Some desperate glory.

I slept well but woke early. As is so often the case, fear had come in the last couple of hours before daylight when the night seemed to be at its darkest. I did not even know what was making me afraid. Actually I did. It was partly fear that I would fail with my walk. When it resumed I would have only four days, or at the most five, in which to complete the task. I should be able to cover the distance in that time. But it was the first part which was worrying me; the ascent up the side of the Canigou.

I was concerned because the map suggested that it should only take a couple of hours from the monastery to the Col de Segales. However, the previous afternoon I had gone out for a stroll and had noticed a signpost which indicated that the col was four hours away. It made me think that I would be facing a rough trail. The real concern was that if I got lost and was forced to retreat I would have wasted a day and I would be stranded with the bulk of the Canigou between myself and the coast. I could always walk around the mountain on lower ground, but that would consume a further couple of days and would leave me with no chance of reaching the Mediterranean in time. It would be ridiculous to have walked so far across France and yet to fail; possibly within sight of the sea. But it was a serious possibility. I knew I would have to make rapid progress on the Thursday morning, aiming for Arles-sur-Tech.

So I had woken early because the fear of failure was playing on my mind. But there was a second demon upsetting my

354

slumbers - the fear of success. Just a few days more and I might actually succeed in my project and reach Banyuls, but then I would have to return to "normal" life. I had found courage to do the walk thus far, but soon I would have to find courage to continue living beyond the walk. I did not relish the prospect of completing the expedition. Uncertainty over the future and a host of other concerns crowded in.

Somehow I reasoned that none of these things added up to a sound basis for fear. Then the dawn brought daylight and another dose of worship in the chapel before breakfast, and with that I felt reassured. I had come this far, and therefore I could go on. At Mass later in the day the priest delivered a homily about Christ walking on the water. I was beginning to like this priest – he was a fatherly figure and in his homilies he seemed to have the uncanny knack of talking about whatever I was thinking already. Again he was speaking in French, of course, but the gist of his talk was clear enough. He was saying that for the Jewish people of Jesus' day the Sea of Galilee was a place of fear, full of monsters and demons. As fishermen some of them were earning their living from the surface of the lake, but nevertheless the depths still frightened them. So Jesus came to them walking on the water, treading on their demons, monsters and fears and saying to them "it is I, do not be afraid."

So that was the question which seemed to be confronting me on this, my final day at the monastery. "Why are you afraid?" I added this to the previous day's question, "what do you want?" and filed it away inside my head. If we assume for the moment that God can and does speak to us, these questions seemed to be the main thrust of the message he was addressing to me. Of course that is a big assumption for people to make today, yet I suspect that God is probably speaking to us most of the time. The problem is that we are not listening. Or we are tuned-in to the wrong wavelength, distracted like Martha by the pressures of the day and rendered deaf by the tyranny of the urgent. I reckoned that these questions would probably stay with me when I came to leave the little community at St.Martin, and I would take them with me along with a few photographs and notes, a couple of booklets and some icons which I had purchased as souvenirs.

During the day I spent some time in the chapel, kneeling on a cushion and concentrating on a wooden statue of the Virgin and Child, which was standing on a table about twenty feet away. In fact I think it was a copy of a similar but larger wooden carving downstairs in the crypt, and the one in the crypt had itself been carved to replace a magnificent work of art which had been stolen some years earlier. As I stared at the statue I allowed my imagination to wander, and I thought about the "Canigou illusion" I had experienced a couple of days previously. As I walked towards the mountain I had the impression that it never drew closer, but just grew larger. What about my statue? The Virgin and the infant Jesus looked benign and harmless. I could patronise them, if I liked, or I could choose to ignore them for that matter. After all, they were only eighteen inches high.

But suppose that was an illusion too? I estimated that the statue was twenty feet away, and indeed there was a wall – the curved stone wall of the chapel – behind it. I let my imagination take away the wall. The statue still looked twenty feet away and eighteen inches high. But suppose, as I moved towards it, that it did not get any closer but just grew larger? What if the apparent size of my little statue was an illusion, and what I could actually see was thousands of miles away, and enormous? What if it was millions of miles away out in space and truly massive, far larger than the earth? Then my attitude would be different. The benign Virgin and Child would be huge and intimidating, and would command the attention and respect of a mere worm such as myself. And what if they were further away again, in fact several light years away, and were actually the size of some of the nebulae, those vast clouds of dust and gas which are sometimes glimpsed through the Hubble telescope and which are light years across and have stars forming inside them even now?

It was a curious thought. In one sense a silly train of thought. But in another sense a perfectly reasonable one. After all, if the figures depicted in that wooden statue truly exist, and if they are those whom the Catholic Faith proclaims them to be, then they are in a very real way bigger than the Eagle Nebula, larger than our whole cluster of galaxies and greater than the universe itself. And even if I cannot perceive them directly as such, they can certainly see me in all of my miserable wretchedness.

If time and space are themselves contained within God, then He is present at all times and in all places. They are all equally accessible to Him; equally immediate; equally "now" and "here." For such a God one day is the same as a thousand years. Jesus is the same, yesterday, today and tomorrow, because for Him all of them are equally "today." A million light years is no distance and an aeon of time is no obstacle, if you are holding them in the palm of your hand. Such a Great Unknown is awesome. How much more awesome if that Unknown chooses to make itself Known, expressing Himself through an incarnation and choosing a specific point in space and time to reveal Himself in material form. Again it comes back to the scandal of the particular, that God should choose to come in one time and place as one form of animal life, as a human being in the shape of Jesus of Nazareth.

From our perspective, having to respond to that unique initiative, it is impossible to grasp the mystery fully. We cannot begin to understand how He could empty Himself of some of His divine attributes for a season of thirty years or so in order to live a fully human life.

357

Yet maybe there is a sense in which, even in shedding Himself of some of His divine attributes, the Incarnation was actually the most fulfilling thing that God could do. To look at it in a stupidly anthropocentric way, it must be a lonely job - being God. How much more exciting to come as one of the creatures whom He had allowed to evolve within His universe, and to show Himself to them as one of their own. And not just to reveal Himself, but to raise their humanity into the realms of the divine. I realised that one of the subtexts for my whole expedition across France had been the quest to find faith – or to retain faith – when so many of our experiences can suggest to us that life is pointless, cruel and absurd. Faced with the reality of a world which is both savage and comical I usually felt that the more convincing responses were to do with the Incarnation.

I allowed my thoughts to drift back into the chapel, and to adjust to its more immediate dimensions. All was still, and the wooden statue appeared to be only twenty feet away. It was once again, as far as I could see, about eighteen inches tall. On odd occasions, in a good time of prayer, I have felt as though time was standing still, and felt that space ceased to be normal. My feet, normally about sixty inches away from my head, could seem to be hundreds of miles away. It doesn't happen often, probably because I don't often pray seriously enough for long enough, but it is odd on those occasions when you sense that in God's sight the dimensions of the room in which you are praying might actually be infinitely larger or smaller than you normally perceive them to be. But then again it is not so odd, if we ourselves are really only thoughts in the mind of the Creator.

And what is "prayer" in any case? I knew I was no expert on it, and not even very good at it. But I realised that for many people, prayer means asking God for things. That certainly has its place, and I would not want to belittle it, but if prayer consists solely of supplication then the whole exercise is seriously reduced and appears rather infantile. Surely our relationship with God ought to be on a deeper level than that. At the very least it needs to involve praise and adoration, thanksgiving and gratitude, confession and remorse. Not just a shopping-list of requests. Prayer should not be about me pestering God as though I can coax Him into changing His mind. It is surely more about Him changing me – getting me to live in accordance with His will. (And, incidentally, if that happens then I am more likely to request things which accord with His genuine pleasure in any case).

Maybe that is one way to learn to pray. Just talk to God. Tell Him what is on your mind. And go on telling Him, until eventually you reach the point where you have run out of things to say. And then you have to shut up and listen to Him, and that is when the real prayer begins. When we listen to Him.

At rock bottom it comes full circle, back to that tricky question – "what do you really want?" Or, to slant it slightly differently, "what do you really need?" Let us suppose that we accept for a moment the proposition that God actually exists in some meaningful sense; which I take to mean that He is a "person" as opposed to being a nebulous entity or simply some sort of codeword for our human values and aspirations. If He truly exists and has acted to create and redeem human beings, what then is our deepest need? Surely it must be to establish communication with such a God; to hear from Him and, better still, to hear that He loves us. To feel that we are enfolded in His love is surely our deepest longing, however cleverly we might try to disguise that need and hide it from other people or even from ourselves. Indeed, we humans are inclined to invest extraordinary amounts of time, energy and money in doing almost anything to hide from God and from His love, seeking to clutter our lives with any number of distractions and obstructions in the hope that these will protect us from Him. Why are we so afraid of that which is our deepest need?

At dinner on that Wednesday evening I felt pangs of sadness. In the morning I would be leaving this little community at St.Martin, and leaving with warm memories of a special place and special people. Or maybe it would be more accurate to say that I had met perfectly normal people, but people for whom God was a serious reality in their midst. I asked them how I should pay for my stay, and was told that there was no charge, but that if I wanted to make a donation there was a box in a discreet corner in the refectory. After dinner I slipped into the refectory and located the box, simultaneously discovering that the bank notes in my wallet added up to a nice round number. Deciding to follow the example of Saint Martin with his cloak I put half of my money in the box and kept the other half for myself.

It was still not nine o'clock, and I did not fancy returning to my room quite yet. The sky was darkening as I slipped back into the chapel, and since early evening thunder had been rumbling; a muffled barrage of heavy artillery which was out of sight but clearly firing somewhere beyond the ridges of the gorge and striking high up on the Canigou massif.

The chapel was totally dark, except for the glow of the little red lamp above the tabernacle where it flickered away, guarding the reserved sacrament. Suddenly I felt afraid again. Just two hours earlier I had been in this very place, but it had been brightly lit and it had been filled with about forty people singing their praise as part of the Mass. Now I was back here again, but this time there was nobody between me and God. With difficulty I fumbled my way into one of the pews. It was unnerving being here, for I did not feel totally alone.

Then, after a few minutes of sitting in silence, I realised that I *was not* alone. One of the nuns was praying in silence on the other side of the chapel. Somehow I had sensed her presence and felt the gravity of another person, even before my ears detected the faint sound of her breathing. Gradually my eyes adjusted to the darkness, and I could make out the outline of a figure deep in the shadows.

After another ten minutes or so the nun got up and left, and shortly afterwards so did I. The monastery is a strange place. At first sight it appears tranquil. Yet it is a harsh environment. It takes all the values and assumptions of our modern world and stands them on their heads. It is a place which can strip you naked before God, if you will allow it to. Potentially it is a place of white-hot intensity and searing pain. As such it can sound ferociously threatening, yet it can also be a gateway to liberation. At first sight a monastery looks like a prison, but many of the inmates will testify that it is actually a pathway to true freedom.

As I returned to my room torrential rain began to fall, cooling and cleansing the night air. I lay awake for a while, and it was peaceful and comforting to hear the rain rattling against the roof and window. I wondered whether one day I too would become a monk.

My anxiety about the forthcoming day had led me to consider setting out early, before the service of *laudes* and before the monastery had been roused from its slumbers by the chapel bell. However, on reflection I had decided that it might look ungracious towards my hosts if I skulked off under the cover of darkness. Besides, missing breakfast would count against me on a day when lunch was likely to consist of a handful of biscuits and a couple of chocolate bars. Studying my map in more detail I had come to accept that Arles-sur-Tech was an unrealistic target for the day's hike. The fearsome initial ascent to the Col de Segales appeared to be five to six kilometres long, with a height gain of 3000 feet. All of it would be on steep wooded hillsides following a trail which might not be well marked. Even if I beat the signposted time of four hours it would still leave me with a long traverse around the Canigou massif to the Refuge de Cortalets, and from there it would be a

361

further six or seven hours down to Arles. And all of this when four out of the previous five days had been devoid of physical exercise. The only realistic option would be to stop at the *refuge* that night, and proceed to Arles the on the following day, which would be a Friday.

All of this was logical enough, but it meant that I would probably still be walking towards Banyuls on the following Monday, with my flight leaving Perpignan on the Tuesday. It was cutting things a little too close for comfort. Throughout my expedition I had fancied the idea of reaching Banyuls with a couple of days to spare, so that I could laze around and celebrate my triumph. But on reflection I figured that it might be a good thing to avoid too much time in Banyuls. I had a suspicion that once the walk had finished I would feel pretty flat and maybe quite depressed. It is often the way when you have spent a lot of time and effort in building up to something significant, such as a family wedding or an important sporting event for example. Even if the occasion is a success the aftermath can feel like a disappointment, for the adrenaline and energy have suddenly gone and depression kicks in. Maybe it would not be such a bad thing to reach Banyuls on the Monday, send a couple of postcards, dip my feet in the sea and then catch a train up to Perpignan.

So in the end I left the monastery in a civilised fashion, having attended worship and eaten breakfast. I was still underway by 9.15am. I grimaced as I stepped out of the main door and it snapped shut behind me, for it reminded me of Patrick Leigh-Fermor's experience. In essence he had written that he found it difficult to adjust to life in the monastery, but ten times harder to adjust back in the opposite direction when he eventually left the institution to return to the world outside. I grimaced for a second time a few seconds later as I passed the sign saying that the Col de Segales was four hours away.

Generally in the mountains you find that if the locals have erected such a sign it is best to believe it.

The path was steep and twisting, but I felt strong and was soon gaining height without undue stress. Maybe the four days of rest since my arrival in Prades the previous Friday had done me good. My main concern was the track, for if I lost it I knew I would be in trouble. There is nothing as tiring as thrashing around in woodland on a hillside when you are lost, as I had found when I attempted to take a short cut out of Gourette three weeks earlier. However, this path seemed to be clearly defined for most of the way, and the frequent markings in yellow or red paint were a tremendous aid to navigation, besides being a great encouragement. Powered by adrenaline and my latent anxiety I stormed upwards, determined to get to the col as quickly as possible, and scrambling over a variety of treetrunks and rocks as the path cut back and forwards across the mountainside.

Eventually I came to a junction in the pathways, and broke into a broad grin as I spotted a familiar symbol; two short lines of paint, one red and one white, parallel to each other and about four inches long. I was reunited at last with my old friend, the GR10. The "col" itself was something of a disappointment, being little more than a junction in the wooded pathways rather than a distinct geographical feature. I did not waste time scouting around but turned north immediately and followed the path along a contour. It was pleasant to be ambling on level ground for once, and glancing down I could make out Vernet-les-Bains, far below and about five miles away to the north-west. Then, to my amazement, the monastery became visible, perched on the edge of its gorge, nearly two miles away and some 3000 feet below my vantage point.

I struggled on, working my way north and then east on a level or descending trail. By early afternoon I had passed the little hut marked as the Refuge de Bonne-Aigue and I was ascending once more, heading for a point below the Pic-du-Joffre. By this stage I was feeling weak and tired, with little of the energy of the morning. Indeed, I realised that the morning's effort had drained me for the day. The decision to stop at the Refuge de Cortalets was clearly a wise one, and it looked even wiser when my water ran out with an hour of walking still to go.

I hauled myself wearily up a steep section of the track towards a cluster of boulders, and found that another view was opening out to the north. Prades looked ridiculously tiny, seven or eight miles away. It was strange to think that I had friends from Surrey down there, and I wondered whether I ought to wave, but even if they were standing in the open looking up at the mountain we would never have seen each other at that distance. They would have been invisible: smaller than the ants at my feet. Even the Abbey of St.Michel-de-Cuxa looked minute. I could just make out its position, at the end of a long straight stretch of road, but curiously I could not see the great square tower which is normally its distinguishing feature.

Behind me to the south rose the great bulk of Canigou itself, and ranges of mountains were visible to the south-west, west and round to the north. I seemed to be above them, or at least level with most of their summits. The horizon was sharply defined against the pale azure of the sky as it led out into the infinity of space, and above my head it appeared a deeper blue, punctuated by the occasional cloud. It was one of the best views I had enjoyed on the entire expedition, and I found it impossible to gaze at it and simultaneously take seriously the proposition that God does not exist.

But then I looked to the north-east and I blinked a couple of times, slowly realising what I could see. It was only a thin line, and I could not even tell whether it was yellow or white or grey in the haze. But it was definitely there, thirty or forty miles away. I could see a beach, and beyond it the water of the

Mediterranean Sea. In an instant optimism flooded through my veins – it looked like I was really going to succeed after all. It had been a desperately hard exercise at times, over the previous five-and-a-half weeks, but deep down I had never really doubted that I would win. Yet it was shocking and overwhelming, to get this sudden visual proof that I really was approaching my goal, and that victory was within my grasp.

Somebody was coming down the path ahead of me, so I sorted out my kit and set off once more. Of course there was still hard work to do. It was roughly fifty miles to Banyuls, which is located on something of a promontory jutting out into the Mediterranean, and it would probably take four days to get there. Of course it was possible that an accident – a twisted ankle or whatever – could rob me of my triumph even at this stage. But the path I was climbing, which had been so wearisome only thirty minutes earlier, suddenly seemed to have no gradient at all. As I approached the Refuge de Cortalets I paused again to take in the view of the imposing Canigou, the sacred mountain of the Catalans, with its summit looking tantalisingly close from my foreshortened perspective.

It would have been good to ascend this, the last great summit in the Pyrenean chain at just over 9000 feet. But the task would have required greater time and energy than I had available, so I contented myself by gazing up at it, just as I had with the first great peak in the range, La Rhune, some thirty-nine days earlier. In fact the first recorded ascent of Canigou had been made in the 13th century by Pedro III of Aragon. He tried to keep his trip secret, as in those days climbing the mountain would have been considered a scandalous and probably blasphemous thing to do. Again it is a reminder that the Alps and Pyrenees were out of bounds to all but a handful of shepherds, chamois hunters and crystal gatherers until relatively recently, and the concept of using the mountains for sport and recreation only really dates from the 19th century.

The Canigou is symbolic of the unity between French Catalonia and Spanish Catalunya, and every year on the Eve of the Feast of John the Baptist a great fire is lit on its peak and carried down by torches to light bonfires in the surrounding villages. However, it is also a dangerous place: roughly three hundred people have died on it, mostly in electrical storms and air crashes. The hazard for aircraft is that their navigational instruments are confused by the magnetism of the iron ore deep within the mountain. In fact during the 16th century iron ore mined in Catalonia was in demand throughout Europe, and with wood available for charcoal and water for power (at least during the winter) the Catalans had got most of the ingredients required to start an industrial revolution. However, my mind was drawn more readily to the dangers for aircraft. In a few days time I should be taking off from the airport in Perpignan, just a few miles away to the north. These gloomy thoughts reminded me of a snatch of conversation I had heard back in the villa in Prades. One of the Home Counties set had been lamenting the death of a friend:

"Well what happened to him?" somebody asked.

"Oh, the usual sort of thing. He was a playboy aviator who flew into a mountain."

The Refuge de Cortalets, run by the Club Alpin Francais, turned out to be quite a luxurious establishment, with a staff cooking and serving meals besides running a bar. My shower was cold, but only because I had got into it before I realised that one had to buy a token and feed it into a box to trigger three minutes of warm water. Dinner was an excellent four courses with soup, meat and pasta, cheese and dessert, and I ate it sitting at a table with a French couple and their schoolgirl daughter. They seemed to speak no English at all, and my French improved dramatically even during this one meal as I dredged up long-forgotten vocabulary from my subconscious. Wine added to the convivial atmosphere as I polished off my own bottle and helped them to finish theirs. In the monastery I had not missed alcohol at all, but after seven hours of walking this drink was more than welcome. After dinner I took a brief stroll outside. An icy wind was blowing down from the Canigou, whilst in the distance Perpignan was illuminated by the last rays of the sinking sun.

Friday was another day, and indeed a new month. I recorded the fact in my diary, remembering that the last time I had started a new month I had been at the Chalet d'Iraty, about to embark on the short walk down to Larrau. It felt like a very long time ago. This coming day, the first of August, I would descend to Arles-sur-Tech, and beyond that it was only three days to Banyuls.

From the Chalet de Cortalets I headed east, circling around the Canigou massif on footpaths and vehicle tracks which, for the most part, followed a level contour. Out to the east the ascending sun was reflecting off the surface of the Mediterranean. After a few hours there was a stiff little climb towards the Col de la Cirere, and for no apparent reason my right knee decided to hurt on the uphill strides. I didn't think it could be too serious, as it wasn't hurting on the level or downhill stretches, but nevertheless it was painful and a little worrying. Eventually I reached a bar and restaurant at the Auberge de Batere. Perusing the menu, which was painted on the wall, I decided to order an omelette, partly for the sake of variety and partly in the hope of getting something tasty and nutritious.

"We can't do omelette today," said the girl behind the bar.

"Okay. In that case I guess I'll have the *plat du jour*, please."

"The *plat du jour* is finished."

"I see. So what exactly have you got?"

"The *assiette des charcuteries*."

"That sounds fine. I'll have one of those, then."

The *assiette* turned out to be very good – a plate of various cold meats with pate and gherkins thrown in for good measure and plenty of bread. The next problem was drink, as the choice seemed to consist of wine and it came in glazed jugs in multiples of half a litre. The prospect of cold *rose* was enticing, so I opted for one of those. Almost a pint of wine is quite a lot at lunchtime, so I told myself it was compensation for several days of temperance at the monastery. France can have that sort of effect upon a man: the culture is sufficiently seductive to convince you that drinking large amounts of fermented grape in the middle of the day is both natural and healthy. To soak up the alcohol I rounded off my meal with a slice of *tarte aux pommes* and a large *café au lait*.

Hillwalking whilst drunk can be an interesting experience, though probably not one to be recommended. I experienced no pain or discomfort during the first part of the descent to Arles-sur-Tech, but I did have one or two difficulties with navigation. Just a few minutes after lunch I reached the so-called Col de la Descargue, which in reality was little more than a bend in the road. The GR10 was poorly marked at this corner, but after a short search I realised that the proper route ran down a gully to the left of a low hilltop. From there the path descended for the next three hours, partly on rocks, partly on vehicle tracks and mostly on dust, picking its way through rough and scrubby vegetation. The temperature, which had been high at lunchtime, rose yet further with every kilometre of the descent, and by the time I reached Arles my water had run out and thirst was asserting itself.

The most famous feature in Arles is the so-called Holy Tomb in the courtyard of the 11th century Benedictine abbey in the centre of the town. The marble coffin could date back as far as the fourth century, and is held by many to be miraculous owing to its ability to fill with water when there is no apparent source. The water itself is reckoned by some to have healing

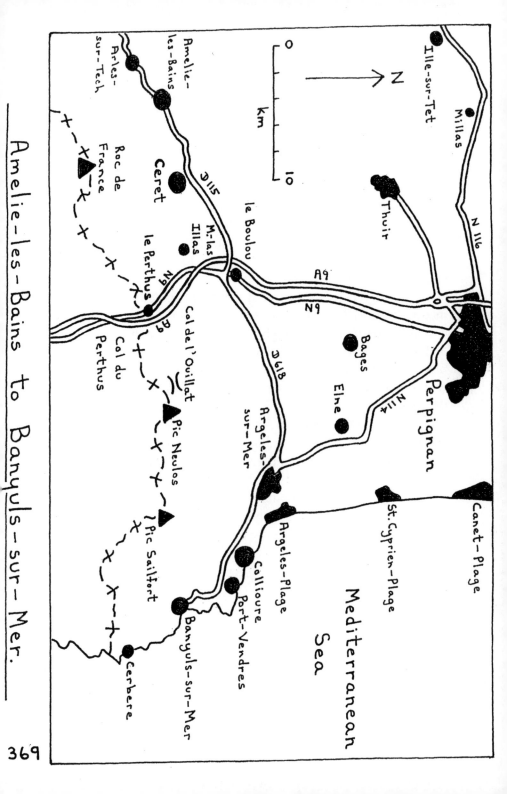

Amelie-les-Bains to Banyuls-sur-Mer.

369

properties. These phenomena are popularly linked to the tomb's use, during the 10th century, as a temporary resting place for the bones of two martyrs which had been brought to Arles from Rome. Various enquiries and scientific investigations have failed to account for the source of the water, which may be produced in volumes of over one hundred gallons per year.

By this stage I felt that any water, holy or not, would help my cause no end. At a bar I asked whether they served iced tea, and when the waitress answered in the affirmative I startled her by ordering two of them. After that it took a few minutes to establish that there was only one hotel in Arles, and it was already full. This was not good news, for the next hotels were in Amelie-les-Bains and it was several miles down the road. In a small supermarket I bought four litres of water, two apples and a couple of bars of chocolate, plus a fresh packet of biscuits and some peanuts. If the hotels in Amelie were full I would need these provisions to survive a night or two out on the hills.

It took an hour to walk to Amelie, weighed down by my extra food and water. The first hotel I tried was full, but at the second one I struck oil and secured a tiny room on the third floor. It had everything I needed, which was a shower and a bed. Moreover my morale had risen during the walk along the main road, as I had realised that I could turn my failure to find accommodation in Arles to my advantage. If I was prepared to walk on roads and country lanes for most of the next day, a Saturday, I could go through Ceret and Maureillas-las-Illas to pick up the GR10 again in le Perthus. I could then cross the motorway at the wretched Col de Perthus and a further couple of hours ascent should get me to the *gite d'etape* at Col de l'Ouillat. In this way I would effectively have completed two days of the GR10 route in one, and it would leave me with the prospect of reaching the Mediterranean on the Sunday evening after all.

It was a bold plan, and possibly a sound one, but it led to a miserable day of toil on the Saturday. I made a good start, and reached Maureillas-las-Illas in only three hours. I celebrated by sitting at a table on a narrow pavement outside a bar on the shady side of a street, consuming a glass of water flavoured with peach syrup. But then things began to go wrong. I made a stupid navigational error as I left the village, following a signpost to le Perthus without realising that it was for motorists rather than pedestrians. The road led me across country and briefly under the A9 motorway before it looped back and deposited me on another main road, the N9. I had little choice other than to follow this for a kilometre or so, until I could get off it and rejoin my original route on country lanes. Yet even this was difficult, and I soon reached a point where none of the lanes on my map seemed to correspond to the reality on the ground. So I was back onto the N9 for the last three or four kilometres to le Perthus, plodding along the narrow verge. It was a miserable way to walk – hot, noisy and dangerous – and it was depressing to get a close-up view of the mass of litter and rubbish which had been tossed into the gutters beside the road.

Eventually I approached le Perthus and stopped at a wayside dining area to restock my water supplies and buy a couple of tins of iced tea. A woman who was serving drinks from a caravan took it on herself to correct my French pronunciation. For a moment I felt irritated and flushed with anger, but then I realised she was only trying to be helpful. She was telling me that when I said "*merci beaucoup*" I was getting the final syllable wrong, and I was actually saying "*cou*" which is the French for "neck" but also the slang for "anus." In retrospect I wished somebody had pointed this out to me six weeks earlier. I had just walked across France, thinking I was saying "many thanks," but in fact saying "thank you, beautiful arse" to virtually every person I had met.

Six hours out from Amelie-les-Bains and I was back on the GR10 route, passing under the motorway for the second time and ascending a lane. The frontier toll-booths at the Col du Perthus looked pretty much how I remembered them from the 1980's. The place had not changed and it certainly had not improved. As the afternoon grew yet hotter I plodded onwards, but in spite of drinking plenty of water my strength was ebbing away. It took the best part of three hours to get from le Perthus to the *gite* at the Col d'Ouillat, and it reminded me increasingly of the ghastly last stage to Montsegur two weeks previously. That march, coincidentally also on a Saturday afternoon, had left me on the floor a couple of times, and the climb towards Col d'Ouillat likewise saw me lying down, feeling weak and slightly sick. After a few minutes of rest I struggled up, heaved the rucksack onto my shoulders one more time, and staggered to the *gite* where I sat on a shady terrace and revived myself by sipping cool drinks.

In fact I had landed in a good spot for the final night of the expedition. I seemed to have half of a house to myself, with my own bedroom, a shower easily accessible, and even a clothes-horse on a sunny balcony to make the drying of kit that much easier. On expeditions it is often the simplest pieces of equipment, combined with a little thought, which can improve one's condition no end and help to boost morale.

I ate my dinner on the terrace as the sun sank. I was virtually the only customer. In the bar a large television screen was showing the opening matches of the French football season, and my eye was drawn continually to a boring first half between Paris St.Germain and Bastia. The view in the opposite direction was more edifying, as the sun slipped behind the Canigou and the prominent Roc de France. The Fort de Bellegarde was visible on high ground just beyond the village of le Perthus, and I could just make out the trucks on the motorway at the Col du Perthus, three or four miles away and far below. Private cars were too small to be visible at that distance.

I found it difficult to sleep that night, for the events of the previous six weeks kept playing over and over in my mind. I could remember each day's route and where I had stayed each night. I could not recall every bend on every path or road, but with a little concentration I could visualise what I had seen in pretty well every kilometre, and that was without referring to my maps. My journey across France was a real line in time and space: it had started at a specific point on the earth's surface and subsequently I had walked every inch of the way. At the same time I reflected sadly that in another sense my line no longer existed. Nobody would see it painted along the ground. Its only existence now was as a series of mental images inside my head.

Outside the bedroom window the night was still and clear. There were countless stars in the inky void of space and the moon, currently over the Canigou massif to the west, looked impossibly bright. I watched the stars for a while, aware that I was merely a few grains of dust staring into infinity.

Sunday 3rd August 2003 was a day I approached with a whole mixture of emotions. One part of me just wanted to get the job finished. At any rate the part of me below the knees seemed to feel that way. Another part felt sad at the prospect of the walk ending, and yet another part was apprehensive at the thought of what might lie beyond the walk.

I packed my rucksack for the final time, and realised that I had developed an affection for this great green monster after all. It had served me well, and I smiled as I heaved it onto my back. "Come on," I said, awarding it the honour of personification. "Let's go to the Mediterranean."

Six weeks ago we had been on the beach at St.Jean-de-Luz. Therefore this Sunday morning was the forty-third day of my walk. When I deducted the rest-days it was actually the thirty-fifth day of walking. I would cross France two days faster than my aggregate time in the 1980's, and with the various detours to Roncesvalles, St.Girons and Montsegur I had definitely covered a greater distance this time. Set against that was the fact that more of my current expedition had been on country lanes and slightly flatter ground, so in theory that should have made it slightly easier. "Easier!" I thought – "what a ridiculous word!" It had been anything but easy. Later I would try to measure the distance from my maps and from calculations of the time spent walking. It was impossible to get a totally accurate result but my estimates suggested I had covered at least 600 miles during the six weeks. Of course that bald statistic said nothing about the ascents or descents, the surfaces on the paths or the temperatures: it had been one of the hottest summers ever recorded in the south of France.

If I had envisaged the final day of the journey as a triumphal progress, or some sort of cake-walk into Banyuls, then I was soon to be disillusioned. At breakfast the proprietor of the *gite* told me that it was going to be even hotter than the previous day. I set off and struggled up through the woods behind the huts, coming out on a lane which led further uphill to a radio installation. It was an ugly monstrosity of a place, surrounded by fences and barbed wire. Even at this early stage in the day I was aware of the salty, leathery smell of my own sweat. From the radio facility on Pic Neulos it was a case of following the ridge, past the Pic-des-Pradets and Pic-des-Quatre-Termes to the Pic-de-la-Carbassere. The Pyrenees are a cruel test. Even on the last day you are still going uphill, or rather going up and down in short stages, which is even more tiring. I felt weak and paused to eat an apple. It turned out to be my last food because the biscuits I was carrying proved to be inedible. I could only have chewed and swallowed them if I had had access to masses of extra water. Of the latter I had started out carrying five pints and I was rationing it as best I could whilst the temperature soared. Even on the ridge there was little by way of a cooling breeze, though for some of the time the path ran through woods and the trees provided a merciful shade. At one point I stopped to rest in the shade of a lone tree, and estimated that I still had five hours to go to Banyuls-sur-Mer. I wished I could simply get those five hours over and done. I also remembered how, on the first day of the walk, I had stopped after five hours on La Rhune and laid down to rest in the shade of a lone tree. I was bemused by this curious symmetry, and wondered whether I should ascribe it to some higher consciousness which had been guiding my expedition.

The slog up to Pic Sailfort was a hard one, but at least at the top I was rewarded with my first sighting of Banyuls. It was far below and still three or four hours away. I took advantage of the shade provided by a scrubby bush, and sank down for another rest. My water supply was now perilously low. I rested for a few minutes, but with nothing to eat it was not doing anything to restore my energy, so I soon set off downhill. I was aware that the descent from the Sailfort would involve some tricky navigation, and if I made a mistake and came down the wrong ridge it could add hours to the ordeal. Fortunately, after some initial difficulties, I found that the markings for the GR10 were reasonably clear and frequent, and they led down a rugged spur onto a ridge where the path ran level in an easterly direction. By now the heat was suffocating and the thin Mediterranean vegetation gave only a modicum of shade. I began to fear that heat exhaustion was a real possibility. If I collapsed here then the death at the end of the expedition might yet be more than metaphorical. I ploughed on regardless, for there was nothing to be gained by stopping, but weakness forced me to rest again before I reached the Col des Gascons.

The cheek and perversity of the Pyrenees were appalling: the route had already allowed me a glimpse of the finishing-line at Banyuls and yet even now I was still being compelled to go uphill. There was no remote possibility of pleasure in this sort of walking. With my body drained of water and energy it was simply an exercise in survival. Indeed, it occurred to me that nobody in their right mind would go hillwalking in this sort of climate for its own sake. I had only endured the last few days since the monastery for the simple reason that I had to, if I was to complete my traverse of the mountains from one coast to the other. A fully sane person would have surrendered long ago.

On the map the Col des Gascons looked reasonably substantial, and I dared to hope that on this blazing Sunday afternoon the gods would be in a merciful mood and would have opened a café or positioned an ice-cream van there. Any facility that sold cold drinks would be wonderful. But there was nothing at the col except a couple of bends on a tarmac road. From the col the GR10 continued east, down through vineyards, but I decided to follow the road into Banyuls. I knew this would increase the distance slightly, but by making the navigation simpler it might save time, as well as providing a flat surface on which to walk. I no longer had the physical or mental strength to mess around in fields or vineyards. But as long as I followed that thin ribbon of tarmac I knew it would lead me home. I struggled on, feeling weaker all the time. Shortly after 3 o'clock my water finally ran out. I had drunk my five pints in six hours, but I had still dehydrated badly. A sensation of sickness began to wash over me, presumably because my stomach had shrunk with little food or water inside, but at the same time I felt that if I were to drink anything it would probably make me ill. Meanwhile the sun was trying to burn my shoulders even through the fabric of my tee-shirt, and it seemed to be succeeding.

Eventually the road led me down into the outskirts of the town. It even brought me to the Celliers des Templiers factory where they produce the famous Banyuls wine. Apparently this is a rich sweet substance rather like port, but it is drunk cold, as an aperitif. I saw signboards advertising trips around the premises, so I staggered into the foyer, thinking there might be refreshments on sale to visitors as they waited for the next guided tour. A trio of men, who seemed startled by my appearance, told me that nothing was available but that I should try a camping site further down the hill. The camping site had a bar area, but it was closed. Across the road was a large empty car park in front of a supermarket. The supermarket was closed, but next door to it there was a vending machine emblazoned with the logo of a famous drinks company.

Feverishly I rolled three fifty-cent coins into the machine and pressed the button for a tin of orangeade. Out rolled a can of cola. But I was thankful. It was liquid, and it was cold. I knew I must have been in a bad way because the cola actually tasted good. The sugar and gas in the drink seemed to settle my stomach and gave me renewed energy. I tried to buy a second tin but the machine rejected my coins several times over. Maybe I had bought the last drink available.

I plodded on towards the town centre, and after a further fifteen minutes I came upon a small supermarket which was open. I grabbed a litre of water from the fridge and three-quarters of a litre of iced tea. Outside on the pavement I discovered that in my haste I had bought lemonade, not water, but it didn't matter. There was a bench outside the supermarket, but as it was in the sun I gave the benefit of it to my rucksack whilst I sat on the flagstones in the shade. The iced tea, with its peach flavour, was delicious. Having drunk all of it I found I had the strength to buy some water and I began to nibble at my biscuits.

For the last few hours I had barely thought about reaching the Mediterranean. My sole preoccupation had been to get to Banyuls and find the fluids which I was craving. The town had looked pretty from above, with a mass of red roofs and plenty of sailing boats and motorboats visible against the deep blue of the sea. This was the Vermillion Coast, and as it was the first Sunday in August the beaches and bars were packed with holidaymakers.

Refreshed by my intake of liquid I remembered that technically I still had not reached the coast. I continued along the street as it curved around to the right. The end came suddenly, as it always does on these occasions. I came to a roundabout which, according to a monument, was named after "Marshal Leclerc (1902-1947)." I decided that if the height of fame is to have a roundabout named after you then it is better not to be famous. The building on the corner had a mural of tiles on it, showing a crude map of the Pyrenees and proclaiming that this was the end of the GR10 long-distance footpath. Next to it I saw the last of those little parallel lines, one red and one white, daubed high up on a lamp-post.

I slipped into a bar for another drink - this one would be in celebration. Whatever else might happen in my life I had walked the length of the Pyrenees in one go, and nobody could ever take that away from me. I also bought a few postcards and stamps. I had promised I would send one to Philippe – the Belgian I had last seen in St.Jean Pied-de-Port five weeks earlier – if and when I reached the Mediterranean. I sent one to my brother Graham, then one to my mother, and finally one to Douglas. This last card recited the barest details of the walk: "Departed St.Jean-de-Luz, 08.56, Sunday 22nd June 2003. Arrived Banyuls-sur-Mer, 16.45, Sunday 3rd August." Then I added a quotation from Henry the Fifth at Agincourt: "and gentlemen in England now a-bed, shall think themselves accursed they were not here."

That boy Shakespeare knew how to write.

I posted my cards and took extra care crossing the road. It would be too ironic to get run over at this stage. Beyond the roundabout I seemed to be next to some sort of kiosk administering a children's crazy-golf course. In a shaded area elderly ladies with small dogs sat on benches under the palm trees. I swung off my rucksack and took out my camera to record the scene on the beach, which was now only feet away on the other side of a low wall. Half a dozen young people were playing volleyball in front of me, and off to the right I could see parents and infants gathered around a Bouncy Castle. The beach, which had more gravel than sand, was heavily populated. There was no tide to worry about, of course, and forty yards away a thick belt of deckchairs, parasols and sunbathers marked the water's edge.

I found myself wishing that these thousands of people had not been there. Throughout the expedition I had imagined my arrival at the coast, and I had built up a mental picture of it as a quiet and private thing, with hardly anybody else around. Of course this was ridiculous, as I was heading for a Mediterranean resort and it was August. But I still found the crowds were a shock. The whole panoply of life seemed to be spread out before me. Somewhere on this beach and throughout the town babies would be crying; families with sulky teenagers would be arguing; young couples would be making love and one or two people would be dying. But I did not belong with any of them. I knew nobody in this place and nobody knew me. As I stood there with my rucksack I was like an intruder from another planet, observing life as it passed by. I had descended from the mountains but I could equally well have come down from Mars.

In 1700 Louis XIV had accepted the throne of Spain on behalf of his grandson Philip V; an event which triggered the War of the Spanish Succession. Louis had said at the time

379

"maintenant il n' y a plus de Pyrenees" ("now there are no longer any Pyrenees"). The sentiment was true for me too. I had no more Pyrenees to face. No more lung-bursting, limb-aching, foot-burning, soul-searing ascents to make, all of them against the weight of my own body and rucksack. Just forty yards of sand and gravel remained, and beyond that everything was blue.

Yet there will always be more Pyrenees. Some are large and some less so. They jostle each other, a crazy mixture of ridges and canyons with valleys running in all directions. It adds up to a pretty accurate metaphor for the messiness of life. A metaphor which I had been living for the last six weeks, ever since I had emerged from that ocean of non-being and begun my journey on the Atlantic shore. And here the journey would end, on another shoreline with a vast expanse of water before me. I thought about T.S.Eliot's words in "Little Gidding" – quoted so often that they have become somewhat hackneyed, and yet they remain forceful – "the end of our travelling is to return to where we began, and to know the place for the first time."

Walking across France was the best thing I ever did in life. And it was probably the worst too. Of course it was a crazy thing to do. But it was magnificent.

Did I know myself any better as a result of my walk? I supposed so.

Did I know God any better? Possibly.

Was I any closer to making sense out of this bittersweet thing we call life? No, definitely not. The questions only multiply and deepen. The apostle Paul wrote that "we see through a glass darkly, but then face to face." It is possible that beyond death the mysteries will be resolved. Or maybe they will deepen yet further. Or maybe when we die it will just all go dark. In any event it is only death that can bring perfect freedom. Of course it is possible that God does not exist and that death will lead us into darkness, but I for one think that is unlikely. I think it is far more likely that when I die I shall see Him face to face, and at last I shall know as I am known.

The volleyball landed at my feet and I lobbed it back to one of the players. Having snapped off a last couple of pictures I put the camera away. For the final time I heaved the giant green rucksack onto my shoulders and adjusted the straps to settle its weight against my back. But this time there was a strange stinging sensation in my eyes, and I realised that hot tears of joy were coursing down through the dust and sweat on my cheeks. I blinked them away with a smile and took a couple of deep breaths.

And then I walked into the sea.